408   50

SPANISH

DICTIONARY

D0581558

COLLINS
TRAVEL
GEM

SPANISH

D I C T I O N A R Y

COLLINS
London and Glasgow

First published 1986

© William Collins Sons & Co Ltd 1986

latest reprint 1988

ISBN 0 00 459437-1

Consultant
Luis Sainz Blanco

Other Travel Gem
Dictionaries:

French

German

Italian

Portuguese

Yugoslav

Greek

Printed in Great Britain

Your TRAVEL GEM DICTIONARY will prove an invaluable companion on your holiday or trip abroad. In a genuinely handy pocket or handbag format, this two-way practical dictionary has a double aim. First, it is your key to understanding the foreign words and phrases you are likely to encounter when travelling in mainland Spain or any of her islands. Second, it contains an essential English wordpack with translations and pronunciations.

Understanding foreign signs and notices

With over 6000 Spanish words and phrases selected for their relevance to the needs of the traveller, your Travel Gem Dictionary provides essential help towards understanding the basic vocabulary of Spanish, and all those important notices, traffic signs, menus and other mystifying items surrounding you on your trip abroad.

Beyond survival communication

In addition, a practical English wordlist of over 3000 items with Spanish translations and clear pronunciations allows you to venture beyond basic communication and provides the ideal complement to your Travel Gem Phrase Book, also in this series.

Enjoy your trip!

Notes to help you

You will find that some words *(adjectives and nouns)* are listed with an ending in brackets. This ending is used when the noun is *feminine* — i.e. is used with **la** instead of **el**, or is marked *(f)*, in the dictionary. The adjective takes the same ending as the noun — i.e. if the noun is feminine, then the adjective will also be feminine. Thus the entry **gordo(a)** shows that both **gordo** and **gorda** mean "fat". Most words are made feminine by simply changing the basic *(masculine)* form from **o** to **a**.

Spanish alphabetical order is different from English alphabetical order, so we have used English order for maximum clarity.

Each translation is followed by its pronunciation (see next page for the pronunciation guide).

To make a word plural in Spanish, you simply add **s**.

Pronunciation Guide

In the pronunciation system used in this book, Spanish sounds are represented by spellings of the nearest possible sounds in English. Hence, when you read out the pronunciation - the line in *italics* after each phrase or word - sound the letters as if you were reading an English word. The syllable to be stressed is shown in **heavy italics**. The following notes should help you:

	REMARKS	EXAMPLE	PRONOUNCED
e	midway between *gate* and *get*	**puede**	***pwe**-de*
o	midway between *goat* and *got*	**cola**	***ko**la*
y	as in *yet*	**tiene**	***tye**-ne*
th	as in *thick*	**centro**	***then**tro*
kh	as in Scottish *loch*	**juego**	***khwe**go*
ly	as in *million*	**lleno**	***lye**no*
ny	as in *onion*	**niño**	***nee**nyo*

Spelling in Spanish is very regular and, with a little practice, you will soon be able to pronounce Spanish words from their spelling alone. The only letters which are unlike English are:

v, w	as *b* in *bed*	**curva**	***koor**ba*
c	before *a, o, u* as in *cat*	**caja**	***ka**kha*
	before *e, i* as *th* in *thin*	**centro**	***then**tro*
g	before *a, o, u* as in *got*	**gato**	***ga**to*
	before *e, i* as *ch* in *loch*	**girar**	*khee**rar***
h	silent	**hombre**	***om**-bre*
j	as *ch* in *loch*	**jueves**	***khwe**-bes*
ll	as *lli* in *million*	**callo**	***ka**lyo*
ñ	as *ni* in *onion*	**niño**	***nee**nyo*
z	as *th* in *thin*	**zumo**	***thoo**mo*

The letter *r* is always rolled; the double *r* is rolled even more strongly. Spanish vowels are single sounds: when you find two together, pronounce both of them in quick succession as in **aceite** *a-**the**-ee-te*.

SPANISH - ENGLISH

A

a: **a la estación** to the station; **a las 4** at 4 o'clock; **de lunes a viernes** from Monday to Friday; **a 30 kilómetros** 30 kilometres away; **a la izquierda/derecha** on/to the left/right
abadejo *m* haddock
abadía *f* abbey
abajo below, downstairs; **hacia abajo** downward(s); **el de abajo** the bottom one
abandonar to give up
abeja *f* bee
abeto *m* fir (tree)
abierto(a) open; on (*water supply*)
abogado *m* lawyer
abolladura *f* dent, bump
abonado(a) *m/f* subscriber
abonados *mpl* subscribers; season-ticket holders
abonar to credit; **abonarse** to subscribe; to buy a season ticket
abono *m* subscription; season ticket
abonos *mpl* deposits
abrazo *m* hug; **un fuerte abrazo** with best wishes (*on letter*)
abrebotellas *m* bottle opener
abrelatas *m* can-opener
abrigo *m* coat; **el abrigo de pieles** fur coat
abril *m* April
abrir to open; to turn on (*water*); **abrir (con llave)** to unlock; **abrir por aquí** open here
abrochar to fasten
absceso *m* abscess
absoluto(a) absolute; **en absoluto** not in the least
abstener: **absténgase de visitas turísticas durante la celebración del culto** please do not visit the church during services
abuela *f* grandmother
abuelo *m* grandfather; **los abuelos** grandparents
aburrido(a) boring; **estoy aburrido** I'm bored
acabado(a) complete; finished
acabar to finish; to complete
academia *f* academy; school

acampar to camp
acaso perhaps
acceso *m:* **acceso andenes** (to) platforms; **acceso prohibido a peatones** no pedestrians; **acceso vías** to platforms
accesorios *mpl* accessories
accidente *m* accident; **el accidente corporal** injury
acedía *f* heartburn
aceite *m* oil; **el aceite bronceador** suntan oil; **el aceite del coche** car oil; **el aceite de oliva** olive oil; **el aceite para niños** baby oil
aceituna *f* olive; **las aceitunas aliñadas** olives seasoned with a variety of herbs
acelerador *m* accelerator
acelerar to speed up; to accelerate
acelgas *fpl* chard; **las acelgas en menestra** boiled chard, fried with potatoes, garlic and egg
acera *f* pavement
acercarse to approach
ácido *m* acid
acogida *f* welcome
acomodador(a) *m/f* usher, usherette
acompañar to accompany
acondicionador de pelo *m* hair conditioner
aconsejar to advise
acordarse de to remember

acortar to shorten
acostarse to go to bed; to lie down
acotado: acotado de pesca fishing restricted
actividad *f* activity
activo(a) active; energetic
acto *m* act; **en el acto** while you wait
actor *m* actor
actriz *f* actress
actual present(day)
acuerdo *m* agreement; **estar de acuerdo con alguien** to agree with somebody; **ponerse de acuerdo** to come to an agreement
acuse de recibo *m* receipt
adecuado(a) suitable
adelantado(a) advanced; **por adelantado** in advance
adelantar to overtake; to advance (*money*)
adelante forwards; ahead
adelgazar to slim
además in addition
adentro indoors; **ir adentro** to go inside
adiós goodbye
administración *f* management; manager's office
admitirse: no se admiten cambios goods cannot be exchanged; **no se admiten cheques** no cheques; **no se admiten comidas de fuera** food purchased elsewhere

may not be consumed on the premises; **no se admiten devoluciones** no refunds will be given; **no se admiten propinas** please do not tip the staff; **no se admiten tarjetas de crédito** no credit cards accepted; **se admiten huéspedes** accommodation available

adobado(a) marinated in garlic, vinegar and herbs

adolescente *m/f* teenager

adonde where

adorno *m* decoration; ornament

adquirir to acquire

aduana *f* customs

aduanero *m* customs officer

adulto(a) grown-up; **para adultos** adult

advertir to warn

aéreo(a) air; aerial

aerobús *m* air bus

aerodeslizador *m* hovercraft

aerolínea *f* airline

aeropuerto *m* airport

afeitadora *f* electric razor

afeitarse to shave; **la máquina de afeitar** electric razor

afilado(a) sharp

afuera outside

afueras *fpl* outskirts; the suburbs

agencia *f* agency; **la agencia de la propiedad**

inmobiliaria estate agent; **la agencia de seguros** insurance company; **la agencia de viajes** travel agency

agente *m* agent; **el agente de tráfico** traffic warden; **el agente de viajes** travel agent

agitado(a) rough

agitar to shake; **agítese antes de usar** shake well before use

agosto *m* August

agotado(a) sold out; out of stock

agradable pleasant

agradecer to thank; **agradecer a alguien** to thank someone

agradecido(a) grateful

agricultor *m* farmer

agridulce sweet and sour

agrietarse to crack

agrio(a) sour

agua *f* water; **el agua destilada** distilled water; **el agua del grifo** tap water; **el agua mineral** mineral water; **el agua no potable** not drinking water; **el agua potable** drinking water; **el agua de seltz** soda water; **sin agua** neat

aguacate *m* avocado; **el aguacate con gambas** avocado stuffed with prawns

aguacero *m* shower (*rain*)

aguardar: aguarde su turno please wait your turn

agudo(a) sharp; pointed

aguja f needle; **la aguja e hilo** needle and thread; **la aguja (palada)** swordfish; **la aguja a la plancha** grilled swordfish

agujero m hole

ahí there

ahogarse to drown

ahora now; **por ahora** for the time being

ahorrar to save

ahumado(a) smoked

aire m air; **al aire libre** open-air

aire acondicionado m air-conditioning

ajedrez m chess

ají m chilli

ajillo m: **al ajillo** in a garlic sauce

ajo m garlic; **el ajo blanco** cold soup made with garlic, almonds, bread, olive oil, vinegar and water; **el ajo de las manos** boiled potatoes and red peppers mixed with a garlic, oil and vinegar dressing

ajustado(a) tight (clothes)

al = "a + el"

ala f wing

a la carta à la carte

alarma f alarm; **la alarma de incendios** fire alarm; **prohibido hacer uso de las alarmas sin causa justificada** do not use the alarm except in case of emergency

alba f dawn

albahaca f basil

albaricoque m apricot

albergue m hostel; **el albergue de carretera** state-run roadside hotel; **el albergue de juventud** youth hostel

albóndiga f meatball

álbum m L.P.

alcachofa f artichoke; **las alcachofas con jamón** artichokes fried with chopped ham

alcalde m mayor

alcance m reach; **manténgase fuera del alcance de los niños** keep out of reach of children

alcaparras fpl capers

alcoba f bedroom

alcohol m alcohol; **el alcohol desnaturalizado** methylated spirits; **sin alcohol** soft

alcohólico(a) alcoholic (drink)

aldea f village

alegre happy

alegría f joy

alejado(a) de away from

alemán(mana) German

Alemania f Germany

alergia f allergy

alérgico(a) a allergic to

aletas *fpl* flippers
alfarería *f* pottery
alfiler *m* pin
alfombra *f* carpet
algas *fpl* seaweed
algo something; **¿algo más?** anything else?
algodón *m* cotton; **el algodón hidrófilo** cotton wool
alguien somebody; someone
algún, alguno(a) some, any; **alguna vez** ever
Alicante *m* strong, full-bodied red wine
aliento *m* breath
alimentación *f* grocery shop
alimentar to feed
alimento *m* food; **los alimentos infantiles** baby foods; **los alimentos de régimen** diet foods
alioli *m* garlic-flavoured mayonnaise
alivio *m* relief
allá there
allí there
all i oli *m* garlic-flavoured mayonnaise
almacén *m* store; **los grandes almacenes** department stores
almeja *f* clam; mussel; **las almejas a la marinera** steamed clams with a parsley, olive oil and garlic sauce
almendra *f* almond; **las almendras garrapiñadas**

sugar-coated almonds
almíbar *m* syrup
almohada *f* pillow
almohadón *m* bolster
almuerzo *m* lunch
alojamiento *m* accommodation
alpargata *f* espadrille
alpinismo *m* mountaineering
alquilar to rent; to hire; **se alquila** to let
alquiler *m* rent; rental; **el alquiler de coches sin conductor** self-drive car hire; **el alquiler de coches con conductor** chauffeur-driven car hire
alrededor de around
alrededores *mpl* outskirts
alternador *m* alternator
alto(a) high; **alta tensión** high voltage
altoparlante *m* loudspeaker
altura *f* altitude; height; **de 6 metros de altura** 6 metres high
alubia *f:* **las alubias blancas** butter beans; **las alubias pintas** red kidney beans
alumno(a) *m/f* pupil
ama de casa *f* housewife
amable pleasant; kind
amanecer *m* dawn
amargo(a) bitter
amarillo(a) yellow
amarrar to moor
ambiente *m* atmosphere

ambos(as) both
ambulancia f ambulance
ambulatorio m National Health clinic
americana f jacket
americano(a) American
amigdalitis f tonsillitis
amigo(a) m/f friend
amistoso(a) friendly
amontillado m a medium dry sherry
amor m love
amortiguador m shock absorber
amperio m amp
ampliación f enlargement
ampolla f blister
amueblado(a) furnished
amueblar to furnish
análisis m analysis; **el análisis de sangre/orina** blood/urine test; **los análisis clínicos** medical tests
ananás f pineapple
ancas fpl: **las ancas de rana** frog's legs
ancho(a) broad; wide
anchoa f anchovy
anchura f width
ancla f anchor
Andalucía f Andalusia
andaluz(a) Andalucian
andar to walk
andén m platform
anestésico m anaesthetic
anfiteatro m circle (*theatre*)
anfitrión m host
anguila f eel

angula f baby eel
anillo m ring; **el anillo de boda** wedding ring; **el anillo de compromiso** engagement ring
animal m animal
anis m aniseed
anisete m aniseed-flavoured liqueur
aniversario m anniversary
año m year; **Año Nuevo** New Year's Day; **¿cuántos años tiene?** how old are you?
anoche last night
anochecer m dusk
ante m suede
anteayer the day before yesterday
antebrazo m forearm
antena f antenna; aerial
anteojos mpl binoculars
antes before
antiadherente non-stick
antibiótico m antibiotic
antichoque shockproof
anticipado(a) in advance
anticonceptivo m contraceptive
anticongelante m antifreeze
anticuario m antique dealer
antídoto m antidote
antigüedades fpl antiques
antiguo(a) old
antihistamínico m antihistamine
antiséptico m antiseptic
anular to cancel
anunciar to announce; to

advertise
anuncio m advertisement;
notice
anzuelo m hook
apagado(a) off
apagar to switch off; to turn
off
apagón m power cut
aparato m appliance; **los
aparatos de sordo** hearing
aids
aparcamiento m parking-
lot; car park; **el
aparcamiento cubierto**
covered parking; **el
aparcamiento subterráneo**
underground car park
aparcar to park; **¿se puede
aparcar aquí?** can I park
here?; **por favor no
aparcar** no parking
aparecer to appear
apartadero m lay-by
apartado de Correos m
P.O. Box
apartamento m apartment
aparte apart
apdo. see **apartado de
Correos**
apeadero m halt (*railway*)
apellido m surname; **el
apellido de soltera** maiden
name
apenas scarcely
aperitivo m aperitif
apertura f: **apertura de
cuentas** new accounts (*in
banks*)

**apetecer: ¿le apetece un
café?** do you feel like a
coffee?
apetito m appetite
apio m celery; **el apio nabo**
celeriac
aplauso m applause
aplazar to postpone
apoplejía f stroke (*illness*)
apostar to bet
apoyabrazos m armrest
apoyacabezas m headrest
apoyarse en to lean on
aprender to learn
aprendiz m trainee; **el
aprendiz de conductor**
learner(-driver)
apretar to press; to push
**aprovechar: ¡que
aproveche!** enjoy your meal!
aproximado(a) approximate
apto U (*film*)
apurarse to hurry;
¡apúrate! hurry up!
aquel that; **aquél** that one
aquella that; **aquélla** that
one
aquellas those; **aquéllas**
those ones
aquello that
aquellos those; **aquéllos**
those ones
aquí here; **por aquí, por
favor** this way please; **venga
aquí** come over here; **está
aquí de vacaciones** he's
over here on holiday
árabe m/f Arab

araña f spider
árbitro m referee (*sports*)
árbol m tree; **el árbol de Navidad** Christmas tree
arcén m verge; hard shoulder
arco m arch
arco iris m rainbow
arder to blaze; **la casa está ardiendo** the house is on fire
ardilla f squirrel
ardor de estómago m indigestion; heartburn
área f: **el área de servicio** service area; **área oficial** staff only
arena f sand
arenque m herring
argot m slang
arma f weapon; **las armas de fuego** firearms
armar to assemble; to pitch
armario m cupboard; wardrobe
armería f hunting and fishing gear
arquitecto m architect
arrancar to switch on
arranque m starter
arrebatar to snatch
arreglar to arrange
arreglo m arrangement
arrendamiento m lease
arrendatario(a) m/f tenant; lessee
arriba upstairs; **hacia arriba** upward(s); **de arriba** overhead
arroyo m stream

arroz m rice; **el arroz abanda** a mixture of cooked fish and shellfish served with rice boiled in fish stock; **el arroz blanco** plain boiled rice; **el arroz a la cubana** rice topped with fried egg and banana; **el arroz a la española** rice cooked in fish stock, chicken livers, pork and tomatoes; **el arroz con leche** rice pudding; **el arroz a la levantina** rice with shellfish, onions, artichokes, peas, tomatoes and saffron; **el arroz a la milanesa** fried rice with onion, chicken livers, ham, tomatoes, peas and grated cheese; **el arroz murciano** rice with pork, tomatoes, red peppers and garlic; **el arroz a la primavera** boiled rice and vegetables served with a hot hollandaise sauce
arrugado(a) creased
arruinar to ruin; to wreck (*plans*)
arte f art
arteria f artery
artesanía f craft shop; **de artesanía** handmade
artesanías fpl crafts
artesano m craftsman
articulación f joint (*of body*)
artículo m: **artículos de fumador** smoker's requisites; **artículos del**

hogar household goods; **artículos de tocador** toiletries; **artículos de ocasión** bargains; **artículos de piel** leather goods; **los artículos de viaje** travel goods

artificial artificial

artista *m/f* artist

artritis *f* arthritis

asadero de pollos *m* roast chicken take-away

asado *m* roast meat

asado(a) roast

asaltar to mug; to assault

asalto *m* raid

asar to roast; **asar a la parrilla** to grill

ascender to amount to; **asciende a 5000 pesetas** it amounts to 5000 pesetas

ascensor *m* lift

asegurado(a) insured

asegurar to insure

aseos *mpl* toilets

así thus; in this way

asiento *m* seat

asistencia *f:* **asistencia técnica** repairs

asistir a to attend

asma *f* asthma

asno *m* donkey

asociación *f* association

asomarse: es peligroso asomarse do not lean out of the window

áspero(a) rough

aspirador *m* vacuum cleaner

aspirina *f* aspirin

asunto *m* subject; matter

atacar to attack

atajo *m* short cut

ataque *m* attack; fit; **el ataque cardíaco** heart attack

atar to tie up

atasco *m* blockage; traffic jam

atención *f:* **atención a su luz** mind your lights; **atención, obras** drive carefully – roadworks ahead; **atención al tren** look out, trains

aterrizaje *m* landing; **el aterrizaje forzoso** emergency landing

aterrizar to land (*plane*)

Atlántico *m* Atlantic Ocean

atomizador *m* spray

atrás behind; **hacia atrás** backwards; **mirar hacia atrás** to look behind

atrasado(a) late

atrasar to hold up

atraso *m* delay

atravesar to pierce; to cross

atreverse a to dare to

atropellar to run down/over

A.T.S. *see* **Ayudante**

atún *m* tuna fish; **el atún encebollado** casseroled tuna fish with onion, tomato, garlic, parsley and walnuts; **el atún a la vinagreta** casseroled tuna fish with onions, garlic, parsley, lemon

juice and vinegar
audífono m hearing aid
aumentar to increase
aumento m rise; increase
aun even
aunque although
auricular m receiver
auriculares mpl headphones
auténtico(a) genuine
auto m car
autoadhesivo(a) self-
adhesive
autobús m bus
autocar m coach
autolavado m car wash
automático(a) automatic;
el coche automático an
automatic
automotor m short-distance
diesel train
automovilista m/f motorist
autopista f motorway; **la
autopista de peaje** toll road
autor m author
autorizado(a) authorized;
**autorizado subir y bajar
viajeros** no stopping except
to set down or pick up
passengers
autoservicio self-service
autostop m: **hacer autostop**
to hitch-hike
autostopista m/f hitchhiker
auxilio m help; **Auxilio en
Carretera** police breakdown
patrol
avance m trailer (film)
avanzar to advance

Av., Avda. see **avenida**
ave f bird
avellana f hazelnut
avena f oats
avenida f avenue
avería f breakdown; **la
avería del motor** engine
trouble; **en caso de avería,
diríjanse a...** in case of
breakdown, contact...
averiarse to break down
aves fpl poultry; **aves y caza**
poultry and game
avión m aircraft; aeroplane;
en avión by air
avisar to inform
aviso m notice; warning
ayer yesterday
ayuda f help
Ayudante m: **Ayudante
Técnico Sanitario (A.T.S.)**
male nurse
ayudar to help; **¿puede
ayudarme?** can you help
me?
ayuntamiento m town hall
azafata f air hostess
azafrán m saffron
azúcar m sugar
azucarado(a) sweet
azucena f lily
azul blue; **azul marino** navy
blue

B

baca f roof rack
bacalao m cod; **el bacalao**

encebollado stewed cod with onion and beaten eggs; **bacalao al pil-pil** garlic-fried cod

bahía f bay

bailador(a) m/f dancer

bailar to dance

baile m dance

bajamar f low tide

bajar to go down; to fall; **bajar la radio** to turn down the radio

bajo(a) low; short; soft; **más bajo** lower

balandro m sailing boat

balanza f scales

balcón m balcony

balneario m spa

balón m ball

baloncesto m basketball

bañador m swimming costume; bather

bañarse to go swimming; **prohibido bañarse** bathing prohibited; **prohibido bañarse sin gorro** bathing caps must be worn

banca f bank

bancario(a) bank

banco m bench; bank

banda f ribbon; band (musical)

bandeja f tray

bandera f flag

banderilla f cocktail stick

bañera f bath(tub)

baño m bath; bathroom; **con baño** with bath

bar m bar

baraja f pack (of cards)

barandilla f banisters

barato(a) cheap; **más barato** cheaper

barba f beard

barbería f barber's

barbero m barber

barbilla f chin

barca f boat; **la barca de pasaje** ferry

barco m ship, boat; **el barco a vela** dinghy

barquillo m ice-cream cone

barra f bar; counter; **la barra de labios** lipstick

barrer to sweep

barrera f barrier; crash barrier

barriga f stomach

barrio m district; suburb; **el barrio chino** red light district

barro m mud

báscula f scales

base f basis; base

bastante enough; quite; rather; **bastante agua** enough water

bastar to be enough; **basta** that's enough

basura f rubbish

basurero m rubbish dump

bata f dressing gown

batata f sweet potato

batería f battery

batido m batter; **el batido de leche** milkshake

batidora *f* mixer
batir to beat
baúl *m* trunk
bautismo *m* baptism
bayeta *f* dishcloth
bebé *m* baby
beber to drink
bebida *f* drink; **las bebidas alcohólicas** liquor; **la bebida no alcohólica** soft drink
béisbol *m* baseball
belleza *f* beauty
berberecho *m* cockle
berenjena *f* aubergine
berro *m* watercress
berza *f* cabbage
besar to kiss
beso *m* kiss
besugo *m* sea bream; **el besugo a la donostiarra** grilled sea bream served with an oil, garlic and lemon juice sauce
betún *m* polish
biberón *m* baby's bottle
biblioteca *f* library
bicicleta *f* bicycle; **ir en bicicleta** to cycle
bien well; **está bien** that's all right; **muy bien** (that's) fine
bienes *mpl* property; possessions
bienvenida *f* welcome
bienvenido(a) welcome
biftec *m* steak
bifurcación *f* fork (*in road*)
bigote *m* moustache

bikini[1] *m* bikini
bikini[2] *m* toasted ham and cheese sandwich
bilingüe bilingual
billar *m* snooker
billete *m* ticket; **el billete de banco** bank note; **el billete de ida** one-way ticket; **el billete de ida y vuelta** return ticket; **un billete de segunda clase** a second-class ticket; **un billete turístico** a tourist ticket; **los billetes de cercanías** local tickets; **los billetes de largo recorrido** long distance tickets
bistec *m* steak
bisutería *f* imitation jewellery (*shop*)
bizcocho *m* spongecake; **el bizcocho borracho** sponge cake filled with brandy or rum; **el bizcocho borracho de Guadalajara** sponge ring filled with brandy or rum and whipped cream; **los bizcochos de soletilla** sponge fingers
blanco(a) white; **en blanco** blank; **por favor dejar en blanco** please leave blank; **un blanco y negro** black coffee with a spoonful of ice-cream in it
blando(a) soft
bloc *m* pad (*notepaper*)
bloque *m* block (*of stone*); **el**

bloque de pisos block of flats

blusa f blouse

bobina f reel

boca f mouth

bocacalle f intersection; turning; **la segunda bocacalle a la derecha** the second on the right

bocadillo m sandwich; **un bocadillo de jamón** a ham sandwich; **bocadillos** snacks

bocado m mouthful

bocina f horn; **tocar la bocina** to hoot

boda f wedding

bodega f off-licence

boina f beret

boite f nightclub

bola f ball

bolera f bowling alley

boletín m bulletin; **el boletín meteorológico** weather forecast

bolígrafo m ballpoint pen

bollería f bakery

bollo m roll; bun

bolsa f bag; **la bolsa de agua caliente** hot water bottle; **la bolsa de aseo** sponge-bag; **la bolsa de compras** shopping bag; **la bolsa de papel** paper bag; **la bolsa de plástico** plastic bag; **la bolsa de viaje** flight bag

bolsillo m pocket

bolsita f sachet; **la bolsita de té** teabag

bolso m bag (*handbag*); **el bolso de mano** handbag

bomba f bomb; **la bomba de la gasolina** fuel pump

bombero m fireman; **el cuerpo de bomberos** fire brigade; **el coche de bomberos** fire engine

bombilla f light bulb; **la bombilla de flash** flashbulb

bombona f: **bombona de gas** gas cylinder

bombonería f confectioner's

bombones mpl chocolates

bonito m striped tuna

bonito(a) lovely; pretty; nice

bono m voucher

bonobús m season ticket

boquerón m anchovy; **los boquerones en vinagre** pickled anchovies served with olive oil, garlic and parsley

boquilla f cigarette holder

bordado(a) embroidered

borde m edge

bordo m: **ir a bordo** to go aboard; **a bordo del barco** aboard the ship

borracho(a) drunk

borrascoso(a) stormy

bosque m forest; wood

bota f boot; **la bota de esquí** ski boot

botavara f boom (*sailing*)

bote m dinghy; **el bote salvavidas** lifeboat

botella f bottle

botijo *m* jar
botiquín *m* first-aid kit
botón *m* button; knob
botones *m* bellboy
botulismo *m* food poisoning
boxeo *m* boxing
braga-pañales *mpl* all-in-one disposable nappies
bragas *fpl* knickers
braqueta *f* fly (*on trousers*)
brasa: a la brasa barbecued
brazo *m* arm; **el brazo de gitano** Swiss roll
brevas *fpl* early summer figs
bricolaje *m* do-it-yourself (shop)
brillante shiny
brillar to shine; **el sol está brillando** the sun is out
británico(a) British
brocha *f* brush; **la brocha de afeitar** shaving brush
broche *m* brooch
brocheta de ternera *f* beef kebabs
broma *f* joke
bronce *m* bronze
bronceado(a) sun-tanned
broncearse to tan
bronquitis *f* bronchitis
brújula *f* compass
brumoso(a) foggy
bucear to dive
budín *m* pudding
bueno(a) good; fine; **¡buenos días!** good morning!; **¡buenas tardes!** good afternoon!; good

evening!; **¡buenas noches!** good night!
buey *m* ox
bufanda *f* scarf
bufet libre *m* set-price meal when you can eat as much as you want
bujía *f* sparking plug
bulevar *m* arcade; gallery
bulto *m* package; lump (*on skin*)
buñuelo *m* fritter; doughnut; **los buñuelos de viento** small light fritters filled with cream
buque *m* ship
burro *m* donkey
bus *m*: **sólo bus** buses only; **el bus aeropuerto** airport bus
buscar to look for; **ir a buscar** to fetch; **se busca** wanted
butaca *f* stalls; seat; **las butacas de platea/de patio** stalls seats
butano *m* Calor gas
butifarra *f* Catalan sausage
buzón *m* letter box

C

caballa *f* mackerel
caballero *m* gentleman; **Caballeros** Gentlemen, Gents
caballo *m* horse; **montar a caballo** to go riding

cabello *m* hair
caber to fit; **no cabe** it won't go in
cabeza *f* head
cabina *f* cabin; **la cabina telefónica** telephone box; **la cabina pública de télex** public telex machine
cable *m* wire; cable; **el cable de remolque** tow rope; **los cables para cargar la batería** jump leads
cabra *f* goat
cabritilla: de cabritilla kid (*leather*)
cabrito *m* kid (*meat*); **cabrito asado** roast kid
cacahuete *m* peanut
cacao *m* cocoa
cacerola *f* saucepan
cacharrería *f* pottery shop
cachemira *f* cashmere
cada every; each; **cada semana** weekly; **cada uno (c/u)** each (one)
cadena *f* chain
cadera *f* hip
caducado(a) out-of-date
caducidad *f* expiry; **fecha de caducidad** expiry date; best before
caer to fall
caerse to fall down
café *m* café; coffee; **el café cortado** small coffee with a dash of milk; **el café corto** a very milky small coffee; **el café descafeinado**
decaffeinated coffee; **el café exprés** espresso coffee; **café en grano** coffee beans; **el café helado** iced coffee; **el café con leche** white coffee; **café molido** ground coffee; **el café solo** black coffee
cafetera *f* coffeepot
cafetería *f* snack bar
caja *f* box; cashdesk; **la caja de ahorros** savings bank; **la caja de cambios** gearbox; **la caja de cerillas** matchbox; **la caja fuerte** safe; **la caja de pinturas** paintbox; **la caja postal de ahorros** Girobank; **la caja de seguridad** safe
cajero(a) *m/f* teller; cashier; **el cajero automático** cash dispenser
cajetilla *f*: **la cajetilla de cigarrillos** packet of cigarettes
cajón *m* drawer
calabacín *m* courgette; **los calabacines rellenos** stuffed courgettes; **los calabacines glaseados** glazed courgettes
calabaza *f* small pumpkin
calamares *mpl* squid; **los calamares a la marinera** squid casserole with onion, garlic, paprika and olive oil; **los calamares rellenos** squid stuffed with egg, ham and breadcrumbs and served

with a wine sauce; **los calamares a la romana** squid fried in batter; **los calamares en su tinta** squid cooked in their ink

calambre *m* cramp

calcetín *m* sock

calculadora *f* calculator

caldereta *f*: **caldereta asturiana** fish and seafood stewed in sherry and peppers; **la caldereta de cordero** stewed lamb with onion, garlic, parsley and spearmint

caldo *m* soup; **el caldo canario** thick soup made with pork ribs, corn, pumpkin and marrow; **el caldo de cocido** thin soup made with meat, sausage, bacon and vegetables; **el caldo gallego** clear soup with vegetables, beans and pork; **el caldo de verduras** clear vegetable soup

calefacción *f* heating; **la calefacción central** central heating

calendario *m* calendar

calentador *m* heater; **el calentador de agua** water heater

calentar to heat

calentura *f* high fever

calidad *f* quality; **los artículos de calidad** quality goods

cálido(a) warm

caliente hot

callado(a) quiet

calle *f* street; **calle cortada** closed to traffic; **la calle de dirección única** one-way street; **la calle mayor** high street; **la calle sin salida** cul-de-sac

callejero *m* street map

callejón *m*: **callejón sin salida** no through road; cul-de-sac

callista *m* chiropodist

callo *m* corn (*on foot*)

callos *mpl* tripe; **los callos a la madrileña** tripe in a spicy sauce with garlic and chorizo

calmado(a) calm

calmante *m* painkiller

calor *m* heat; **hace calor** it's warm today; **tengo calor** I'm warm

calvo(a) bald

calzada *f* roadway; **calzada deteriorada** uneven road surface; **calzada en mal estado** poor road surface

calzado *m* footwear; **calzados** shoe shop

calzoncillos *mpl* underpants

cama *f* bed; **la cama de campaña** camp bed; **la cama turca** campbed; **las camas gemelas** twin beds; **una cama individual** single bed; **una cama de matrimonio** double bed

cámara f camera; **la cámara de cine** cine camera

camarera f waitress

camarero m barman; waiter

camarón m shrimp

camarote m cabin

cambiar to change; to exchange; **cambiar de marcha** to change gear; **no se cambian los discos** records cannot be exchanged

cambio m change; gear (of car); exchange (rate); **cambio de cheques** cheques cashed; **cambio de sentido** motorway exit; **el cambio sincronizado de velocidades** synchromesh; **compruebe su cambio** check your change; **facilite el cambio** have your change ready; **traiga su cambio preparado** please have your change ready

camilla f stretcher

camino m path; road; **¿cuál es el camino para Londres?** which is the way to London?; **camino cerrado** road closed

camión m truck; lorry; **camión grúa** breakdown lorry

camionero m lorry driver

camioneta f van

camisa f shirt

camisería f shirt shop

camiseta f tee shirt; vest

camisón m nightdress

campana f bell

campeón m champion

camping m camping; camp(ing) site; **hacer camping** to go camping; **el camping gas** calor gas light

campo m field; countryside; **el campo de golf** golf course; **en el campo** in the country

caña f cane; glass of beer; **la caña de cerveza** glass of beer; **la caña de pesca** fishing rod

canal m canal; **el Canal de la Mancha** the Channel

canapé m open sandwich

cancelar to cancel

cancha f: **cancha de tenis** tennis court

canción f song

canela f cinnamon

canelones mpl cannelloni

cangrejo m crab; **el cangrejo de río** crayfish

canguro m babysitter

canoa f canoe

cansado(a) tired

cantante m/f singer

cantar to sing

cantidad f quantity

cantimplora f water bottle

cantina f buffet (in station)

caoba f mahogany

capilla f chapel

capitán m captain

capó m bonnet (car)

cápsulas *fpl* capsules
capuchino *m* cappuccino coffee
cara *f* face
carabineros *mpl* customs police
caracol *m* snail
caramelo *m* sweet; caramel
caravana *f* caravan
carbón *m* coal
carbonada *f* minced beef stewed with tomatoes, onions, potatoes and fruit
carburador *m* carburettor
carburante *m* fuel
cárcel *f* prison
cardenal *m* bruise
carga *f* load; cargo
cargado(a) strong
cargar to load; **cargar en cuenta** to charge to account
cargo *m* charge; **los cargos por entrega** delivery charges; **los cargos por recogida** collection charges; **a cargo del cliente** at the customer's expense
cariñoso(a) affectionate
carnaval *m* carnival
carne *f* meat; flesh; **la carne de cerdo** pork; **la carne de cordero** lamb; **la carne de membrillo** quince jelly; **la carne picada** mince; **la carne de ternera** veal; **la carne de vaca** beef
carnet de conducir *m* driving licence

carnet de identidad *m* identity card
carnicería *f* butcher's
carnicero *m* butcher
caro(a) expensive
carpa *f* carp
carpeta *f* file
carpintería *f* carpenter's shop
carrera *f* career; race; **las carreras de caballos** horse-racing
carrete *m* roll of film
carretera *f* road; highway; **la carretera de circunvalación** ring road; **la carretera comarcal** B-road; **carretera cortada/bloqueada por la nieve** road closed/blocked by snow; **la carretera de doble calzada** dual carriageway; **la carretera local** local road; **la carretera nacional** trunk road; **la carretera secundaria** minor road
carretilla *f* cart; luggage trolley
carril *m* lane (*on road*); **el carril de aceleración** outside lane; **el carril de deceleración** exit lane; **el carril de la izquierda** the outside lane
carrito *m* trolley
carrocería *f* body(work)
carta *f* letter; playing card; menu; **la carta aérea** air

mail letter; **la carta certificada** registered letter; **la carta higiénica** toilet paper; **la carta verde** green card; **la carta de vinos** wine list

cartel m poster

cartelera f entertainments

cartera f wallet

carterista m pickpocket

cartero m postman

cartón m cardboard; **el cartón de cigarrillos** a carton of cigarettes

cartucho m cartridge

casa f home; house; household; **en casa** at home; **la casa de campo** farmhouse; **la casa de huéspedes** boarding house; **casa particular ofrece habitaciones** accommodation available; **la casa de socorro** first-aid post

casado(a) married

casarse to marry

cascada f waterfall

cáscara f peel; eggshell

casco m helmet

casero(a) home-made; **la comida casera** home cooking

caseta f beach hut

casete f cassette

casi nearly; almost

casilla f locker

casillero de consigna m locker

caso m case; **en caso de** in case of; **en caso de reclamaciones diríjanse a...** please address any complaints to...

castaña f chestnut; **las castañas pilongas** dried chestnuts

castaño(a) brown

castañuelas fpl castanets

castellano(a) Castilian

castillo m castle

catalán(ana) Catalonian

catálogo m catalogue

catarro m catarrh; cold

catedral f cathedral

catorce fourteen

causa f cause; **a causa de** because of

causar to cause

cava m Catalan champagne-style sparkling wine

caza f hunting; game

cazador m hunter

cazadora f jerkin

cazuela f casserole; pan; **a la cazuela** casseroled

cebador m choke

cebolla f onion

cebolleta f spring onion

cebollino m chive

cebra f zebra

cecina f cured meat

ceder to give in; **ceder/ceda el paso** give way

C.E.E. f E.E.C.

ceja f eyebrow

célebre famous
céle re quick; fast
celeste light blue
celofán m cellophane
cementerio m cemetery
cemento m cement; concrete
cena f dinner; supper
cenicero m ashtray
centenario m centenary
centeno m rye
centésimo(a) hundredth
centímetro m centimetre
centollo m spider crab
central f: **la central telefónica** telephone exchange
centralita f switchboard
centro m centre; **el centro asistencial** health centre; **el centro de la ciudad** city centre; **el centro comercial** shopping centre; **el centro urbano** city centre
cepillo m brush; **el cepillo de dientes** toothbrush; **el cepillo para el pelo** hairbrush; **el cepillo de uñas** nailbrush
cera f wax
cerámica f ceramics, pottery
cerca near; **cerca de** close to
cercanías fpl outskirts
cercano(a) close
cerdo m pig; pork; **el cerdo simple** pork steak
cereal m breakfast cereal
cerebro m brain
cereza f cherry

cerilla f match
cero m zero
cerrado(a) shut; off (*water supply*); **cerrado por reforma** closed for repairs
cerradura f lock
cerrajería m locksmith's
cerrajero m locksmith
cerrar to close; to block; **cerrar con llave** to lock; **cerramos los sábados por la tarde** closed Saturday afternoons
cerrojo m bolt
certificado m certificate; **el certificado de seguros** insurance certificate; **certificados** registered letters
certificado(a) registered
certificar to register
cervecería f brewery; pub
cerveza f beer; lager; **la cerveza de barril** draught beer; **la cerveza negra** stout
césped m lawn
cesta f shopping basket
cestería f basketwork (shop)
chacinas fpl sausages
chacolí m sparkling, light red or white wine from the Basque Country
chal m shawl
chalé m villa
chaleco m waistcoat; **el chaleco salvavidas** life jacket
chalote m shallot

champán *m* champagne
champaña *m* champagne
champiñón *m* mushroom
champú *m* shampoo
chandal *m* track suit
chanfaina *f* stew of goat's offal with vegetables
chanquetes *mpl* small edible fish similar to whitebait
chapado en oro gold-plated
chaparrón *m* shower (*rain*)
chaqueta *f* jacket
charco *m* pool; puddle
charcutería *f* pork butcher's
charla *f* talk; chat
charol *m* patent leather
chasis *m* chassis
chateaubriand/ chatobrian *m* thick fillet steak covered with bacon rashers and lightly cooked in butter
chato de vino *m* a small glass of wine
cheque *m* cheque; **el cheque de viaje** traveller's cheque
chica *f* girl
chicle *m* chewing gum; **chicle sin azúcar** sugarfree chewing gum
chico *m* boy
chico(a) small
chile *m* chilli
chilindrón: a la chilindrón pot-roasted with tomatoes, peppers, onions and garlic
chillar to scream

chimenea *f* fireplace; chimney
chino(a) Chinese
chipirones *mpl* baby squid
chiquillo(a) small; **el chiquillo** little boy
chirimoya *f* custard apple
chiringuito *m* bar
chispa *f* spark
chiste *m* joke
chistoso(a) funny
chivo *m* kid; goat
chocar to collide
chocolate *m* chocolate; **el chocolate con churros** drinking chocolate with fritters; **el chocolate con leche** milk chocolate; **el chocolate sin leche** plain chocolate; **el chocolate a la taza** drinking chocolate
chocolatería *f* a café where hot chocolate with "churros" is sold
chofer *m* driver
chopitos *mpl* small squid
choque *m* crash; **tener un choque con el coche** to crash one's car
chorizo *m* salami; hard pork sausage
choto *m*: **el choto al ajillo** kid with garlic and oil
chuleta *f* cutlet; **la chuleta de cerdo** pork chop; **las chuletas de cerdo empanadas** pork chops fried in breadcrumbs; **las**

chuletas de cordero lamb chops; **las chuletas de cordero con bechamel** fried lamb chops served with white sauce; **las chuletas de ternera** veal cutlets; **las chuletas de ternera a la parrilla** grilled veal cutlets

chuletón m beef chop; **el chuletón de ternera con salsa Roquefort** large veal chop served with Roquefort cheese sauce

chupete m dummy

churrasco m steak

churrería f fritter shop or stand

churro m deep-fried batter stick sprinkled with sugar and eaten with drinking chocolate

cicatriz f scar

ciclismo m cycling

ciclista m/f cyclist

ciego(a) blind

cielo m sky

cien hundred; **ciento uno(a)** a hundred and one; **cien gramos de** 100 grammes of

cierre m fastener; zip

cierto(a) certain; **cierta gente** some people

ciervo m deer

cifra f figure

cigala f crayfish; **las cigalas cocidas** boiled crayfish; **las cigalas plancha** grilled crayfish

cigarrillo m cigarette

cigarro m cigar

cima f mountain top

cinco five

cincuenta fifty

cine m cinema

cinta f tape; **la cinta adhesiva** adhesive tape; **cinta limpiadora** cleaning tape; **cinta virgen** blank tape

cintura f waist

cinturón m belt; **el cinturón de seguridad** safety belt; seat belt; **el cinturón salvavidas** lifebelt

circo m circus

circuito cicloturista m route for cyclists

circulación f traffic

circular to drive; to walk; **circulen por la otra acera** walk on the other side of the street; **circule a su derecha** keep right; **circula a diario** daily service including weekends

círculo m circle

cirio m candle

ciruela f plum; **la ciruela pasa** prune; **las ciruelas claudias** greengages

cirugía f surgery

cirujano m surgeon

cita f appointment

ciudad f city; town

ciudadano m citizen

clarete m light, red wine

claro(a) light (*bright, pale*);

clear
clase f class
clásico(a) classical
clasificado(a): clasificada S adults only
clavel m carnation
clavo m nail
claxon m horn
cliente m/f customer; client
clima m climate
climatizado(a) air-conditioned
clínica f clinic; nursing home; **la clínica dental** dental surgery
clip m paperclip
club nocturno m night club
cobertor m blanket
cobrador m conductor
cobrar to charge; to cash
cobre m copper
cobro m payment; **cobros** withdrawals
cocer to cook
coche m car; **el coche de alquiler** hired car; **el coche será devuelto en...** car to be returned to...
coche-cama m sleeping car
cochecito de niño m pram
coche-comedor m dining car
coche patrulla m police car
cochinillo m piglet
cocido m chick-pea, meat and vegetable stew
cocido(a) cooked; **insuficientemente**

cocido(a) undercooked
cocina f kitchen; stove; **la cocina española** Spanish cooking; **la cocina eléctrica** electric cooker; **la cocina de gas** gas cooker
cocinar to cook
cocinero(a) m/f cook
coco m coconut
cóctel m cocktail
código m code; **el código de la circulación** Highway Code; **el código postal** post-code
codo m elbow
codorniz f quail; **las codornices asadas** roast quail
coger to catch; to get; **cogimos el tren** we took the train
cojinetes mpl bearings (in car)
col f cabbage; **las coles de Bruselas** Brussels sprouts
cola f glue; queue
colador m sieve
colchón m mattress; **el colchón inflable** air bed; **el colchón neumático** air bed
coleccionar to collect
colegio m college; school
cólera f anger
colgar to hang (up)
coliflor f cauliflower; **la coliflor al ajo arriero** boiled cauliflower served with a garlic, parsley, paprika and

vinegar sauce; **la coliflor en bechamel** cauliflower in a white sauce

colilla *f*: **no tire colillas** do not drop cigarette ends

colina *f* hill

colirio *m* eye-drops

collar *m* necklace

colmado *m* grocer's

colonia *f* eau-de-Cologne

color *m* colour; **color limón** lemon

colorete *m* blusher

columna *f* column; **la columna de dirección** steering column; **la columna vertebral** spine

combustible *m* fuel

comedia *f* comedy

comedor *m* dining room

comenzar to begin

comer to eat

comercial commercial; business

comerciante *m* merchant

comercio *m* trade; business

comestibles *mpl* groceries

cometa *f* kite

cómico *m* comedian

comida *f* meal; food; lunch; **la comida para niños** baby food; **se sirven comidas** meals served; **comidas caseras** home cooking

comienzo *m* beginning

comisaría *f* police station

como how

cómo: ¿cómo? pardon?;

¿**cómo está?** how are you?; ¿**cómo se llama?** what is your name?

comodidad *f* comfort; **las comodidades** amenities

cómodo(a) comfortable

compañía *f* firm; **la compañía de seguros** insurance company

compartimiento *m* compartment

compartir to share

completo(a) inclusive; **completo** no vacancies

comportarse to behave; **compórtese con el debido respeto** please respect this place of worship

composición *f*: **composición de trenes** list of train carriages

compota *f* preserve; **la compota de frutas** stewed fruit

compra *f* purchase; **compras** shopping; **ir de compras** to go shopping

comprar to buy; **se compra oro/plata** gold/silver bought

compraventa we buy and sell anything

comprender to understand

compresas *fpl* sanitary towels

comprobante *m* receipt; voucher

comprobar to check; **compruebe su cambio**

please check your change
compromiso *m* engagement; appointment; **sin compromiso** without obligation
común common
comunicar to communicate; **estar comunicando** to be engaged
con with
coñac *m* cognac; brandy
concesionario *m* agent
concha *f* sea-shell; **la concha de ensaladilla** a small portion of Russian salad, served as a snack
concierto *m* concert
concurrido(a) busy
concurso *m* competition
condición *f* condition; **las condiciones de circulación** road conditions
condimento *m* seasoning
conducción *f* driving
conducir to drive; **conducir por la derecha** drive on the right; **conducir por la izquierda** drive on the left
conductor(a) *m/f* driver
conectar to connect; to plug in
conejo *m* rabbit; **el conejo a la cazadora** wild rabbit casseroled with ham, bacon, onion, garlic, brandy and thyme; **el conejo con caracoles** wild rabbit stewed with snails; **el conejo**

guisado rabbit stew
confección *f:* **de confección** ready-to-wear; **confecciones caballero** menswear; **confecciones niño** childrenswear; **confecciones señora** ladieswear
conferencia *f* conference; **la conferencia a cobro revertido** reversed charge call; **la conferencia interurbana/a larga distancia** long-distance call
confianza *f* confidence
confirmar to confirm
confitería *f* confectioner's
confitura *f* jam
confundir to mix up
congelado(a) frozen
congelador *m* freezer
congrio *m* conger eel; **el congrio asado** conger eel baked with onions and flavoured with cloves; **el congrio en cazuela** conger eel casseroled with carrots, onions, tomatoes, wine, garlic and parsley
conjunto *m* group; outfit (*clothes*)
conmigo with me
conocer to know (*person*); to meet
conocido(a) *m/f* acquaintance
conseguir to obtain; **conseguir comunicar** to get through

consejo m advice
conserje m caretaker
conservar to keep;
consérvese en lugar fresco y seco keep in a cool, dry place; **conserve su billete** please keep your ticket
conservas fpl tinned foods
consigna f left-luggage office
consomé m consommé; **el consomé de ave** chicken consommé; **el consomé de gallina** chicken consommé; **el consomé al jerez** consommé with sherry; **el consomé madrileño** onion soup
constipado m cold
construcción f building
cónsul m consul
consulado m consulate
consultar to consult
consultorio m surgery; doctor's office
consumidor m consumer
consumir to eat; to use; **consumir preferentemente antes de** best before
contacto m contact
contado m: **al contado** cash down
contador m meter
contagiarse de to catch (illness)
contagioso(a) contagious
contaminación f pollution
contar to tell; to count

contener to hold; to contain
contenido m contents
contento(a) pleased
contestar to answer; **contestar el teléfono** to answer the phone
continuar to continue
continuo(a) continuous
contra against; **contra reembolso** cash on delivery
contrabando m smuggling
contrario m opposite; **al contrario** on the contrary
contrato m contract
contraventana f shutter
control m inspection; check; **el control de pasaportes** passport control; **control de la policía** police checkpoint; **control de seguridad** security check
controlar to check
conveniente suitable
convenir to be suitable; to be convenient
convento m convent; monastery
conversación f conversation
copa f cup; **la copa de helado** mixed ice-cream; **la copa de vino** wineglass
copia f copy; print
coquinas fpl small cockles
corail m intercity train
corazón m heart
corbata f tie
corcho m cork
cordero m lamb; mutton; **la**

pierna de cordero leg of lamb; **el cordero asado** roast leg of lamb; **el cordero en chilindrón** roast lamb with tomato, onion, pepper, garlic, parsley and paprika sauce

cordillera f mountain range

cordón m shoelace

corona f crown

correa f leash; strap; **la correa del ventilador** fanbelt

correcto(a) proper; right

correo m mail; **por correo** by post; **mandar por correo** to post; **por correo aéreo** by air mail

correos m post office

correr to run

correspondencia f mail

corrida de toros f bullfight

corriente f power; current; **la corriente de aire** draught

corsetería f corsetry; lingerie

cortado(a) off (milk); sour

cortar to cut; to turn off

cortarse to cut oneself; **cortarse el pelo** to have a haircut

corte m cut; **el corte de helado** ice-cream wafer; **el corte de pelo** haircut

cortina f curtain

corto(a) short

cosa f thing; **las cosas** stuff

cosecha f harvest; vintage

coser to sew

cosméticos mpl cosmetics

costa f coast

costar to cost

costilla f rib; **la costilla de cerdo** pork chop

costo m cost; expense

costura f sewing; seam

cotizaciones fpl exchange rate

coto m: **coto de caza** hunting by licence; **coto de pescado** fishing by licence

crecer to grow

crecimiento m growth

crédito m credit; **a crédito** on credit

creer to believe; **creo que sí** I think so

crema f cream; **la crema de afeitar** shaving cream; **la crema bronceadora** suntan lotion; **la crema catalana** caramel custard; **la crema de champiñones/espárragos** cream of mushroom/asparagus soup; **la crema dental** toothpaste; **la crema labial** lip salve; **la crema limpiadora** cleansing cream; **la crema de manos** hand cream; **la crema de menta** crème de menthe; **la crema nutritiva** nourishing cream; **la crema para el pelo** conditioner

cremallera f zip

crepé m pancake

crimen *m* crime

crisis *f* crisis

cristal *m* glass; window pane; crystal

cristalería *f* glassware (*shop*); glazier's

croqueta *f* croquette; **las croquetas de camarones** shrimp croquettes

cruce *m* intersection; crossroads; **un cruce de línea** crossed line

cruce giratorio *m* roundabout

crucero *m* cruise; **hacer un crucero** to go on a cruise

crucigrama *m* crossword puzzle

crudo(a) raw

cruz *f* cross

cruzar to cross; **prohibido cruzar las vías** do not cross the railway line

cuaderno *m* exercise book

cuadrado(a) square

cuadro *m* picture; painting; **a cuadros** check; **el cuadro de servicios** timetable

cuajada *f* curd; **la cuajada con miel** curd with honey

cuál which one

cualquier whichever

cualquiera anybody at all

cuando when; **¿cuándo?** when?

cuánto(a) how much; **¿cuánto tiempo?** how long?; **¿cuántos(as)?** how many?

cuarenta forty

cuarentena *f* quarantine

cuarta *f* top (gear)

cuarto *m* room; quarter; **el cuarto de baño** bathroom; **el cuarto de estar** living room; **un cuarto de hora** a quarter of an hour; **las 6 menos cuarto** a quarter to 6; **las 6 y cuarto** a quarter past six

cuarto(a) fourth

cuatro four

cubalibre *m* rum and coke

cubertería *f* cutlery

cubierta *f* deck

cubierto(a) covered; indoor; **los cubiertos** cutlery; **cubierto no. 3** menu no. 3

cubo *m* bucket; pail; **el cubo de la basura** dustbin; **el cubo de flash** flashcube

cubrecama *m* bedspread

cubrir to cover

cuchara *f* spoon; tablespoon

cucharilla *f* teaspoon

cuchillo *m* knife

cucurucho *m* ice-cream cornet

cuello *m* neck; collar

cuenta *f* bill; account (*at bank, shop*); **la cuenta bancaria** bank account; **la cuenta de gastos** expense account; **cuentas corrientes** current accounts; **pagar la cuenta** to check out

cuentakilómetros *m* milometer

cuento *m* story

cuerda *f* string; rope

cuero *m* leather

cuerpo *m* body

cuesta *f* hill; **cuesta arriba/abajo** uphill/downhill

cuestión *f* issue

cueva *f* cave

cuidado *m* care; **¡cuidado!** look out!; **al cuidado de (a/c)** care of, c/o; **cuidado con el perro** beware of the dog

cuidar to look after; **cuidar niños** to babysit; **cuide la compostura** please respect this place of worship

culo *m* bottom, backside

culpa *f* fault; **yo no tengo la culpa** it's not my fault

cultivar to grow

cumbre *f* summit

cumpleaños *m* birthday; **¡feliz cumpleaños!** happy birthday!

cumplido *m* compliment

cumplir to obey; **hoy cumple 20 años** it's his 20th birthday today

cuna *f* cradle; cot

cuñada *f* sister-in-law

cuñado *m* brother-in-law

cuneta *f* roadside

cupón *m* coupon

cupón-respuesta *m* reply coupon

cura *m* priest

curarse to heal

curva *f* bend; curve; **la curva muy cerrada** hairpin bend; **curvas peligrosas en 2 km** dangerous bends in 2 kilometres

D

damas *fpl* draughts

damasquinado(a) inlaid

dañar to damage

dañino(a) harmful

daño *m* damage

dar to give; **dar algo a alguien** to give someone something

dársena *f* dock

dátil *m* date (*fruit*)

datos *mpl* data

de of; from; **1,000 pesetas de gasolina** 1,000 pesetas worth of petrol

debajo under; underneath

deber to owe; **¿cuándo debe llegar?** when is it due to arrive?

debido(a) due

débil weak (*person*)

decidido(a) determined

decidir to decide

décimo(a) tenth

decir to say; to tell

declaración *f* statement

declarar to declare; **nada que declarar** nothing to

declare; **¿algo que declarar?** anything to declare?

declive m slope; **fuerte declive** steep hill

decoración f decoration; home furnishings

dedo m finger; **el dedo del pie** toe

defecto m fault; defect

defectuoso(a) faulty

defensa f defence

deformar to change shape; to warp; **no deforma** will not lose its shape

defunción f funeral

degustación f sampling; **degustación de vinos** wine-tasting

dejar to let; **dejar de hacer algo** to stop doing something; **dejen libre el portón** keep clear; **dejar caer** to drop; **dejen las bolsas a la entrada** please leave your shopping bags at the entrance

del = "**de** + **el**"

delante de in front of

delantero(a) front

delgado(a) slim; thin

delicado(a) delicate

delicioso(a) delicious

demás rest; **todos(as) los/las demás** all the rest

demasiado(a) too much; **es demasiado grande** he's too big

demorar to delay

demostrar to show

denominación f: **denominación de origen** label guaranteeing the quality of wine

dentadura postiza f dentures

dentífrico(a) tooth; **el dentífrico** toothpaste

dentista m/f dentist

dentro (de) inside; **dentro de un mes** in a month's time

departamento m compartment; **departamento extranjero** foreign department

depender de to depend on

dependiente(a) m/f sales assistant

deporte m sport

deportista m/f sportsman/sportswoman

deportivo(a) sporty; sports

depósito m deposit; **el depósito de gasolina** petrol tank

depreciarse to lose value; to depreciate

deprimido(a) depressed

depurador de agua m water purifier

derecha f right(-hand side); **a la derecha** on/to the right

derecho m right; **el derecho a** the right to; **los derechos de aduana** customs duty; **libre de derechos de**

aduana duty-free
derecho(a) right; straight;
  derecho a casa straight
  home
derramar to spill
derretirse to melt
derribar to knock over
derrumbamiento m
  landslide
desabrochar to unfasten
desacuerdo m disagreement
desafilado(a) blunt
desagradable unpleasant
desaguadero m drain
desagüe m drainpipe
desanimado(a) discouraged
desaparecer to disappear
desarrollar to develop
desastre m disaster
desayuno m breakfast
descafeinado(a)
  decaffeinated
descalzo(a) barefoot
descansar to rest
descanso m rest; half-time
descarga f shock (electric)
descargado(a) flat
descenso m descent;
  descenso peligroso steep
  hill
descolgar to pick up; to lift
desconcertado(a)
  embarrassed
descondensador m demister
desconectar to switch off
descongelar to defrost; to
  thaw; to de-ice
desconocido(a) unknown;

strange
describir to describe
descubierto(a) bare
descubrir to discover; to
  find out
descuento m discount; **con
  descuento** at a discount;
  **por favor, no pidan
  descuento** no discounts
  given
desde since; from; **desde
  ayer** since yesterday; **desde
  que** ever since
desdichado(a) unhappy
desear to want; to desire
desechos mpl refuse
desembarcadero m quay
desembarcar to land; to
  disembark
desembocadura f:
  **desembocadura de una
  calle** road junction
desenchufado(a) off;
  disconnected
deseo m desire; wish
desesperado(a) desperate
desfile m parade
desgastar to wear out
desgaste m wear and tear
desgracia f misfortune;
  accident; **por desgracia**
  unfortunately
desgraciado(a) unlucky
deshacer to undo; **deshacer
  las maletas** to unpack
desierto(a) deserted
desinfectante m disinfectant
desinfectar to disinfect

desinflado(a) flat (*deflated*)
deslizarse to glide
desmaquillador *m* make-up remover
desmayarse to faint
desnatado(a) skimmed
desnivel *m* unevenness
desnudar to undress
desnudarse to get undressed
desnudo(a) naked; nude
desobedecer to disobey
desobediente disobedient
desocupado(a) free
desocupar to vacate
desodorante *m* deodorant; **el desodorante en barra** stick deodorant; **el desodorante líquido** roll-on-deodorant
desorden *m* mess
desordenar to make a mess of
despacho *m* office; **el despacho de billetes** ticket office; **el despacho de pan** bakery
despacio slowly; **cierren despacio** close gently
despedida *f* farewell
despedir: despedir a alguien en la estación to see someone off at the station
despedirse to say good-bye
despegue *m* takeoff (*of plane*)
despejado(a) clear; cloudless
despensa *f* larder
desperfecto *m* fault; **desperfectos** damage

despertador *m* alarm (clock)
despertarse to wake up
despierto(a) awake
después after; afterward(s)
destapar to uncover; to uncork
desteñir: no destiñe fast colours
destilería *f* distillery
destinatario *m* addressee
destino *m* destination
destornillador *m* screwdriver
destornillar to unscrew
destruir to destroy
desván *m* attic
desventaja *f* disadvantage; handicap
desvestirse to undress
desviación *f* diversion
desviar to divert
desvío *m* detour; **hacer un desvío** to make a detour; **desvío provisional** temporary detour
detallado(a) itemized; detailed
detalle *m* detail; **en detalle** in detail; **al detalle** retail
detención *f* arrest
detener to arrest
detenerse to pause
detergente *m* detergent; washing-up liquid
deteriorado(a) shop-soiled
detrás (de) behind
deuda *f* debt
devaluación *f* devaluation

devolución *f* repayment; refund; **no se admiten devoluciones** no refunds will be given

devolver to give back; to put back; **devolver el dinero** to repay; **este teléfono no devuelve cambio** this phone does not give change

día *m* day; **todo el día** all day; **el día comercial** weekday; **el día festivo** bank holiday; **el día de fiesta** public holiday; **el día hábil** working day; **el día inhábil** non-working day; **el día laborable** working day; **el día de mercado** market-day; **el día de semana** weekday; **el día de trabajo** working day

diabético(a) *m/f* diabetic

diagnóstico *m* diagnosis

diagrama *m* diagram

dialecto *m* dialect

diamante *m* diamond

diapositiva *f* slide (*photo*)

diario *m* newspaper

diario(a) daily

diarrea *f* diarrhoea

dibujo *m* picture; drawing; **dibujo animado** cartoon

diciembre *m* December

diecinueve nineteen

dieciocho eighteen

dieciséis sixteen

diecisiete seventeen

diente *m* tooth; **los dientes**

postizos false teeth

diez ten

diferencia *f* difference

diferente different

difícil difficult

dificultad *f* difficulty

dínamo *f* dynamo

dinero *m* money; **el dinero (contante)** cash; **el dinero suelto** small change

dios *m* god

diplomático *m* diplomat

dirección *f* direction; address; steering; **la dirección local** local address; **la dirección particular** home address; **la dirección permanente** permanent address; **dirección prohibida** one-way; **dirección única** one-way

directo(a) direct; **el tren directo** through train

director *m* director; president (*of company*); **el director de banco** bank manager; **el director gerente** managing director; **el director de hotel** hotel manager

directora *f* headmistress; manageress

dirigirse a to go towards; to speak to

disco *m* record; disc; **el disco dislocado** slipped disc; **el disco de estacionamiento**

parking disc
discoteca f disco
discrecional optional
disculpa f excuse
disculparse to apologize
discusión f argument
discutir to discuss; to argue
diseño m pattern; design;
  diseños exclusivos
  exclusive designs
disfraz m mask; fancy dress
dislocar to dislocate
disminución f decrease
disminuir to decrease;
  disminuir la marcha to
  reduce speed
disolver to dissolve
disparador m trigger;
  shutter release
disparar to shoot
disponible available
dispositivo m gadget;
  **dispositivo interuterino
  (D.I.U)** I.U.D.
dispuesto(a) ready;
  arranged
disputa f quarrel; dispute
distancia f distance; **a corta
  distancia del mar** within
  easy reach of the sea
distinguir to distinguish
distinto(a) different
distribuidor m distributor;
  **el distribuidor
  automático** vending
  machine
distrito m district; **el
  distrito postal** postal

district
D.I.U. *see* **dispositivo**
diversión f fun
diverso(a) various
divertido(a) amusing
divertirse to enjoy oneself
dividir to divide
divieso m boil (*on skin*)
divisa f foreign currency
divorciado(a) divorced
divorcio m divorce
doblado(a) dubbed
doblar to turn
doble double; **un whisky
  doble** a double whisky
doce twelve
docena f dozen
doctor m doctor
documentación f papers; **la
  documentación (del
  coche)** car logbook
documental m documentary
documento m document
dólar m dollar
doler to hurt; to ache
dolor m ache; pain; **el dolor
  de barriga** stomach ache; **el
  dolor de cabeza** headache;
  el dolor de espalda
  backache; **el dolor de
  garganta** sore throat; **el
  dolor de muelas** toothache;
  el dolor de oídos earache
doloroso(a) painful
domicilio m home address
dominar to control
domingo m Sunday
don m Mister

donación f donation
donde where; **¿de dónde eres?** where are you from?; **¿dónde va?** where are you going?
dorada f sea bream
dormido(a) asleep
dormir to sleep
dormitorio m bedroom
dorso m back; **véase al dorso** P.T.O.
dos two; **dos veces** twice
dosis f dose; dosage
dossier m file
droga f drug
drogadicto(a) m/f drug addict
droguería f shop selling household cleaning articles
ducha f shower; **tomar una ducha** to have a shower; **con ducha** with shower
duda f doubt
dudar to doubt
dueño m owner
dulce sweet; **el dulce** sweet
duodécimo(a) twelfth
duque m duke
duración f: **de larga duración** long-life
durante during; **durante la noche** overnight
durar to last; **¿cuánto tiempo dura el programa?** how long is the programme?
duro(a) tough; hard

E

echado(a) lying (state)
echar to pour; to throw
echarse to lie down; **echarse a perder** to go bad
economía f economy
económico(a) economic; economical
edad f age (of person); **la edad mínima** age limit
edición f edition
edificio m building
edredón m eiderdown; quilt
educación f education
educado(a) polite
efectivo m: **pagar en efectivo** to pay cash
efecto m effect; **los efectos personales** belongings
eficaz effective
eje m axle
ejecutivo m executive
ejemplar m copy (of book)
ejemplo m example; **por ejemplo (p. ej.)** for example
ejercicio m exercise
ejército m army
el the
él he; him
elástico m elastic
elección f election; choice
electricidad f electricity; electrical appliances shop
electricista m electrician
eléctrico(a) electric(al)
electrodomésticos mpl

electrical appliances
elefante m elephant
elegante smart; stylish
elegir to choose
elenco m list; table
elepé m L.P.
elevado(a) high
elevador m elevator
ella she; her
ellas they
ello it
ellos they
embajada f embassy
embajador m ambassador
embalar to pack
embalse m reservoir
embarazada pregnant
embarcadero m jetty
embarcarse to embark; to
board
embargo m embargo
embarque m boarding
emboquillado(a) tipped
emborracharse to get
drunk
embotellamiento m traffic
jam; hold-up
embrague m clutch (of car)
embutidos mpl sausages
emergencia f emergency
emisora f radio station
emitido: emitido por
issued by
empanada f Cornish pasty;
las empanadas de carne
small meat and vegetable pies
eaten hot or cold
empanadilla f pasty with

savoury filling;
empanadilla de salchicha
sausage roll
empanado(a) fried in
breadcrumbs
empaquetar to package
emparedado m open
sandwich
emparrillado(a) grilled
empaste m filling
empezar to begin
emplasto m plaster
empleado(a) m/f employee
emplear to use; to spend
empleo m employment; use
empresa f enterprise;
project; firm
empujar to push; **empuje**
push
en in; into; on; **en avión/
tren/coche** by air/train/car
enaguas fpl petticoat
enamorado(a) in love
encaje m lace
encantado(a) delighted
encantador(a) charming
encargado de in charge of
encargar to order
encargo m: **encargos para
casa** special orders accepted
encendedor m cigarette
lighter
encender to switch on; to
light; **encender una cerilla**
to strike a match; **encender
las luces** switch on
headlights
encendido m ignition

encendido(a) on
enchufar to plug in
enchufe *m* plug; point;
socket; **el enchufe múltiple**
adaptor
encía *f* gum
encima de onto; on top of;
por encima de beyond
encogerse to shrink; **no
encoge** will not shrink
encontrar to find
encontrarse to meet
encrucijada *f* crossroads
encuentro *m* meeting
encurtidos *mpl* pickles
endeudarse to get into debt
endibias *fpl* endives
enemigo *m* enemy
energía *f* energy
enero *m* January
enfadado(a) angry
enfadarse to lose one's
temper
énfasis *m* emphasis; stress
enfermedad *f* disease; illness
enfermera *f* nurse
enfermería *f* infirmary;
first-aid post
enfermo(a) sick; ill
enfrente de opposite
enfriamiento *m* chill
enfriar to chill
engordar to get fat
engranado(a) in gear
engrasar to lubricate
engrase *m* lubrication
¡enhorabuena!
congratulations!

enjuague *m* rinse
enlace *m* connection; **coger
el enlace** to make a
connection; **el enlace de la
autopista** motorway
junction
enlazar to connect; **este
tren enlaza con el tren de
las 16.45** this train connects
with the 16.45
enmarcar to frame
enojado(a) angry
enorme enormous
ensaimada *f* sweet bun
ensalada *f* salad; **la
ensalada de aguacates**
avocado salad; **la ensalada
de anchoas** anchovy, boiled
eggs and vinaigrette salad; **la
ensalada de endibias**
endive salad with Roquefort
cheese dressing; **la ensalada
de frutas** fruit salad; **la
ensalada de lechuga y
tomate** green salad; **la
ensalada mixta** mixed
salad; **la ensalada verde**
green salad
ensaladilla *f:* **la
ensaladilla rusa** Russian
salad
enseñanza *f* teaching;
education
enseñar to teach; to show;
**por favor, enseñen los
bolsos a la salida** please
show your bag when leaving
entender to understand

entero(a) whole
entierro *m* funeral
entonces then
entrada *f* entrance; ticket;
admission; **el precio de
entrada** admission fee;
entrada libre admission
free; **entrada prohibida** no
entry; **entrada por delante**
entrance at the front;
entradas starters
entrantes *mpl* starters
entrar to go in; to come in;
entrar en to enter; **antes de
entrar, dejen salir** let
passengers off first
entre among; between
entreacto *m* interval
entrecot *m* rib steak; **el
entrecot grillé** grilled rib
steak
entrega *f* delivery; **la
entrega de equipajes**
baggage reclaim; **la entrega
de lista** poste restante;
entrega en el acto while-
you-wait; **entrega de
paquetes** parcels to be
collected here
entregar to deliver
entremeses *mpl* hors
d'oeuvres; **los entremeses
de jamón en tacos** diced
Spanish ham; **los
entremeses variados**
assorted hors-d'oeuvres
entresuelo *m* mezzanine
entretener to amuse; to

entertain
entretenido(a) amusing
entusiasmado(a) excited
entusiasmo *m* enthusiasm
envase *m* container; **envase
no retornable** non-
returnable bottle
envenenamiento *m:*
**envenenamiento de la
sangre** blood poisoning
enviar to send
envidioso(a) jealous;
envious
envío *m* shipment
envoltura *f* wrapping
envolver to wrap
epidemia *f* epidemic
epilepsia *f* epilepsy
equilibrio *m* balance;
perder el equilibrio to lose
one's balance
equipaje *m* luggage;
baggage; **la reclamación de
equipajes** baggage claim; **el
equipaje de mano** hand-
luggage; **el equipaje
permitido** luggage
allowance
equipo *m* team; equipment;
kit (*sports*)
equitación *f* horseriding
equivocación *f* mistake
equivocado(a) wrong;
mistaken
eres you are
erizo de mar *m* sea urchin
error *m* error; mistake
es he/she/it is; you are

esa that (*feminine*); **ésa** that one

esas those (*feminine*); **ésas** those ones

esbelto(a) slim

escabechado(a) pickled

escabeche *m* spicy marinade; **en escabeche** pickled; in a marinade; **el escabeche de pescado** marinated fish

escala *f* stopover

escalar to climb

escaldar to scald

escalera *f* flight of steps; stairs; ladder; **la escalera de incendios** fire escape; **la escalera mecánica** escalator; **la escalera de tijera** stepladder

escalón *m* step (*stair*); **el escalón central** ramp; **escalón lateral** steep verge

escalope *m* escalope; **los escalopes de ternera** veal escalopes

escama *f* flake; scale (*of fish*); **las escamas de jabón** soap-flakes

escanciador *m* wine waiter

escapar(se) to escape

escaparate *m* shop window

escape *m* exhaust

escarabajo *m* beetle

escarcha *f* frost

escarchado(a) glacé

escarlata scarlet

escarpado(a) abrupt; steep

escayola *f* plaster

escayolar to put in plaster

escenario *m* stage

esclava *f* name bracelet

escoba *f* broom

escobilla (para pipas) *f* pipe cleaner

escocés(esa) Scottish

Escocia *f* Scotland

escoger to choose

escombro *m* mackerel

escombros *mpl* rubbish

esconder to hide

escota *f* sheet (*sailing*)

escribir to write

escrito: por escrito in writing

escritor *m* writer

escritura *f* writing

escuchar to listen; to listen to

escuela (primaria) *f* primary school

escupir: prohibido escupir en el suelo no spitting on the floor

escurrir to wring

ese that (*masculine*); **ése** that one

esencial essential

esfuerzo *m* effort

esmalte *m* enamel; **el esmalte para las uñas** nail polish

esmeralda *f* emerald

eso that

esos those; **ésos** those ones

espacio *m* space

espaguetis *mpl* spaghetti; **los**

espaguetis boloñesa spaghetti bolognese
espalda f back
España f Spain
español(a) Spanish
espantoso(a) dreadful
esparadrapo m sticking plaster
espárrago m asparagus; **los espárragos gigantes** large asparagus; **los espárragos trigueros** wild asparagus
espátula f spatula
especial special; particular
especialidad f speciality
especialista m consultant
especias fpl spices
especie f kind; **una especie de judía** a kind of bean
espécimen m specimen
espectáculo m entertainment; show; **el espectáculo de variedades** variety show
espectador(a) m/f spectator
espejo m mirror; **el espejo retrovisor** rear-view mirror
espera f wait
esperanza f hope
esperar to hope; to wait (for); **espero que sí/no** I hope so/not
espeso(a) thick
espetos mpl barbecued sardines
espina f fishbone; spine
espinaca f spinach; **las espinacas con pasas y piñones** spinach with raisins and pine kernels
espinazo m spine
espinilla f shin
esponja f sponge
esposa f wife
esposo m husband
espray m spray
espuma f foam; **la espuma de afeitar** shaving foam
espumoso(a) frothy; sparkling; **el espumoso** sparkling wine
esq. see **esquina**
esquí m skiing; ski; **el esquí acuático** water-skiing; **hacer esquí acuático** to go water-skiing
esquiador(a) m/f skier
esquiar to ski
esquina f street corner; **esquina (esq.) Goya y Corrientes** on the corner of Goya St. and Corrientes St.
esta this; **ésta** this one
establecimiento m shop
estación f (railway) station; season; stop; bus station; **la estación de autobuses** terminal (buses); **la estación de servicio** petrol station; **la estación de metro** underground station; **la estación marítima** port
estacionado(a) parked
estacionamiento m parking
estacionar to park
estadio m stadium; football

ground

estado *m* state; **el estado del tiempo** weather conditions

Estados Unidos (EE.UU.) *mpl* United States

estampilla *f* postage stamp

estancia *f* stay

estanco *m* tobacconist's (shop)

estanquero(a) *m/f* tobacconist

estaquilla *f* tent peg

estar to be (*temporary state*); **está Ud en lugar sagrado** this is a place of worship

estas these; **éstas** these ones

estatua *f* statue

este[1] this; **éste** this one

este[2] *m* east

esterilizar to sterilize

estilo *m* style

estilográfica *f* fountain pen

estimado(a): estimada Señora Dear Madam; **estimado Señor Smith** Dear Mr Smith

esto this

estofado *m* stew; **el estofado de vaca con patatas** beef stew with potatoes

estómago *m* stomach

estorbar to get/be in the way (of)

estornudar to sneeze

estornudo *m* sneeze

estos(as) these

estrangulador *m* choke (*of car*)

estrecho(a) narrow

estrella *f* star

estreñido(a) constipated

estreñimiento *m* constipation

estreno *m* première; new release; **el estreno de gala** grand première

estropeado(a) out of order

estructura *f* structure

estudiante *m/f* student

estudiar to study

estudio *m* studio

estufa *f* stove

estúpido(a) stupid

etapa *f* stage; phase

etiqueta *f* label; ticket; tag; **de etiqueta** formal

Europa *f* Europe

europeo(a) European

evidente obvious

evitar to avoid

exacto(a) accurate; exact; precise

examen *m* examination; **el examen de conducir** driving test

examinar to examine

excelente excellent

excepción *f* exception

excepto except (for); excepting

excesivo(a) unreasonable

exceso *m* excess; **el exceso de equipaje** excess baggage; **el exceso de velocidad** speeding

exclusivo(a) exclusive

excursión f tour; excursion; outing; **la excursión en autocar** coach trip; **la excursión a pie** hike
excursionismo m hiking
exigir to demand
existir to exist
éxito m success
expedición f expedition
expedido(a) issued
expedidor m: **el expedidor del telegrama** the sender of the telegram
expedir to send
experiencia f experience
experimentado(a) experienced
experto m expert
explicación f explanation
explicar to explain
exponer: no exponer a los rayos solares do not expose to sunlight; **no exponer a temperaturas superiores a...** do not expose to temperatures above...
exportación f export
exportar to export
exposición f exhibition; show
exposímetro m exposure meter
expreso m express train
exprimidor m lemon-squeezer
exquisito(a) delicious
extender to stretch; to extend; to spread

extensión f extension
exterior outside
externo(a) outside; external
extintor m fire extinguisher
extranjero(a) m/f foreigner; **en el extranjero** abroad
extraño(a) peculiar; odd; strange
extremidad f limb
extremo m end

F

fabada f Asturian dish made of beans, pork sausage and bacon
fábrica f factory; **la fábrica de cerveza** brewery
fabricación f manufacturing; **la fabricación en serie** mass production
fabricante m manufacturer
fácil easy
facilidades fpl easy terms
facilitar to make easy; to supply; **facilite el cambio** please have your change ready
factor m guard
factura f receipt; bill; **la factura desglosada** itemized bill
facturación f: **la facturación de equipajes** luggage check-in
faisán m pheasant
falda f skirt; **la falda**

escocesa kilt; **la falda pantalón** culottes; **la falda plisada** pleated skirt

fallar to go wrong; to fail

fallo m failure

falso(a) false

falta f defect; shortage

faltar to be missing

fama f reputation

familia f family

famoso(a) famous

farmacéutico(a) m/f chemist

farmacia f chemist's shop; **la farmacia de guardia** duty chemist

faro m headlamp; headlight; lighthouse; **el faro antiniebla** fog-lamp

farol m lamppost

favor m favour; **por favor** please

f.c. see **ferrocarril**

febrero m February

fecha f date; **fecha de caducidad** valid until; best before; **fecha de expedición** date of issue

felicidad f happiness

felicitaciones fpl congratulations

feliz happy

felpudo m doormat

femenino(a) feminine

feo(a) ugly

feria f trade fair; fun fair

feroz fierce

ferretería f hardware store

ferretero m ironmonger

ferrobús m local train

ferrocarril (f.c.) m railway; **por ferrocarril** by rail

festín m feast

festivos mpl public holidays

fiambre m cold meat; **el fiambre variado** slices of assorted cold meats

fianza f security

fiar: no se fía no credit given

fibra f fibre; **la fibra de vidrio** fibre-glass

ficha f chip (in gambling); token; counter

fideos mpl spaghetti; noodles; **fideos a la catalana** thick soup with pork rib, bacon, onion, tomato, garlic and noodles

fiebre f fever; **tener fiebre** to have a temperature; **la fiebre del heno** hay fever

fiesta f party; public holiday

figón m bar; economical restaurant

fijador m styling mousse

fijar to fix; to fasten

fijo(a) fixed; firm; set

fila f row

filatelia f collector's stamp shop

filete m fillet; **el filete de lomo (de vaca)** rump steak; **los filetes de lenguado** rolled sole baked with wine, mushrooms and butter

filial f branch

film(e) *m* film
filtro *m* filter; **el filtro de aceite** oil filter; **el filtro de aire** air filter; **con filtro** filter-tipped; **sin filtro** plain
fin *m* end; **el fin de semana** weekend; **por fin** at last
final final; **el final** end
financiero(a) financial
finca *f* farm; property
fino *m* light, dry, very pale sherry
fino(a) fine; thin
firma *f* signature
firmar to sign
firme firm; **firme en mal estado** poor road surface; **firme deslizante** slippery surface
flaco(a) thin
flan *m* cream caramel; **el flan de la casa** homemade cream caramel; **el flan con guindas** cream caramel with black cherries; **el flan con nata** cream caramel with whipped cream
flash *m* flashlight
flatulencia *f* wind
flequillo *m* fringe
flete *m* freight; **el flete por avión** air freight
flojo(a) slack; weak (*tea*); mild
flor *f* flower
florero *m* vase
florista *m/f* florist
floristería *f* florist's

flotador *m* rubber ring (*for swimming*)
flotar to float
flúor *m* fluoride
foco *m* spotlight
foie-gras *m* liver pâté
folleto *m* brochure
fonda *f* inn; tavern; small restaurant
Fondillón *m* dark red wine from Alicante
fondo *m* bottom; background; back (*of hall, room*)
fontanería *f* plumbing
fontanero *m* plumber
footing *m* jogging
forastero *m* stranger
forfait *m* lift pass
forma *f* form; shape
formulario *m* form
forro *m* lining
fortaleza *f* fortress
fortuito(a) accidental
fósforo *m* match
foto *f* picture; photo
fotocopia *f* photocopy; **se hacen fotocopias en el acto** photocopies while you wait
fotografía *f* photography; photograph
fotógrafo *m* photographer
fotómetro *m* light meter
fractura *f* fracture
frágil fragile; handle with care
frambuesa *f* raspberry

francés(esa) French
Francia *f* France
franela *f* flannel
franqueo *m* postage
frasco *m* flask
frazada *f* blanket
fregadero *m* sink
fregar to mop; **fregar los platos** to wash up
freiduría *f* fried-fish restaurant
freír to fry
frenar to put on the brakes; to brake
freno *m* brake; **el líquido de frenos** brake fluid; **el freno de pie** foot-brake; **el freno de mano** hand-brake; **los frenos de disco** disc brakes
frente[1] *f* forehead
frente[2]: **en frente** opposite; **frente a** facing; **de frente** head-on
fresa *f* strawberry; **las fresas con nata** strawberries with cream
fresco(a) fresh; crisp; cool
fresón *m* large strawberry
frigorífico *m* refrigerator
frío(a) cold; **sírvase frío** serve chilled; **tengo frío** I'm cold
fritada *f*: **la fritada de pimientos y tomates** fried green peppers, tomatoes, onion and garlic
frito(a) fried; **un huevo frito** a fried egg

fritura *f* mixed fried fish or meat
frontera *f* border; frontier
frotar to rub
fruta *f* fruit; **la fruta escarchada** candied fruit; **la fruta del tiempo** fresh fruit of the season
frutería *f* fruit shop
frutos secos dried fruit and nuts
fuego *m* fire; **fuegos artificiales** fireworks; **¿tiene fuego?** have you got a light?; **prohibido hacer fuego** it is forbidden to light fires
fuente *f* fountain
fuera outdoors; out; **está fuera** he's out
fuera-borda *f* speedboat
fuerte strong; loud
fuerza *f* force; strength
fuga *f* leak (*gas*)
fumador(a) *m/f* smoker; **no fumadores** non-smokers
fumar to smoke; **prohibido fumar** no smoking; **no fumar** no smoking
funcionar to run; to work; **no funciona** out of order
furgón de equipajes *m* baggage car
furgoneta *f* van
fusible *m* fuse
fútbol *m* football

G

gachas *fpl* creamed cabbage and potatoes

gafas *fpl* glasses; **las gafas de bucear** goggles; **las gafas de esquí** ski goggles; **las gafas de sol** sunglasses

galería de arte *f* art gallery

Gales *m* Wales

galés(esa) Welsh

gallego(a) Galician

galleta *f* biscuit; **las galletas saladas** savoury biscuits

gallina *f* hen

gallo *m* cock(erel)

galón *m* gallon

gamba *f* prawn; **las gambas al ajillo** garlic-fried prawns; **las gambas con gabardina** prawns fried with batter; **las gambas al pil-pil** prawns cooked with garlic, oil and red pepper; **las gambas a la plancha** grilled prawns

gamuza *f* chamois (leather)

ganado *m* cattle

ganador(a) *m/f* winner

ganar to win; to earn

ganas *fpl*: **tener ganas de hacer algo** to feel like doing something

ganga *f* bargain

ganso *m* goose

garaje *m* garage

garantía *f* guarantee

garantizado guaranteed

garantizar to guarantee

garbanzo *m* chickpea

garganta *f* throat

gargantilla *f* choker

garrafa *f* decanter

gas *m* gas; **el gas butano** Calor gas; **con gas** fizzy; **sin gas** non-fizzy

gasa *f* gauze; nappy

gaseosa *f* lemonade; fizzy drink

gasfitero *m* plumber

gasoil *m* diesel fuel

gasóleo *m* diesel oil

gasolina *f* petrol; **gasolina normal** 3-star petrol; **gasolina super** 4-star petrol

gasolinera *f* petrol station

gastar to spend; to use

gasto *m* expense; **los gastos** expenditure

gastrónomo *m* gourmet

gato *m* cat; jack (*for car*)

gaviota *f* seagull

gazpacho *m* cold soup made with tomatoes, onion, cucumber, green peppers and garlic

generación *f* generation

género *m* type; material; **los géneros de punto** knitwear

generoso(a) generous

gente *f* people

gerente *m/f* manager/ manageress

gesto *m* gesture

gimnasio *m* gym(nasium)

ginebra *f* gin

ginecólogo(a) m/f
gynaecologist
girar to turn; **girar** twist
giro m: **giros y
transferencias** drafts and
transfers; **el giro postal**
money order; postal order
gitano(a) m/f gypsy
glándula f gland
globo m balloon
glorias fpl pastries with an
almond and sweet potato
filling
glorieta f roundabout
gobernador m governor
gobierno m government
gol m goal
golf m golf
golpe m blow; stroke
golpear to hit; to beat; to
bump; **golpearse la cabeza**
to bang one's head
goma f rubber; gum; **la
goma de borrar** rubber; **la
goma de mascar** chewing
gum
goma-espuma f foam
rubber
gordo(a) fat
gorro de baño m bathing
cap
gota f drop; **las gotas
nasales** nose drops
gotear to leak; to drip
grabado m print; engraving
gracias thank you
gracioso(a) funny
grada f tier; **gradas** terraces

gradería f terrace
grado m degree; grade
gramática f grammar
gran see **grande**
granada f pomegranate
Gran Bretaña f Great
Britain
grande large; great; tall;
wide
grandes almacenes mpl
department stores
granero m barn
granizo m hail
granja f farm; milk bar
grano m spot; pimple
grapa f staple
grapadora f stapler
grasa f fat; grease; lubricant
gratén: al gratén with a
cheese and browned
breadcrumb topping
gratinado(a) au gratin
gratis free of charge
grave serious; deep
gravilla suelta f loose
chippings
grelo m young turnip
grieta f crack
grifo m tap
gripe f flu
gris grey; dull
gritar to scream
grito m shout; cry
grosella f red currant; **la
grosella espinosa**
gooseberry; **la grosella
negra** blackcurrant
grosero(a) rude

grúa *f* crane; breakdown van
grueso(a) thick
grupo *m* party; group; **el grupo sanguíneo** blood group
gruta *f* grotto; cave
guante *m* glove
guantera *f* glove compartment
guapo(a) handsome; pretty
guardabarros *m* mudguard
guardacostas *m* coastguard
guardar to put away
guardarropa *m* cloakroom
guardería *f* nursery
guardia *f* guard; **el Guardia Civil** Civil Guard; **Guardia Civil de Carreteras** traffic police; **el guardia de tráfico** traffic warden
guarnición *f*: **la guarnición de legumbres** garnish of vegetables
guerra *f* war
guía *m/f* courier; guide; **la guía telefónica** telephone directory
guinda *f* black cherry
guisantes *mpl* peas
guiso *m* stew
guitarra *f* guitar
gustar to like; to enjoy; **¿le gustaría una taza de café?** would you like a cup of coffee?
gusto *m* taste; pleasure

H

haba *f* broad bean; **las habas a la catalana** broad beans with ham, onions and tomatoes stewed in white wine; **las habas con jamón** broad beans sautéed with diced ham; **las habas a la rondeña** broad beans fried with red peppers, tomatoes, onions and ham
habano *m* cigar
habichuelas *fpl* haricot beans
hábil skilful
habitación *f* room; **la habitación doble** double room; **una habitación individual** a single room
habitante *m* inhabitant
habitar to live (in)
hablar to speak; to talk; **¿habla Ud inglés?** do you speak English?; **se habla inglés** English spoken
hacer to do; to make; **hace calor** it is hot; **hace frío** it's cold; **hacer una foto** to take a photo; **hace sol** it's sunny; **se hacen trajes a medida** suits made to measure; **hacer noche** to stay overnight; **hace una semana** one week ago
hacia toward(s); **hacia adelante** forwards; **hacia**

atrás backwards; **conducir hacia atrás** to reverse
hacienda f farm; ranch
hallar to find
hamaca f hammock
hambre f hunger; **morirse de hambre** to starve; **tengo hambre** I am hungry
hamburguesa f hamburger; **la hamburguesa con guarnición** a hamburger served with chips or vegetables
hamburguesería f hamburger restaurant
harina f flour
hasta until; till; ¡**hasta luego!** see you soon!
hay there is/there are
hecho(a) finished; done; ripe (*cheese*); **hecho a mano** handmade; **poco hecho** underdone; rare; **hecho a la medida** made to measure
helada f frost; **peligro - en heladas** danger - ice on road
heladería f ice-cream parlour
helado m ice-cream; **el helado de mantecado** vanilla ice-cream; **el helado de nata** plain ice-cream; **el helado de turrón** almond ice-cream; **el helado de tutti-frutti** assorted fruit ice-cream; **el helado de vainilla** vanilla ice-cream
helar to freeze
hélice f propeller

helicóptero m helicopter
hemorragia f haemorrhage
hemorroides fpl haemorrhoids
heno m hay
herbolario m health food shop
herida f injury; wound
herido(a) injured
hermana f sister
hermanastra f stepsister
hermanastro m stepbrother
hermano m brother
hermético(a) air-tight
hermoso(a) beautiful
herpes fpl shingles
herramienta f tool
hervido(a) boiled
hervidor m kettle
hervir to boil
hidropedal m pedal boat
hielo m ice; **con hielo** on the rocks
hierba f grass; herb
hierbabuena f mint
hierro m iron
hígado m liver; **el hígado con cebolla** fried calf's liver with onions; **el hígado de ternera salteado** sautéed calf's liver served with a wine, parsley, butter and garlic sauce
higiénico(a) hygienic
higo m fig; **los higos chumbos** prickly pears; **los higos pasos** dried figs
hija f daughter

hijastra *f* stepdaughter
hijastro *m* stepson
hijo *m* son
hilas *fpl* lint
hilo *m* thread; linen
hincha *m* fan
hinchazón *f* swelling
hipermercado *m* superstore
hípica *f* showjumping
hipo *m* hiccups
hipódromo *m* racecourse
historia *f* story; history
hogar *m* fireplace; home; household goods
hoja *f* leaf; blade; sheet of paper; **la hoja de afeitar** razor blade
hojaldre *m* puff pastry
hola hullo; hello
hombre *m* man; **el hombre de negocios** businessman
hombro *m* shoulder
hondo(a) deep
honrado(a) honest
hora *f* hour; **¿qué hora es?** what's the time?; **las horas de oficina** opening hours; **hora prescrita de llegada** time due; **hora prevista de llegada** expected arrival time; **las horas puntas** rush hour; **las horas de recogida** times of collection
horario *m* timetable; **el horario de salidas** departure board; **el horario de caja** opening hours; **el horario atención al**

público opening hours
horario(a) hourly
horchata de chufa *f* cold drink made from almonds
horizonte *m* horizon
hormiga *f* ant
hormigón *m* concrete
hornillo *m*: **el hornillo de camping gas** camping stove
horno *m* oven; **al horno** baked; roasted
horquilla *f* hairpin
hortalizas *fpl* vegetables
hospedaje *m* hostel
hospedería *f* hostel
hospital *m* hospital
hostal *m* bed and breakfast
hotel *m* hotel
hoy today
hueco(a) hollow
huelga *f* strike
huérfano(a) *m/f* orphan
huerta *f* orchard
hueso *m* bone; stone (*in fruit*)
huésped *m* host; guest
huéspedes *mpl* guest house
huevas *fpl* roe; **las huevas de bacalao** cod roe; **las huevas de merluza** hard hake roe
huevería *f* poultry shop
huevo *m* egg; **el huevo hilado** garnish made with egg yolk and sugar; **el huevo pasado por agua** soft-boiled egg; **los huevos de aldea** free-range eggs; **los huevos con chorizo** baked eggs with

Spanish sausage; **los huevos duros** hard-boiled eggs; **los huevos escalfados** poached eggs; **los huevos a la española** stuffed eggs with a cheese sauce; **los huevos a la flamenca** baked eggs with ham and peas; **los huevos fritos** fried eggs; **los huevos fritos al nido** eggs fried in thick slices of bread; **los huevos con migas** fried eggs with fried breadcrumbs; **los huevos con patatas** fried eggs and chips; **los huevos al plato** baked eggs; **los huevos revueltos** scrambled eggs

humedad *f* moisture

húmedo(a) wet; damp

humo *m* smoke

humor *m* mood; **de mal humor** in a bad temper; **de buen humor** in a good mood

hundirse to sink

huracán *m* hurricane

I

ida *f* departure; **de ida y vuelta** return

idea *f* idea

identificar to identify

idioma *m* language

iglesia *f* church

igual even; equal; **me da igual** I don't care

ileso(a) unhurt

ilimitado(a) unlimited

iluminación *f* lighting

imán *m* magnet

impaciente impatient; eager

impar odd; **impares** parking allowed on odd days of month

impedir to prevent

imperdible *m* safety pin

impermeable waterproof; **el impermeable** raincoat

importación *f* import

importante important

importar: no importa it doesn't matter

importe *m* amount; **el importe exacto** exact amount; **el importe final** final total; **el importe de la factura** the amount of the bill

imposible impossible

imprescindible vital

impresionante amazing; impressive

impreso *m* form

impresos *mpl* printed matter; **impresos certificados** registered printed matter

imprevisto(a) unexpected

impuesto *m* tax; **el impuesto sobre la renta** income tax; **el impuesto al valor añadido (I.V.A.)** V.A.T.

incapacitado(a) disabled

incendio *m* fire (*accident*); **en caso de incendio rompan el cristal** break

glass in case of fire
inclinar to tip (tilt)
inclinarse to lean
incluido(a) included; including
incluir to include
incluso(a) included; including
incómodo(a) uncomfortable
inconsciente unconscious
inconveniente m trouble; problem
incumplimiento m: **el incumplimiento de contrato** breach of contract
indemnización f compensation
independiente independent; self-contained
indicaciones fpl directions
indicador m gauge; **el indicador de dirección** indicator
indicativo m dialling code; **el indicativo de la población** dialling code of the town
índice m index; index finger
individual individual; single
industria f industry
infarto m heart attack
infección f infection
infeccioso(a) infectious
inferior inferior; lower
inflable inflatable
inflador m air bed pump
inflamable inflammable
inflamación f inflammation

inflamado(a) inflamed
inflar to inflate
información f information (office)
informaciones fpl information desk
infracción f offence; **la infracción de tráfico** traffic offence
ingeniero m engineer
ingenioso(a) clever
Inglaterra f England
inglés(esa) English; **en inglés** in English; **se habla inglés** English spoken
ingreso m entrance; **ingresos** deposits
inmediatamente at once; immediately
inmobiliaria f estate agent's
inmueble m property
innecesario(a) unnecessary
inocente innocent
inoculación f inoculation
inodoro m toilet
inoportuno(a) inconvenient
inoxidable stainless; rustproof
inquieto(a) worried
inquilino m tenant
inscribirse to check in
insecticida m insecticide
insecto m insect
insistir to insist
insolación f sunstroke
insólito(a) unusual
insoportable unbearable
inspección f inspection;

survey
instalación *f*: **la instalación sanitaria** plumbing; **las instalaciones deportivas** sports facilities
instalarse to move in; to settle in
instante *m* moment; **al instante** right away
instituto *m* institute; **el instituto de belleza** beauty salon; **el instituto de segunda enseñanza** secondary school
instrucciones *fpl* directions; instructions
instrumento *m* instrument
insulina *f* insulin
insulto *m* insult
integral: pan integral wholemeal bread
íntegro(a) complete
inteligencia *f* intelligence
intención *f* intention; **tener la intención de hacer algo** to intend to do something
intentar to attempt
interés *m* interest
interesante interesting
interior inside
intermedio *m* interval
intermitente *m* indicator; **el intermitente de emergencia** hazard lights
internacional international
intérprete *m* interpreter
interrumpir to disturb; to interrupt

interruptor *m* switch
interurbano(a) long-distance
intoxicación *f*: **la intoxicación por alimentos** food poisoning
intransitable blocked; closed to traffic
introducir to introduce; to insert; **introduzca monedas** insert coins
inundación *f* flood
inútil useless
inválido *m* invalid
inventario *m* stocktaking; inventory
invernadero *m* greenhouse
invertir to invest
investigación *f* research
invierno *m* winter; **los deportes de invierno** winter sports
invitación *f* invitation
invitado(a) *m/f* guest
invitar to invite
inyección *f* injection
inyectar to inject
ir to go
Irlanda *f* Ireland
irlandés(esa) Irish
irrompible unbreakable
irse to go away; to leave
isla *f* island
itinerario *m* route; schedule
I.V.A. *see* **impuesto**; **I.V.A. incluido** VAT included
izquierda *f* left; **torcer hacia la izquierda** to turn

left
izquierdo(a) left; **el lado izquierdo** the left side

J

jabalí m wild boar
jabón m soap; **el jabón líquido** liquid soap; **el jabón en polvo** washing powder; soap powder; **el jabón de tocador** beauty soap
jacinto m hyacinth
jamás never
jamón m ham; **el jamón de Jabugo** Andalucian cured ham; **el jamón serrano** cured ham; **el jamón de Trevélez** a mild cured ham from Granada
jaqueca f migraine
jarabe m syrup; **el jarabe para la tos** cough syrup
jardín m garden; **el jardín botánico** botanical gardens; **jardín zoológico** zoo
jardinero m gardener
jarra f jug; **la jarra de cerveza** glass of beer
jaula f cage
jefe m chief; head; boss; **el jefe de cocina** chef; **el jefe de estación** station master; **el jefe de tren** guard
jengibre m ginger
jerez m sherry
jeringa f syringe

jersey m sweater; pullover
jornada f day
joven young
joya f jewel; **las joyas** jewellery; **las joyas de fantasía** costume jewellery
joyería f jeweller's
joyero m jeweller; jewel box
jubilado(a) m/f pensioner
judías fpl beans; **las judías blancas** white haricot beans; **las judías con chorizo** white haricot beans cooked with sausage, potatoes and onion; **las judías encarnadas a la madrileña** red haricot beans with bacon, garlic, onion and sausage; **las judías salteadas con gambas** sautéed beans with prawns; **las judías salteadas con jamón** sautéed beans with ham; **las judías verdes** French beans; **las judías verdes a la riojana** boiled green beans with sausage, bacon, onion and fried pork chops
judío(a) Jewish
juego m game; **el juego de cartas** card game; **un juego de tenis** a game of tennis; **prohibidos los juegos de pelota** ball games prohibited
juerga f party
jueves m Thursday
juez m judge

jugador(a) *m/f* player; **el jugador de golf** golfer
jugar to play; to gamble; **jugar bien al golf** to be good at golf
jugo *m* juice
juguete *m* toy
juguetería *f* toy shop
julio *m* July
jumbo *m* jumbo jet
Jumilla *m* dry red wine from Murcia
junio *m* June
juntarse to gather
junto(a) together; **¿están juntos?** are you together?
jurar to swear
justicia *f* justice
justo(a) fair
juvenil junior
juventud *f* youth
juzgar to judge

K

kilo *m* kilo; **un kilo de** a kilo of
kilogramo *m* kilogramme
kilometraje *m* = mileage; **kilometraje ilimitado** unlimited mileage
kilómetro *m* kilometre
kilovatio *m* kilowatt

L

la the; her; it
labio *m* lip

laborable working (*day*); **laborables** weekdays; **laborables de 9 a 20 h** in force weekdays from 9am to 8pm
laboratorio *m* laboratory
labrador *m* farmer
laca *f* hair spray
lado *m* side; **al lado de** beside
ladrón *m* thief; burglar
lago *m* lake
lágrima *f* tear
lampa *f* spade
lámpara *f* lamp; **la lámpara indicadora** pilot light; **la lámpara fluorescente** fluorescent light
lampistería *f* electrical repairs
lana *f* wool; **de lana** woollen; **pura lana virgen** pure new wool; **lanas** wool shop
lancha *f* launch; **la lancha motora** speedboat; motorboat; **la lancha de socorro** lifeboat
langosta *f* lobster
langostino *m* large prawn
lanolina *f* lanolin
lápiz *m* pencil; **el lápiz de color** crayon; **el lápiz de labios** lipstick; **el lápiz para cejas** eyebrow pencil
largo(a) long; **a largo plazo** long-term
largometraje *m* feature film

laringitis f laryngitis
las them; the
lasaña f lasagna
lástima f: ¡qué lástima!
what a pity!
lastimar to hurt
lastimarse to be injured; to
hurt oneself
lata f can (container); tin; en
lata tinned; canned
lateral side
Latinoamérica f Latin
America
latinoamericano(a) Latin
American
lavable washable
lavabo m lavatory; washbasin
lavadero m laundry room
lavado(a): lavado(a) a la
piedra stonewashed; lavado
en seco dry-cleaning;
lavado y engrase car wash
and oil put in; lavado y
marcado shampoo and set
lavadora f washing machine
lavandería f laundry; la
lavandería automática
launderette; laundry
lavaparabrisas m
windscreen washer
lavaplatos m dishwasher
lavar to wash
lavarse to wash oneself
laxante m laxative
le him; you; to him/her/it/you
leche f milk; con leche white
(coffee); la leche
condensada condensed

milk; la leche desnatada
skimmed milk; la leche
entera full cream milk; la
leche evaporada evaporated
milk; la leche fresca fresh
milk; la leche frita thick
slices of custard fried in
breadcrumbs; la leche
hidratante moisturizer; la
leche de larga duración/
uperizada long-life milk; la
leche merengada milk and
egg sorbet; la leche en
polvo dried milk
lechería f dairy
lechero m milkman
lechón m sucking pig
lechuga f lettuce
leer to read
legumbres fpl vegetables;
pulses
lejano(a) distant
lejía f bleach
lejos far
leña f firewood
lencería f lingerie; linen;
draper's
lengua f language; tongue; la
lengua en salsa de nueces
tongue with a walnut and
wine sauce; la lengua de
ternera en salsa picante
cooked veal tongue oven-
baked and with a butter,
onion, gherkin and caper
sauce; las lenguas de gato
sponge fingers
lenguado m sole; lemon sole;

el lenguado meunière fried sole baked in the oven with butter and lemon sauce; **el lenguado a la plancha** grilled lemon sole; **los lenguados rellenos** fillet of sole stuffed with shrimps or prawns

lente f lens; **las lentes de contacto** contact lenses

lentejas fpl lentils

lento(a) slow

Léon m light dry wine from Northern Spain

león m lion

leotardos mpl tights

les them; you; to them/you

letra f letter (of alphabet)

letrero m notice

levantar to lift

levantarse to get up; to rise

ley f law

libertad f freedom

libra f pound (currency, weight); **la libra esterlina** sterling

libre free; vacant; for hire (taxi); **libre de impuestos** tax-free; **dejen libre el portón** keep clear

librería f bookshop

librito m: **el librito de papel de fumar** packet of cigarette papers

libro m book; **el libro de bolsillo** paperback; **existe libro de reclamaciones** a complaints book is provided

licencia f licence; degree; **la licencia de conducir** driving licence

licor m liqueur; **los licores** spirits

liebre f hare; **la liebre estofada con judías** hare stew with French beans

ligero(a) light (not heavy)

lima f file; lime; **el zumo de lima** lime juice; **la lima de uñas** nailfile

límite m limit; boundary; **el límite de velocidad** speed limit

limón m lemon

limonada f lemon drink

limpiador(a) cleaning; cleansing

limpiaparabrisas m windscreen wiper

limpiar to clean; to polish; **limpiar en seco** to dry-clean

limpieza en seco f dry cleaning

limpio(a) clean

línea f line; **la línea está cortada** the line is dead; **las líneas aéreas** airlines

lino m linen

linterna f torch

lío m fuss; **armar un lío** to make a fuss

liquidación f liquidation; **liquidación total** clearance sale; closing down sale

líquido m liquid; **el líquido**

de frenos brake fluid
lisa f grey mullet
liso(a) plain
lista f list; **la lista de
correos** poste restante; **la
lista de espera** waiting list;
la lista de precios price
list; **la lista de vinos** wine
list
listo(a) ready; clever;
listo(a) para comer ready-
cooked
litera f bunk; berth;
couchette; **litera reservada**
reserved berth; **literas** bunk
beds
litoral m coast
litro m litre
llama f flame
llamada f call; **la llamada
automática** direct-dialled
call; **la llamada
interurbana** long-distance
call; **la llamada telefónica**
telephone call; **la llamada a
través de la operadora**
operator-dialled call; **la
llamada urbana** local call
llamar to call; **llamar por
teléfono** to telephone
llamarse to be called; **me
llamo Paul** my name is Paul
llano(a) flat; even
llanta f tyre
llave f key; **la llave de
contacto** ignition key; **la
llave inglesa** spanner; **la
llave maestra** master key;

la llave de socorro
emergency handle; **se hacen
llaves en el acto** keys made
while you wait
llavero m key ring
Lleg. see **llegada**
llegada f arrival; **llegadas
(Lleg.)** arrivals; **llegada
nacional** domestic flights
(arrival)
llegar to arrive; to come
llenar to fill; to fill in/out
lleno(a) full; **lleno de** full of
llevar to bring; to wear; to
carry; to take; **para llevar**
to take away
llorar to cry
llover to rain
llovizna f drizzle
llueve it's raining
lluvia f rain
lluvioso(a) rainy; wet
lo it; him
lobo m wolf
local m: **el local** premises;
bar; **local climatizado** air-
conditioned premises
localidad f place; **las
localidades** tickets
loción f lotion; **la loción
contra los insectos** insect
repellent; **la loción para
después del afeitado**
aftershave (lotion); **la loción
desmaquillante** make-up
removal lotion
loco(a) mad; crazy
lograr to get; to manage

lombarda f red cabbage
lomo m: **el lomo de cerdo** loin of pork; **el lomo relleno** stuffed loin of pork
lona f canvas
loncha f slice; **en lonchas** sliced
Londres m London
longaniza f red sausage
longitud f length
loro m parrot
los them; the
loza f crockery
lubina f bass; **la lubina cocida** boiled bass; **lubina a la flor de tomillo** bass seasoned with thyme
lubricantes mpl lubricants
luces see luz
lucio m pike
lugar m place; **el lugar de nacimiento** place of birth; **el lugar de expedición** issued in; **en lugar de** instead of
lujo m luxury; **de lujo** de luxe
lujoso(a) luxurious
luna f moon; **la luna de miel** honeymoon
lunes m Monday
lustrar to polish
luz f light; **apagar la luz** to put out the light; **encender la luz** to put on the light; **las luces de detención** brake lights; **las luces de estacionamiento** parking lights; **las luces**

laterales/de posición side lights; **la luz de marcha atrás** reversing light; **la luz roja** red light; **la luz trasera** rear light

M

macarrones mpl macaroni; **los macarrones al gratén** macaroni in cheese browned in the oven; **los macarrones con tomate** macaroni with tomato sauce
macedonia (de frutas) f fresh fruit salad
maceta f flowerpot
madera f wood; **de madera** made out of wood; wooden
madrastra f stepmother
madre f mother
madrugada f dawn; early morning
maduro(a) ripe; mature
maestro(a) m/f primary schoolteacher
magnetófono m tape recorder
magnífico(a) magnificent; great
mahonesa f mayonnaise
maicena f cornflour
maíz m maize; **el maíz en la mazorca** corn-on-the-cob
mal[1] m evil; **el mal de alturas** mountain/air sickness
mal[2] see malo

Málaga *m* sweet, dark dessert wine
mala hierba *f* weed
malestar *m* discomfort; annoyance
maleta *f* case; suitcase
maletero *m* boot (*of car*)
Mallorca *f* Majorca
malo(a) bad
Malta *f* Malta
malva mauve
mamá *f* mum(my)
mañana tomorrow; **la mañana** morning; **mañana por la mañana** tomorrow morning
mancha *f* stain; mark
Mancha *f* the English Channel
mandar to send; **mandar por correo** to post
mandarina *f* tangerine
mandíbula *f* jaw
mandos *mpl* controls
manejar to drive
manera *f* manner; way
manga *f* sleeve
mango *m* handle; mango
manguera *f* hose
manicura *f* manicure
manitas *fpl*: **las manitas de cerdo** pig's trotters
mano *f* hand; **a mano** by hand; **de segunda mano** used; **las manos de cerdo** pig's trotters
manopla *f* facecloth
manso(a) tame

manta *f* blanket; **la manta eléctrica** electric blanket; **la manta de viaje** travelling rug
mantel *m* tablecloth
mantelería *f* table linen
mantener to support; to maintain; **por favor mantengan las puertas despejadas** please do not block the doors; **manténgase en posición vertical** this way up; keep upright; **manténgase fuera del alcance de los niños** keep out of reach of children; **mantenga limpia la ciudad** keep your city tidy
mantequería *f* grocer's
mantequilla *f* butter
manual *m* handbook
manzana[1] *f* apple; **las manzanas al horno** baked apples; **las manzanas rellenas** stuffed apples
manzana[2] *f* block (*area, distance*)
manzanilla *f* camomile tea; dry, sherry-type wine
mapa *m* map; **el mapa de carreteras** road map
maquillaje *m* make-up
máquina *f* machine; **la máquina de coser** sewing machine; **la máquina de afeitar** electric razor; **la máquina de escribir** typewriter; **la máquina de**

fotos camera
maquinaria f machinery;
**maquinaria pesada en
movimiento** heavy
machinery on the move
maquinilla de afeitar f
razor
maquinista m engine driver
mar m sea
maravilloso(a) wonderful;
marvellous
marca f make; brand
marcar to dial; to mark
marcha f march
marcha atrás f reverse gear;
en marcha atrás in reverse
(gear)
marcharse to leave
marco m frame
marea f tide; **la marea baja**
low tide; **la marea alta** high
tide
mareado(a) dizzy; **estar
mareado** to be seasick
mareo m seasickness;
giddiness
marfil m ivory
margarina f margarine
margarita f daisy
marido m husband
marina f navy
marinera: a la marinera
in a fish or seafood sauce
marinero m sailor
mariposa f butterfly
mariscos mpl seafood;
shellfish
marisquería f seafood

restaurant
mármol m marble
marrón brown
marroquí Moroccan
marroquinería f leather
goods; leather goods shop
Marruecos m Morocco
martes m Tuesday; **el
martes de carnaval** Shrove
Tuesday
martillo m hammer
marzo m March
más more; plus; **más allá de**
beyond
masaje m massage
masajista m/f masseur/
masseuse
masculino(a) masculine
mástil m mast
matador m bullfighter
matar to kill
materia f material; subject
material m material; **de
material** leather
Maternidad f Maternity
Hospital
matinal morning
matrícula f registration
number
matrimonio m marriage;
married couple
matrona f midwife
máximo m maximum
mayo m May
mayonesa f mayonnaise
mayor senior; elder;
mayores de 18 años over-
18s

mayoría f majority; **la mayoría de la gente** most people

mayorista m wholesaler

mayúscula f capital letter

mazapán m marzipan

mazo m mallet

me me; to me

mecánico m mechanic

mecha f wick; **ponerse mechas** to have one's hair streaked

mechero m lighter

medallones mpl: **los medallones de ternera** small sirloin of veal steaks

media f stocking

mediano(a) medium; middling

medianoche f midnight; **a medianoche** at midnight; **las medianoches** small slightly sweet buns

mediante by means of

medicina f medicine; drug

médico m doctor; **el médico odontólogo** dentist

medida f measurement; size; **a la medida** made-to-measure

medio(a) half; **el medio** the middle; **el medio ambiente** the environment; **a medio camino** halfway; **la media hora** half an hour

mediodía m midday; noon; **a mediodía** at midday

medios mpl means

medir to measure; **¿cuánto mide?** how tall are you?

Mediterráneo m: **el Mediterráneo** the Mediterranean (Sea)

medusa f jellyfish

mejilla f cheek

mejillón m mussel; **los mejillones en escabeche** tinned mussels in a spicy sauce; **los mejillones a la marinera** mussels in white wine; **los mejillones al vapor** steamed mussels; **los mejillones vinagreta** mussels in vinaigrette sauce

mejor better; best

mejora f improvement

mejorana f marjoram

mejorar to improve; to get better

melaza f molasses; treacle

melocotón m peach; **los melocotones en almíbar** tinned peaches; **los melocotones naturales** fresh peaches

melón m melon; **el melón con jamón** melon with cured ham

membrillo m quince

memoria f memory

menaje m kitchen utensils; **el menaje de cocina** kitchenware; **el menaje de hogar** household goods

mendigo m beggar

menestra f vegetable stew

menor least; **menores** all ages (*at cinema*)

Menorca *f* Minorca

menos minus; less; except; **niños de menos de 10 años** children under 10

mensaje *m* message

mensajero *m* messenger

mensual monthly

menta *f* mint; peppermint

mente *f* mind

mentir to tell a lie

mentira *f* lie

mentolado(a) mentholated

menú *m* menu; **menú fijo** table d'hôte

menudencias *fpl* offal; giblets

menudillos *mpl* giblets

menudo(a) small; **a menudo** often

mercado *m* market; **el mercado de divisas** foreign exchange market

Mercado Común *m* Common Market

mercancías *fpl* goods; **mercancías peligrosas** dangerous goods

mercería *f* haberdasher's

merendar to have a snack

merendero *m* open-air snack bar

merengue *m* meringue

meridional southern

merienda *f* tea (*meal*); picnic

merluza *f* hake; **la merluza cocida con vinagreta** hake boiled and served with vinaigrette sauce; **la merluza imperial** boiled hake served with vegetables and mayonnaise; **la merluza a la plancha** grilled hake; **la merluza a la romana** hake fried in batter; **la merluza en salsa verde** hake in parsley sauce; **la merluza con sidra** hake baked with clams, onions and cider; **la merluza a la vasca** hake casseroled with clams and asparagus

mermelada *f* jam; **la mermelada de naranjas** marmalade

mero *m* grouper; **el mero emparrillado** grilled grouper

mes *m* month

mesa *f* table

mesón *m* reasonably priced restaurant

meter to put

método *m* method

métrico(a) metric

metro *m* metre; underground

mexicano(a) Mexican

México *m* Mexico

mezcla *f* mixture; motorbike petrol

mezclarse to mix

mezquita *f* mosque

mi my

mí me

microbio m germ
microbús m minibus
micrófono m microphone
miedo m fear; **tener miedo** to be scared
miel f honey
mientras while
miércoles m Wednesday
migas fpl fried breadcrumbs
migraña f migraine
mil thousand
miligramo m milligramme
mililitro m millilitre
milímetro m millimetre
militar military
milla f mile
millón m million
millonario m millionaire
mimbre m wicker
mimbrería f wickerwork
mina f mine (for coal etc)
miniatura f miniature
mínimo m minimum
ministerio m ministry; **el Ministerio de Asuntos Exteriores** Foreign Office
ministro m minister
minusválido(a) handicapped
minuto m minute
mío(a) my; **el/la mío(a)** mine
miope short-sighted
mirada f look
mirador m viewpoint
mirar to look at
mis my
misa f mass

mismo(a) same
misterio m mystery
mitad f half; **a mitad de precio** half-price
mixto(a) mixed
mochila f rucksack
moda f fashion; **modas** clothes shop; **moda infantil** children's clothes
modales mpl manners
modelo m model; style; make; **modelo a cumplimentar para solicitar moneda extranjera** fill out this form when ordering foreign currency; **modelos exclusivos** exclusive models
modista f dressmaker
modo m way; manner; **modo de empleo** directions for use
mojado(a) wet
mojama f salted tuna
mojarse to get wet
moldeador m soft perm
molestar to bother; to annoy; **no molestar** do not disturb
molestia f bother; nuisance
molido(a) ground
molino m mill; **el molino de viento** windmill
mollejas fpl sweetbreads
momento m instant; moment
monasterio m monastery
moneda f currency; coin; **introduzca monedas** insert

coins; **la moneda
extranjera** foreign currency
monedero *m* purse
monja *f* nun
monje *m* monk
mono *m* monkey
mono(a) pretty
montaña *f* mountain
montañismo *m*
mountaineering
montar to ride; **montar a
caballo** to ride a horse;
montar en bicicleta to ride
a bicycle
montilla *m* a dry sherry
montón *m*: **un montón de** a
lot of
monumento *m* monument
mora *f* mulberry; blackberry
morado(a) purple
moraga *f*: **moraga de
sardinas** barbecued sardines
morcilla *f* black pudding
mordedura *f* bite
morder to bite
moreno(a) dark(-skinned)
morir to die
morros *mpl* pig's or calf's
cheeks; **los morros y sesos
de ternera a la vinagreta**
calf's cheeks and brains
cooked and served with a
vinaigrette sauce and capers;
**los morros de ternera a la
vizcaína** calf's cheeks cooked
with onions, red peppers and
garlic
mosca *f* fly

moscarda *f* bluebottle
Moscatel *m* sweet white wine
mosquitero *m* mosquito net
mostaza *f* mustard
mosto *m* grape juice
mostrador *m* counter
mostrar to show; to
demonstrate
motivo *m* reason
motocicleta *f* motorbike
motociclista *m/f*
motorcyclist
motoneta *f* motor scooter
motor *m* engine; motor
mousse *f* mousse; **la mousse
de chocolate** chocolate
mousse; **la mousse de
limón** lemon mousse
mover to move
movimiento *m* motion;
movement
mozo *m* porter
muchacha *f* girl; maid
muchacho *m* boy
muchedumbre *f* crowd
mucho(a) a lot (of); much;
very; **me gusta mucho** I
like it very much
muchos(as) many
mudar to change
mudo(a) dumb
mueble *m* piece of furniture;
los muebles furniture
(shop)
muela *f* tooth
muelle *m* quay; pier; spring
muerte *f* death
muerto(a) dead

muestra f exhibition; sample

mujer f woman; wife; **la mujer de la limpieza** cleaning lady; **la mujer de negocios** businesswoman

muleta f crutch

multa f fine

mundo m world

muñeca f wrist; doll

murciélago m bat (*animal*)

muro m wall

músculo m muscle

museo m museum

música f music

musical m musical instruments shop

músico(a) m/f musician

muslo m thigh

musulmán(ana) Muslim

muy very

N

nabo m turnip

nácar m mother-of-pearl

nacer to be born

nacimiento m birth

nación f nation

nacional national

nacionalidad f nationality

nada nothing; **no veo nada** I can't see anything; **de nada** don't mention it

nadador(a) m/f swimmer

nadar to swim

nadie no one; nobody

naipe m playing card

naranja¹ f orange

naranja² orange (*colour*)

naranjada f orangeade

naranjado(a) orange

narciso m daffodil

nariz f nose

nata f cream; **la nata batida** whipped cream

natación f swimming

natillas fpl egg custard; **las natillas de la casa** homemade egg custard

natural natural; unsweetened

naturista nudist

náusea f nausea

navaja f pocketknife; penknife

navegar to sail

Navidad f Christmas; **el día de Navidad** Christmas Day

neblina f fog

nebuloso(a) foggy

necesario(a) necessary

necesitar to need; **se necesita** needed

negar to deny

negarse to refuse

negativo m negative

negocios mpl business

negro(a) black

nervio m nerve

nervioso(a) tense; nervous

neumático m tyre

nevar to snow

nevera f refrigerator

ni nor; **ni...ni** neither...nor

nido m nest

niebla f fog; mist

nieta f granddaughter

nieto *m* grandson
nieve *f* snow
nilón *m* nylon
niña *f* girl; baby girl
ningún, ninguno(a) none;
  en ninguna parte nowhere
niño *m* boy; baby; **los niños**
  children; **los niños también**
  pagan children pay full price
níspero *m* medlar
nivel *m* level; standard
no no; not
no. *see* **número**
no alcohólico(a)
  nonalcoholic
noche *f* night; **de una noche**
  overnight; **esta noche**
  tonight
nochebuena *f* Christmas Eve
nochevieja *f* New Year's Eve
nocivo(a) harmful
no fumador *m* non-smoker
nombre *m* name; **el nombre**
  de pila first name
noreste *m* northeast
normal normal; ordinary
noroeste *m* northwest
norte *m* north
nosotros(as) we; us
nota *f* note; mark
notar to notice
notaría *f* solicitor's office
notario *m* notary; solicitor
noticiario *m* news bulletin;
  newsreel
noticias *fpl* news
novela *f* novel
noveno(a) ninth

noventa ninety
novia *f* bride; girlfriend;
  fiancée
noviembre *m* November
novio *m* bridegroom;
  boyfriend; fiancé
nube *f* cloud
nublado(a) cloudy
nudillo *m* knuckle
nudo *m* knot
nuera *f* daughter-in-law
nuestro(a) our
nueve nine
nuevo(a) new
nuez *f* nut; walnut; **la nuez**
  moscada nutmeg; **las**
  nueces con nata y miel
  walnuts with cream and
  honey
núm *see* **número**
numerado(a) numbered
número *m* number; size;
  issue; **el número del**
  abonado the subscriber's
  telephone number; **el**
  número de matrícula
  registration number; **el**
  número de teléfono
  telephone number; **coja su**
  número take a number
nunca never
nutrir to feed

O

o or; **o...o...** either...or...
obedecer to obey
obispo *m* bishop

objetivo *m* camera lens; **el objetivo granangular** wide-angle lens; **el objetivo zoom** zoom lens

objeto *m* object; **los objetos de valor** valuables; **los objetos de regalo** gifts

oblongo(a) oblong

obra *f* work; **la obra de teatro** play; **la obra de arte** work of art

obras *fpl* road works

obrero *m* workman; **obreros trabajando** men at work

observar to watch

obstáculo *m* obstacle

obstrucción *f* blockage

obstruir to block; **por favor no obstruyan las puertas** please stand clear of the doors

obtener to obtain

obturador *m* shutter (*camera*)

occidental western

océano *m* ocean

ochenta eighty

ocho eight

ocio *m* spare time

octavo(a) eighth

octubre *m* October

ocupado(a) engaged; busy

ocurrir to happen

odio *m* hatred

oeste *m* west

ofensivo(a) rude

oferta *f* offer; special offer

oficial official

oficina *f* office; **la oficina**
de objetos perdidos lost property office; **la oficina de turismo** tourist office

Oficina de Correos *f* the Post Office

oficio *m* church service; occupation

ofrecer to offer; **se ofrece/ofrécese** offered

oído *m* hearing; ear

oír to hear

ojo *m* eye; **¡ojo!** careful, look out; **ojo, pinta** wet paint

ola *f* wave

oler to smell

olla *f* pot; **la olla de garbanzos** chick-pea, bacon and cabbage stew; **la olla podrida** spicy hotpot; **la olla a presión** pressure cooker

olmo *m* elm

olor *m* smell

oloroso *m* cream sherry

olvidar to forget

ombligo *m* navel

ómnibus *m* bus; stopping train

once eleven

onda *f* wave; **la onda corta** short wave; **la onda larga** long wave; **la onda media** medium wave

onza *f* ounce

ópera *f* opera

operación *f* operation

operador(a) *m/f* telephone operator

opinar: opino que... I think that...

opinión f view; opinion

oporto m port wine

oportunidad f opportunity; **oportunidades** bargains

oprimir to press

óptica f optician's

óptico m optician

óptimo(a) excellent

opuesto(a) opposite

orden f command; **por orden de la dirección** by order of the management

oreja f ear

orfebrería f gold/silver work

organización f organization

organizado(a) organised

organizador m steward

organizar to organize

oriental eastern; oriental

orilla f shore; **la orilla del mar** seaside

orín m rust

orinal de niño m potty

ornamento m ornament

oro m gold; **de oro** gold

orquesta f orchestra

oscuro(a) dark; dim

oso m bear

ostra f oyster

otoño m autumn

otro(a) other

ovalado(a) oval

oveja f sheep

oxidado(a) rusty

P

pabellón m: **el pabellón de deportes** sports centre

paciente m/f patient

padre m father; **los padres** parents

paella f rice dish of chicken, shellfish, garlic, saffron and vegetables

pagado(a) paid; **pagado por adelantado** paid in advance

pagar to pay for; to pay; **pagar al contado** to pay cash

pagaré m I.O.U.

página f page

pago m payment; **pago(s) al contado** cash only accepted

pague: pague en caja please pay at the cashdesk

país m country

paisaje m scenery; **paisajes pintorescos** scenic route

paja f straw

pájaro m bird

pajita f drinking straw

pala f shovel; spade

palabra f word

palacio m palace

palanca f lever; **la palanca de cambio** gear lever

palco m box (in theatre)

pálido(a) pale

palillo m toothpick

palmera[1] f palm-tree

palmera[2] f small sweet puff

pastry

palmito *m* palm heart

palo *m* stick; mast; **el palo de esquí** ski stick; **el palo de golf** golf club

paloma *f* pigeon; dove

palta *f* avocado pear

pan *m* bread; loaf of bread; **el pan de centeno** rye bread; **el pan de higos** dried figs with spices; **el pan integral** wholemeal bread; **el pan de molde** sliced bread; **el pan tostado** toast; **el pan de nueces** walnut and raisin cake

pana *f* corduroy

panadería *f* bakery

panadero *m* baker

pañal *m* nappy; **los pañales de usar y tirar** disposable nappies

panecillo *m* roll

paño *m* flannel; cloth; **el paño higiénico** sanitary towel

panqueque *m* pancake

pantalla *f* screen; lampshade

pantalones *mpl* pair of trousers; trousers; **el pantalón de sport** casual trousers; **el pantalón vaquero** jeans; **los pantalones cortos** shorts

pantys *mpl* tights

pañuelito *m:* **los pañuelitos**

mojados baby wipes

pañuelo *m* handkerchief; **el pañuelo de papel** tissue (*handkerchief*)

papa *f* potato; **las papas fritas** chips; French fries

papá *m* dad(dy)

papel *m* paper; **el papel de cartas** writing pad; **el papel de envolver** wrapping paper; **el papel de escribir** stationery; **los papeles de fumar** cigarette papers; **el papel higiénico** toilet paper; **el papel pintado** wallpaper; **el papel timbrado** paper with official stamp

papelera *f* waste paper basket; **use las papeleras** please use the litter bins provided

papelería *f* stationer's

paperas *fpl* mumps

papilla *f* baby cereal

paquete *m* packet; parcel

paquetería *f* haberdasher's

par[1] *m* pair; **un par de** a couple of; **pares sueltos** odd pairs

par[2]: **un número par** an even number; **pares** parking allowed on even days of month

para for; towards

parabrisas *m* windscreen

paracaídas *m* parachute

parachoques *m* bumper

parada _f_ stop; **la parada de autobús** bus stop; **la parada discrecional** request stop; **la parada de taxis** taxi rank

parador _m:_ **el parador nacional** state-run inn

paragolpes _m_ bumper

paraguas _m_ umbrella

paraíso _m_ gallery (_theatre_)

paralizado(a) paralysed

parar to stop

parcela _f_ plot of land

parecer to seem; to look

parecido(a) similar

pared _f_ wall

pareja _f_ pair

pariente _m/f_ relation

parlamento _m_ parliament

párpado _m_ eyelid

parque _m_ park; **el parque de atracciones** amusement park; **el parque de bomberos** fire station; **el parque infantil** children's playground

parquímetro _m_ parking meter

parra _f_ vine

parrilla _f_ grill; **a la parrilla** grilled

parrillada _f_ grilled meat or fish; barbecue

parroquia _f_ parish church

parte[1] _f_ part

parte[2] _m_ report; **el parte meteorológico** weather forecast

particular particular; private

partida _f_ departure

partido _m_ political party; match (_sport_); round of golf

partir to depart

pasa _f_ raisin; currant

pasado(a) off (_meat_); past; **pasado mañana** the day after tomorrow; **muy pasado** well done; **poco pasado** rare; **la semana pasada** last week

pasaje[1] _m_ alleyway

pasaje[2] _m_ ticket; fare

pasajero(a) _m/f_ passenger

pasamano _m_ handrail

pasaporte _m_ passport; **el pasaporte familiar** joint passport

pasar to pass; to spend (_time_); **pasarlo bien** to have a good time; **pase sin llamar** enter without knocking

pasarela _f_ gangplank

pasatiempo _m_ hobby

Pascua _f_ Easter

pase _m:_ **los pases de favor** complimentary tickets

paseo _m_ walk; avenue; promenade; **el Paseo Colón** Columbus Avenue; **dar un paseo** to go for a walk; **dar un paseo en coche** to go for a drive

pasillo _m_ corridor; passage; gangway

paso _m_ step; pace; **el paso**

elevado footbridge; **el paso de ganado** cattle crossing; **el paso inferior** subway; **el paso a nivel** level crossing; **el paso de peatones** pedestrian crossing; **el paso sin guarda** open level crossing; **el paso subterráneo** subway; **los pasos de contador** telephone meter units; **prohibido el paso a personal no autorizado/a toda persona ajena** no unauthorised personnel allowed

paso(a) dried

pasta f pastry; pasta; **las pastas** pastries; spaghetti; **la pasta dentífrica** toothpaste; **la pasta de dientes** toothpaste

pastel m cake; **los pasteles** pastries; **el pastel de tortilla** omelettes of different flavours in layers separated by mayonnaise

pastelería f cake and confectionery shop; cakes and pastries

pastilla f tablet (*medicine*); **la pastilla de jabón** bar of soap; **las pastillas para el mareo** seasickness tablets

pastor m minister

patada f kick

patata f potato; **las patatas al ajillo** potatoes fried with garlic and parsley; **las patatas en ajo pollo** potatoes cooked in a sauce made with garlic, almonds, bread, parsley and saffron; **las patatas bravas** hot spicy potatoes; **las patatas fritas** French fries; **las patatas fritas a la inglesa** crisps; **las patatas al gratén con queso** potatoes and ham with cheese sauce browned under grill; **las patatas guisadas** potatoes cooked with pork ribs, paprika and onion; **las patatas a la riojana** fried potatoes in a spicy pepper and chilli sauce

patinaje m skating; ice-skating

patinazo m skid

patines mpl roller skates

patio m patio; courtyard

pato m duck; **pato a la naranja** duck in orange sauce

patrón m pattern

patrulla f patrol

pavo m turkey; **el pavo trufado** turkey with truffle stuffing

paz f peace

P.D. P.S.

peaje m toll

peatón m pedestrian; **peatón, en carretera circula por tu izquierda** pedestrians should keep to the left

peces *mpl* fish

pecho *m* breast; chest

pechuga *f* breast (*poultry*);
la pechuga de pollo
chicken breast

pedazo *m* bit; piece

pediatra *m/f* paediatrician

pedicuro *m* chiropodist

pedido *m* order; request

pedir to ask for

pedregoso(a) stony

pegamento *m* gum

pegar to stick (on)

peinado *m* hair-style

peinar to comb

peine *m* comb

p. ej. *see* ejemplo

peladilla *f* sugared almond

pelar to peel

peldaño *m* doorstep; stair

pelea *f* fight

peletería *f* furrier's

película *f* film; la película
de miedo horror film

peligro *m* danger; peligro
de incendio danger of fire;
peligro de muerte danger -
keep out; peligros diversos
danger

peligroso(a) dangerous; no
peligroso(a) safe

pelo *m* hair

pelota *f* ball

peltre *m* pewter

peluca *f* wig

peluquería *f* hairdresser's;
barber's; la peluquería de

caballeros barber's

peluquero(a) *m/f* hairdresser

pena: ¡qué pena! what a
pity!

pendiente *m* earring

pene *m* penis

Penedés *m* good quality table
wine and sparkling white
wine

penicilina *f* penicillin

pensar to think

pensión *f* lodgings; boarding
house; bed and breakfast; la
pensión completa full
board; la media pensión
half board

peor worse

pepinillo *m* gherkin

pepino *m* cucumber

pepitoria: a la pepitoria
stewed with onions, tomatoes
and green peppers

pequeño(a) little; small;
slight

pera *f* pear

percebe *m* edible barnacle

percha *f* coat hanger; peg

perder to miss (*train*); to
lose; perder el tiempo to
waste one's time

perderse to lose one's way

pérdida *f* loss

perdido(a) lost

perdiz *f* partridge; la perdiz
a la cazadora partridge
cooked with shallots,
mushrooms, herbs and wine;
la perdiz estofada partridge

stew; **las perdices con
chocolate** partridges in red
wine and chocolate-flavoured
sauce; **las perdices
escabechadas** pickled
partridges
perdón m pardon; ¡**perdón!**
sorry!
perdonar to forgive;
perdonen las molestias we
apologise for any
inconvenience
perejil m parsley
perezoso(a) lazy
perfecto(a) perfect
perforar: no perforar do
not pierce
perfume m perfume
perfumería f perfume shop
periódico m newspaper
periodista m/f reporter;
journalist
período m period;
menstruation
perla f pearl
permanecer to stay;
**permanezcan en sus
asientos** please remain seated
permanencia f stay
permanente f perm
permiso m permission; pass;
permit; **con permiso** excuse
me; **el permiso de
conducir** driving licence; **el
permiso de residencia**
residence permit; **el
permiso de trabajo** work
permit

permitido(a) permitted
**permitir: no se permite
llevar envases a la grada**
no bottles or cans may be
taken onto the stand
pero but
perro m dog; **el perro
caliente** hot dog; **perros no**
no dogs allowed
persianas fpl blinds
persona f person
personal personal; **el
personal** personnel; staff
persuadir to persuade
pertenecer a to belong to
pesadilla f nightmare
pesado(a) heavy
pesar to weigh
pesca f fishing; **la pesca
salada** salted fish
pescadería f fishmonger's
pescadilla f whiting; baby
hake; **las pescadillas al
vino** whiting cooked in wine,
stock and butter and then
oven-baked
pescado m fish
pescador m fisherman
peseta f peseta
pésimo(a) dreadful
peso m weight; **al peso** by
weight
pesquero m fishing boat
pestaña f eyelash
pestiños mpl crisp honey-
fritters
petaca f tobacco pouch
petróleo m petroleum

pez *m* fish; **el pez espada** swordfish
picadillo *m* minced beef
picado(a) chopped; minced
picadura *f* bite (*by insect*); sting; cut tobacco
picante peppery; hot; spicy
picar to itch; to sting
picatostes *mpl* pieces of fried bread usually accompanied by hot chocolate
pichón *m* pigeon
pico *m* peak
pidan: no pidan descuento no discounts given
pie *m* foot
piedra *f* stone; **la piedra preciosa** gem; **las piedras de mechero** flints
piel *f* fur; skin; leather; **la piel de carnero** sheepskin
pierna *f* leg; **la pierna de cordero** leg of lamb
pieza *f* part; **la pieza de repuesto** spare part
pijama *m* pyjamas; fruit dessert with custard
pila *f* battery
píldora *f* pill; the pill; **tomar la píldora** to be on the pill
piloto *m* pilot; captain
pilotos *mpl* sidelights
pimentón *m* paprika
pimienta *f* pepper; **a la pimienta** au poivre
pimiento *m* pepper (*vegetable*); **el pimiento**
verde/rojo green/red pepper; **el pimiento morrón** red pepper; **los pimientos fritos** fried small green peppers; **los pimientos rellenos** stuffed peppers
piña *f* pineapple; **la piña en almíbar** tinned pineapple; **la piña natural** fresh pineapple
pinacoteca *f* art gallery
pinchazo *m* blow-out; puncture
pincho *m:* **el pincho morruno** shish kebab
pino *m* pine
piñones *mpl* pine kernels
pintar to paint
pintor *m* painter
pintura *f* paint; painting
pinza *f* clothes-peg
pinzas *fpl* tweezers
piononos *mpl* small Swiss rolls
pipa *f* pipe
pipirrana *f* a salad of tomatoes, peppers, cucumber, onion, tuna and boiled egg
piragua *f* canoe
piragüismo *m* canoeing
Pirineos *mpl* Pyrenees
pisar to step on; to tread on
piscina *f* swimming pool; **la piscina cubierta** indoor pool; **la piscina para niños** paddling pool
piso *m* floor; flat; **el primer piso** first floor; **piso**

deslizante slippery road

pista f track; **la pista de aterrizaje** runway; **la pista de baile** dance floor; **la pista de esquí** ski run; **la pista de patinaje** skating rink; **la pista de tenis** tennis court

pisto m sautéed peppers, onions, aubergines, tomatoes and garlic; **el pisto manchego** sautéed tomatoes, aubergines, peppers and ham with beaten egg mixed in

pitillera f cigarette case

pitillo m cigarette

pizarra f slate; blackboard

pizca f pinch (of salt etc)

pizza f pizza

placa f number plate

placer m pleasure

plancha f iron (for clothes); **a la plancha** grilled

planeta m planet

plano m plan; town map

plano-guía m: **plano-guía de la ciudad** city plan

planta f plant; sole; **la planta baja** ground floor; **la planta sótano** basement

plástico m plastic

plata f silver; **plata de ley** sterling silver

plataforma f platform

plátano m banana

platea f stalls (theatre)

platería f jeweller's

platija f plaice

platillo m saucer

platino m platinum

platinos mpl contact points

plato m plate; dish (food); course; **el plato del día** set menu; **el plato fuerte** main course; **los platos fríos** cold starters

playa f beach; **la playa naturista** nudist beach

plaza f square; **la plaza del mercado** marketplace; **la plaza de toros** bull ring; **plazas libres** vacancies; parking space available; **plazas limitadas** limited number of seats available

plazo m period; expiry date

plazoleta f square

plazuela f square

pleamar f high tide

plegable folding

plomero m plumber

plomo m lead

pluma f feather; pen; **la pluma estilográfica** fountain pen

población f population

pobre poor

poco(a) little; **un poco** a little; **un poco de** a bit of

pocos(as) a few

poder to be able

podólogo m chiropodist

podrido(a) rotten

policía f police; **el policía** police officer; policeman

polideportivo m sports

centre
polietileno *m* polythene
político(a) political
póliza *f* policy; **la póliza de seguros** insurance policy
pollería *f* poultry shop
pollo *m* chicken; **el pollo al ajillo** garlic-fried chicken; **el pollo asado** roast chicken; **el pollo a l'ast** spit-roasted chicken; **el pollo a la buena mujer** chicken casserole with onions, bacon, potatoes and brandy; **el pollo a la cacerola** chicken casserole; **el pollo a la catalana** sautéed chicken with mussels and prawns, covered with tomato sauce; **el pollo al chilindrón** chicken garnished with tomatoes and peppers; **el pollo estofado** casseroled chicken with potatoes, mushrooms, shallots and brandy; **el pollo a la pepitoria** casseroled chicken in herbs, garlic, almonds and sherry
polvo *m* dust; powder; **el polvo de talco** talcum powder; **los polvos faciales** face powder
pomada *f* ointment
pomelo *m* grapefruit
ponche *m* punch
poner to put; to place; to switch on; **poner a media luz** to dip (*headlights*)

poney *m* pony
popa *f* stern
popular popular
póquer *m* poker
por for; per; through; about; **¿por qué?** why?; **100 km por hora** 100 km per hour; **20 por ciento** 20 per cent; **por supuesto** of course; **por día/semana** per day/week
porcelana *f* china; porcelain
porción *f* helping; portion
por favor please
porque because
porrón *m* glass wine jar with a long spout
porrusalda *f* cod, potato and leek soup
portaequipajes *m* luggage rack; boot
portafolio *m* briefcase
portamonedas *m* purse
portátil portable
portería *f* caretaker's office
portero *m* caretaker; doorman
portón *m* door
Portugal *m* Portugal
portugués(esa) Portuguese
posada *f* inn; lodgings
poseer to own
posible possible
posición *f* position
postal postal; **la (tarjeta) postal** postcard
poste *m* mast; post; **el poste indicador** signpost
posterior back; later

postre m dessert; sweet; **el postre de músico** dessert of assorted nuts and raisins

potable drinkable

potaje m stew; thick vegetable soup; **el potaje de garbanzos** thick chickpea soup; **el potaje de habichuelas** thick haricot bean soup; **el potaje de lentejas** thick lentil soup

pote gallego m stew with potatoes, pig's trotters and ears

potente powerful

práctico(a) convenient; practical

precaución f caution; **precaución, obras** drive carefully, roadworks ahead

precio m price; **el precio del cubierto** cover charge; **el precio de entrada** entrance fee; **el precio fijo** set price; **el precio de oferta** sale price; **el precio del viaje** fare

precioso(a) precious; beautiful

precipicio m cliff

preciso(a) precise; necessary

preferentemente preferably

preferir to prefer

prefijo m dialling code; **el prefijo de acceso a internacional** international dialling code

pregunta f question; **hacer una pregunta** to ask a question

preguntar to ask

premio m prize

prenda f garment

prender to switch on; to turn on

prensa f newspaper stand; **hay prensa extranjera** we sell foreign newspapers

preocupado(a) worried

preparación f preparation

preparar to prepare; to fix

preparativos mpl preparations

presa f dam

presentar to introduce

presentarse to check in

preservativo m condom

presión f pressure; **la presión de los neumáticos** tyre pressure

prestar to lend

presto soon

presupuesto m estimate

prevención f precaution

prima f cousin

primario(a) primary

primavera f spring

primer, primero(a) first; **en primera** in first gear; **los primeros auxilios** first aid; **viajar en primera** to travel first class

primo m cousin

princesa f princess

principal main; principal

príncipe m prince

principiante *m/f* beginner
principio *m* beginning
prioridad de paso *f* right of way
prisa *f* rush; haste; **tener prisa** to be in a hurry
prismáticos *mpl* binoculars
privado(a) personal; private
proa *f* bow (*of ship*)
probable probable; **poco probable** unlikely
probadores *mpl* fitting rooms
probar to try; to sample; to taste
problema *m* problem
procedencia *f* point of departure; **procedencia Madrid** coming from Madrid
procedente de coming from
productos *mpl* produce
profesión *f* profession; job
profesor(a) *m/f* secondary school teacher
profundo(a) deep
programa *m* programme; schedule
prohibición *f* ban
prohibido(a) prohibited; **prohibido estacionarse** no waiting; **prohibido fumar** no smoking; **prohibido el paso** no entry; **prohibido acampar** no camping
prohibir to ban; to forbid; **se prohíbe fumar** no smoking

promedio *m* average
promesa *f* promise
prometer to promise
pronóstico *m* forecast; **el pronóstico del tiempo** weather forecast
pronto soon
propiedad *f* property; **propiedad privada** private
propietario(a) *m/f* owner
propina *f* tip
propio(a) own
proponer to suggest
propuesta *f* proposal; suggestion
prostituta *f* call girl
protección *f* insurance cover; protection; **la protección civil** civil defence
protestante Protestant
provecho *m* benefit
proveer to supply
provincia *f* province
provisional temporary
próximamente: **próximamente en esta sala/en este cine** coming soon
próximo(a) next; **próximo estreno** coming soon
proyecto *m* project; plan
prueba *f* trial; proof; test
público(a) public; **para todos los públicos** U film
puchero *m* stew
pudín *m* pudding
pudrir to rot

pueblo m people; village

puente m bridge; **el puente de peaje** toll bridge

puerro m leek; **los puerros en ensalada** boiled leeks in vinaigrette

puerta f door; gate; **por favor, cierren la puerta** please close the door; **la puerta de embarque** boarding gate

puerto m port; harbour; mountain pass; **el puerto deportivo** marina

pues since; so

puesto m stall; job; **el puesto de flores** flower stall; **el puesto de socorro** first-aid post

pulga f flea

pulgada f inch

pulgar m thumb

pulmón m lung

pulmonía f pneumonia

pulpo m octopus; **el pulpo a la gallega** octopus with peppers and paprika

pulsar to push; **no pulse el botón más que por indicación de la operadora** do not push the button until instructed to do so by the operator

pulsera f bracelet

pulso m pulse

pulverizador m spray

puñetazo m punch

puño m shirt cuff; fist

punta f point; tip

puntapié m kick

puntiagudo(a) sharp; pointed

punto m dot; point; **hacer punto** to knit; **el punto muerto** neutral

puntual punctual

puntualidad f: **se ruega puntualidad** please be punctual

punzada f stitch

puré m purée; **el puré de patatas** mashed potatoes; **el puré de guisantes** thick cream of pea soup; **el puré de verduras** creamed vegetables

puro m cigar

puro(a) pure

Q

que than; **qué** what, which; **¿qué?** what?; **¿qué tal?** how are you?

quedar to remain

queja f complaint

quejarse to grumble; **quejarse de** to complain about

quemado(a) burned; **quemado por el sol** sunburnt

quemadura f burn; **la quemadura del sol** sunburn

quemar to burn

quemarse to burn oneself

querer to love; to want
querido(a) m/f darling
queroseno m paraffin
quesería f cheese and wine shop
queso m cheese; **el queso de bola** a round, mild cheese like Edam; **el queso de Burgos** cream cheese; **el queso de cabra** goat's milk cheese; **el queso de Cabrales** very strong blue cheese; **el queso fresco** curd cheese; **el queso manchego** hard sheep's milk cheese; **el queso con membrillo** cheese with quince jelly eaten as a dessert; **el queso de nata** cream cheese; **el queso de oveja** sheep's milk cheese; **el queso del país** local cheese
quien who; **¿quién?** who?
quilate m carat
quincallería f ironmonger's
quince fifteen
quiniela f football pools
quinientos(as) five hundred
quinto(a) fifth
quiosco m kiosk; **el quiosco de periódicos** newsstand
quisquilla f shrimp
quita-esmalte m nail polish remover
quitamanchas m stain remover
quitar to remove; **quitarse la ropa** to take off one's clothes
quizás perhaps

R

rábano m radish
rabia f rabies
rabino m rabbi
rabo m: **rabo de buey** oxtail
R.A.C.E. see **real**
ración f portion; **las raciones** snacks
radiador m radiator
radio f radio; **por la radio** on the radio; **Radio Nacional Española (RNE)** Spanish National Radio
radio-casete m radio cassette
radiografía f X-ray; **hacer una radiografía** to X-ray
ragout m meat and vegetable stew; **el ragout de cordero** lamb stew
raíz f root
raja f split
rallador m grater
rama f branch
ramo m bunch of flowers
rana f frog
rape m angler fish; **el rape a la malagueña** angler fish baked in a sauce of almonds, tomatoes, parsley and onions
rápido m express train; heel bar
rápido(a) quick; fast
raqueta f racket; bat
raramente seldom

rascacielos m skyscraper
rascar to scratch
rastro m flea market
rata f rat
ratero m pickpocket
rato m (short) time
ratón m mouse
ravioles mpl ravioli
raya f stripe; parting
rayo m beam; ray
razón f reason
real royal; **Real Automóvil Club de España (R.A.C.E.)** Royal Spanish Automobile Club
rebaja f reduction; **rebajas** sales
rebozado(a) cooked in batter
recado m errand; message
recalentarse to overheat
recambio m spare; refill
recepción f reception; reception desk
recepcionista m/f receptionist
receta f recipe; prescription; **con receta médica** a prescription is necessary
recibir to receive
recibo m receipt
recién recently; **recién pintado** wet paint
reciente recent
recipiente m container
reclamación f claim; complaint; **reclamaciones en el acto** any complaints must be made immediately

reclamar to claim
recoger to pick up; **se recoge la basura** rubbish is collected; **recoja aquí su tíquet** take your ticket
recogida f collection
recomendado(a): no recomendada a menores de 13 años not recommended for under-13s
recompensa f reward
reconocer to recognize
recorrer to tour; to travel
recorrido m journey; route; **de largo recorrido** long-distance; **el recorrido en vacío** journey to pick-up point; **el recorrido turístico** tourist route
recortarse: recortarse el pelo to get one's hair trimmed
recreo m leisure; break
recto(a) straight
recuerdo m souvenir; **recuerdos** greetings
recuperable returnable
recuperar to get back
recuperarse to recover
recursos mpl resources
red f net; **Red Nacional de los Ferrocarriles Españoles (RENFE)** Spanish railway network
redactar to draw up; to write
redecilla f luggage rack
redondo(a) round
reducción f reduction

reducido(a) low; limited
reembolso m refund; **contra reembolso** cash on delivery
reemplazo m replacement
reestreno m second run
referencia f reference
reflejo m reflection; rinse
refresco m refreshment; cold drink
refrigeración f air-conditioning
refrigerado(a) air-conditioned
refugio m shelter; island (traffic); central reservation
regalar to give
regaliz m licorice
regalo m gift; present
regata f regatta
regazo m lap
régimen m diet; **estar a régimen** to be on a diet
región f district; area; region
registro m register
regla f rule
regresar to return
regreso m return
regular regular; not bad
reina f queen
Reino Unido m United Kingdom
reír to laugh
rejilla f luggage rack
relación f account; report
relajarse to relax
relámpago m lightning
religión f religion
rellenar to fill in; to stuff;

rellene este cupón fill in this form
relleno(a) stuffed
reloj m clock; watch; **el reloj de pulsera** wristwatch; **el reloj despertador** alarm clock
relojería f watchmaker's; jeweller's
remar to row
remedio m remedy
remitente m sender
remitir to send
remo m oar
remolacha f beetroot; **la remolacha en ensalada** beetroot in vinaigrette
remolcador m tug
remolque m tow rope; trailer
RENFE see red
renta f income
rentable profitable
reorganización f reorganization
reparación f repair; **reparación del calzado** shoes repaired; **reparación de neumáticos** tyres repaired
reparar to repair; to mend
repartir to deliver; to divide
reparto m delivery
repente: de repente suddenly
repentino(a) sudden
repetir to repeat
repollo m cabbage; **el repollo al natural** plain

boiled white cabbage; **el repollo con manzanas** boiled white cabbage with apples

reportaje m report

reposacabezas m headrest

reposición f revival

repostería f pastries

república f republic

repuesto m replacement; **la pieza de repuesto** spare part

repujado(a) embossed

requesón m cottage cheese

requisito m requirement; qualification

resaca f hangover

resbaladizo(a) slippery

resbalar to slip; to slide

rescatar to rescue

rescate m rescue

reserva f reserve; reservation; **la reserva en grupo** block booking; **en reserva** in stock

reservado(a) reserved

reservar to reserve; **se reserva el derecho de admisión** the management reserves the right to refuse admission

resfriado m cold

resfriarse to catch cold

residencia f residence; residential hotel; hostel

resistente hard-wearing

resolver to solve

resorte m spring (coil)

respaldo m chair back

respeto m respect

respiración f breathing

respirar to breathe

responder to answer; to reply; **no se responde de robos** the management accepts no liability for theft

responsabilidad f responsibility

respuesta f answer; reply

restar to deduct; to subtract; to be left

restaurante m restaurant; **el restaurante vegetariano** vegetarian restaurant

resto m the rest; **los restos** remains; **restos de serie** remnants

resultado m result

resultar to turn out

resumen m summary

retales mpl remnants

retener to keep

retirar to withdraw

retirarse: ¡**no se retire!** hold on!

retornable returnable

retrasar to delay; to put off

retrasarse to lose (clock, watch); **el tren se ha retrasado** the train has been delayed

retraso m delay; **sin retraso** on schedule

retrete m lavatory

retroceder to turn back

retrovisor m rear-view

mirror

reumatismo m rheumatism

reunión f meeting; conference

reunirse to meet; to get together

revelar to show; to develop

reventar to burst

reventón m puncture

revés m reverse; **al revés** upside down; **volver algo del revés** to turn something inside out

revisar to check

revisión f service (for car); inspection

revisor m conductor; ticket inspector

revista f magazine; revue; **la revista infantil** comic; **la revista de variedades** variety show

rey m king

rezar to pray

Ribeiro m fresh young wine from the Orense region

ribera f bank

rico(a) rich; wealthy

riesgo m risk

rifa f raffle

rígido(a) stiff

rímel m mascara

rincón m corner; spot

riñón m kidney; **los riñones al jerez** kidneys in sherry sauce; **los riñones salteados** sautéed kidneys served with tomato and wine

sauce

río m river

Rioja m excellent red and white table wine

riqueza f wealth

risa f laugh; laughter

rizado(a) curly

RNE see **radio**

robar to steal; to rob

robo m robbery

roca f rock

roce m graze

rodaballo m turbot

rodaja f slice

rodaje m set of wheels

rodilla f knee

rogar to ask

rojo(a) red

rollo m roll

romana: a la romana fried in batter or breadcrumbs

románico(a) romanesque

romántico(a) romantic

romería f pilgrimage

romero m rosemary

romper to smash; to break

ron m rum

roncar to snore

roñoso(a) mean, stingy

ropa f clothes; **la ropa blanca** bedding; **la ropa de cama** bedding; **la ropa de deporte** sportswear; **la ropa interior** underwear; **la ropa por lavar** washing

rosa rose; pink

rosado m rosé

rosbif m roast beef

rosca *f* doughnut

rosquilla *f* doughnut

rótula *f* kneecap

rotulador *m* felt-tip pen

rozar to scrape; to graze

rubí *m* ruby

rubio(a) fair; blond(e)

rueda *f* wheel; **la rueda trasera** rear wheel; **la rueda de repuesto/recambio** spare wheel

ruega: se ruega no fumar no smoking please; **se ruega paguen en el acto** please pay as soon as you are served; **se ruega puntualidad** please be punctual; **se ruega silencio** silence please; **se ruega no tocar** please do not touch

ruido *m* noise; row

ruidoso(a) noisy

ruinas *fpl* ruins

ruleta *f* roulette

rumbo *m* direction; **con rumbo** bound for

ruta *f* route; **la ruta turística** scenic route

S

S.A. *see* **sociedad**

sábado *m* Saturday

sábana *f* sheet

sabañon *m* chilblain

saber to know

sabor *m* taste; flavour

sabroso(a) tasty

sacacorchos *m* corkscrew

sacapuntas *m* pencil sharpener

sacar to take out; **sacarse una muela** to have a tooth taken out

sacarina *f* saccharin

sacerdote *m* priest

saco *m* sack; **el saco de dormir** sleeping bag

sagrado(a) holy

sal *f* salt; **sin sal** unsalted

sala *f* hall; ward; **la sala de baile** dance hall; **la sala de embarque** departure lounge; **la sala de espera** airport lounge; waiting room; **la sala de fiestas** dance hall; **la sala de televisión** TV lounge

salado(a) savoury; salty

salario *m* wage; wages

salchicha *f* sausage

salchichón *m* salami sausage

saldo *m* balance; **saldos** sale

salero *m* salt cellar

salida *f* exit; departure; socket; **salida de emergencia** emergency exit; **salida de camiones** beware of lorries; **salida nacional** departure - domestic flights; **salida de vehículos** danger - vehicles exiting; **salidas vuelos regulares** departures - scheduled flights

salir to go outside; to come out; to go out

salmón *m* salmon
salmonete *m* red mullet
salón *m* lounge (*in hotel*); **el salón de belleza** beauty parlour; **el salón de juegos** amusement arcade; **el salón de té** teashop; **el salón de peluquería** hairdresser's
salpicadero *m* dashboard
salpicón *m*: **el salpicón de mariscos** prawn and lobster salad
salsa *f* gravy; sauce; dressing; **la salsa bearnesa** thick sauce made with butter, egg yolks, shallots, vinegar and herbs; **la salsa bechamel** white sauce; **la salsa tártara** tartar sauce; **la salsa de tomate** tomato sauce; **la salsa verde** parsley, garlic and onion sauce; **la salsa vinagreta** vinaigrette sauce
saltar to jump; to blow (*fuse*)
salteado(a) sauté, sautéed
salto *m* jump
salud *f* health; ¡**salud**! cheers!
saludar to greet; **le saluda atentamente** yours sincerely
salvaje wild
salvavidas *m* lifebelt
salvia *f* sage
san *m* saint
sanatorio *m* clinic; nursing home
sandalia *f* sandal

sandía *f* watermelon
sanfaina *f* sautéed aubergines, red pepper and onions
sangrar to bleed
sangre *f* blood
sangría *f* iced drink of red wine, brandy, lemonade and fruit
sangüí *m* sandwich
sano(a) healthy
santo(a) *m/f* saint
sarampión *m* measles
sardina *f* sardine; **la sardina arenque** pilchard; **las sardinas a la marinera** sardines cooked with vegetables, garlic and peppers; **las sardinas en pimientilla** sardines cooked with peppers; **las sardinas rebozadas** sardines in batter
sarpullido *m* rash
sartén *f* frying pan
sastre *m* tailor
sastrería *f* tailor's
satisfacer to satisfy
sazón *f* season; **en sazón** in season
se him-/her-/itself; themselves; yourself; oneself
secado a mano *m* blow-dry
secador de pelo *m* hair-drier
secar to dry; **secar por centrifugado** to spin(-dry)
sección *f* department (*in store*)

seco(a) dry; dried (*fruit, beans*)

secretario(a) *m/f* secretary

secreto(a) secret

sector sanitario *m* First Aid

secuestrador *m* hijacker

secuestrar to kidnap; to hijack

secuestro aéreo *m* hijack

secundario(a) secondary; subordinate; minor

sed *f* thirst; **tener sed** to be thirsty

seda *f* silk

sediento(a) thirsty

seguido(a) continuous; **en seguida** straight away; **todo seguido** straight on

seguir to continue; to follow

según according to

segundo(a) second; **de segunda clase** second-class; **de segunda mano** secondhand

seguridad *f* security; reliability; safety

seguro *m* insurance; **el seguro del coche** car insurance; **el seguro contra tercera persona** third party insurance; **el seguro contra todo riesgo** comprehensive insurance

seguro(a) safe

seis six

sello *m* stamp; **poner un sello** to stamp

semáforo *m* traffic lights;

saltarse un semáforo en rojo to go through a red light

semana *f* week; **la semana pasada** last week; **Semana Santa** Holy week; Easter

semanal weekly

semanario *m* weekly paper

semejante alike

semifinal *f* semifinal

semilla *f* seed

seña *f* sign; **las señas** address

señal *f* sign; signal; **la señal de comunicando** busy/ engaged signal; **la señal de socorro** Mayday; **la señal de tráfico** road sign

señalar to point out

sencillo(a) simple; plain

sendero *m* footpath

seno *m* breast

señor *m* gentleman; **Señor (Sr.)** Mr; sir

señora *f* lady; **Señora (Sra.)** Mrs; Ms; Madam

señorita *f* Miss; **Señorita (Srta.) Smith** Miss Smith

sentar to sit

sentarse to sit down

sentido *m* sense

sentimiento *m* feeling

sentir to feel

septentrional northern

se(p)tiembre *m* September

séptimo(a) seventh

sequía *f* drought

ser to be

sereno(a) calm; clear

serie *f* series

serio(a) serious
serpiente f snake
servicio m service; service charge; **servicio incluido** service included; **el área de servicios** service area; **el servicio de autobuses** bus service; **el servicio automático** direct-dialled calls; **el servicio de entrega** delivery service; **servicio discrecional** request stop; **el servicio doméstico** home help; **el servicio de extranjero** foreign department; **el servicio de grúa** towing service; **el servicio de habitaciones** room service; **el servicio de lavandería** laundry service; **el servicio manual** calls through the operator; **el servicio de mesa** extra portions; **el servicio oficial** authorised dealers - repairs; **el servicio de reparto** delivery service; **los servicios de urgencia** emergency services
servicios mpl public conveniences
servilleta f serviette; napkin
servir to serve
sesada f brains
sesenta sixty
sesión f performance; **la sesión continua** continuous performances; **la sesión**

matinal morning performance; **la sesión de noche** late night performance; **sesión numerada** seats bookable in advance; **la sesión de tarde** evening performance; **la sesión vermut** mid-evening performance
sesos mpl brains; **los sesos a la mallorquina** brains served with an onion, vinegar and egg sauce; **los sesos a la romana** brains fried in batter
seta f mushroom
setenta seventy
seto m hedge
sexo m sex
sexto(a) sixth
sí yes
si whether; if
sidra f cider
siempre always
sien m temple (of head)
siéntase: siéntase por favor please take a seat
siento: lo siento I'm very sorry
sierra f mountain range
siesta f siesta; nap
siete seven
siga follow; **siga adelante** carry on; **siga derecho** keep straight ahead; **siga las instrucciones al dorso** follow the instructions overleaf

sigla f symbol
siglo m century
significado m meaning
significar to mean
signo m sign
sigue: sigue Usted en zona de obras you are still in an area of roadworks
siguiente following; next
silenciador m silencer
silencio m silence; **¡silencio!** be quiet!
silencioso(a) silent
silla f chair; **la silla alta para niño** highchair; **la silla plegable** folding chair; **la silla de ruedas** wheelchair; **la silla tijera** deckchair
sillita de ruedas f push-chair
sillón m chair; armchair
simpático(a) nice
simple simple
sin without; **sin embargo** however; **sin falta** without fail
sinagoga f synagogue
sino but
sintético(a) synthetic
síntoma m symptom
sinvergüenza m/f rascal
siquiera even
sírvase: sírvase Ud. mismo please serve yourself; **sírvase frío** serve chilled; **sírvase a temperatura ambiente** serve at room temperature

sirve: no sirve it's no good
sistema m system; **el sistema de refrigeración** cooling system
sitio m place; space; position
situación f situation
situado(a) located; situated
slip m pants; briefs
smoking m dinner jacket
sobrar to be left
sobre[1] on; upon
sobre[2] m envelope; **el sobre de té** teabag
sobrecarga f surcharge
sobrecargo m purser
sobredosis f overdose
sobremarcha f overdrive
sobretodo m overcoat
sobrina f niece
sobrino m nephew
sociedad f society; **Sociedad Anónima (S.A.)** Ltd., plc
socio m member; partner; **no socios** non-members
socorrista m lifeguard
socorro: ¡socorro! help!
sofocante close; stuffy
soga f rope
soja f soya
sol m sun; sunshine; **tomar el sol** to sunbathe
solamente only
solapa f flap
solar sun
soldado m soldier
soleado(a) sunny
solicitar to apply for

solicitud f application
sólo only
solo(a) alone; lonely
solomillo m sirloin; **el solomillo a la broche** spit-roasted sirloin; **el solomillo de cerdo al jerez** ham-stuffed pork fillet roasted with sherry and onion; **el solomillo de jabugo** sirloin of pork; **el solomillo mechado** beef sirloin wrapped in bacon rashers and baked in the oven; **soltar** to let go; to untie
soltero(a) single
solucionar to solve
sombra f shade; shadow; **la sombra de ojos** eye shadow
sombreador m eye shadow
sombrero m hat; sun hat
sombrilla f sunshade; parasol
somnífero m sleeping pill
sonar to ring
soñar to dream
sonido m sound
sonreír to smile
sonrisa f smile; grin
sopa f soup; **la sopa de ajo** garlic soup; **la sopa de cebolla** onion soup; **la sopa de cebolla gratinada** onion soup with cheese topping browned in the oven; **la sopa al cuarto de hora** fish soup with hard-boiled eggs, peas, bacon, garlic and onions; **la**

sopa de fideos chicken noodle soup; **la sopa de pescado** fish soup; **la sopa de picadillo** chicken soup with chopped ham and egg and noodles; **la sopa sevillana** smooth, creamy fish and mayonnaise soup with olives; **la sopa de verduras** vegetable soup
soplar to blow
soportar to bear; to stand
sorbete m water ice
sordo(a) deaf
sorprendido(a) surprised
sorpresa f surprise
sorteo m raffle
sostén m bra
sótano m basement; cellar
soy I am
Sr. see **señor**
Sra. see **señora**
S.R.C. R.S.V.P.
Srta. see **señorita**
stárter m starting motor
su his; her; their; its; **su madre** his/her mother
suave mild; gentle; smooth
súbdito m: **súbdito británico** British subject
subida f climb
subir to rise; to increase; to climb; **subir a** to get on
submarinismo m scuba diving
subterráneo(a) underground
subtítulo m subtitle

suburbio *m* suburb
suceder to occur
suciedad *f* dirt
sucio(a) dirty
sucursal *f* branch
sudar to sweat
sudeste *m* southeast
sudoeste *m* southwest
sudor *m* sweat
suegra *f* mother-in-law
suegro *m* father-in-law
suela *f* sole
sueldo *m* salary; pay
suelo *m* soil; ground; floor
suelto(a) loose; **el suelto**
loose change
sueño *m* sleep; dream; **tengo
sueño** I'm sleepy
suero *m* serum
suerte *f* luck; **¡buena
suerte!** good luck!; **mala
suerte** bad luck
suéter *m* sweater
suficiente enough
suflé *m* soufflé
sufrir to suffer
sugerencia *f* suggestion
sujetador *m* bra
suma *f* total
sumamente extremely
sumar to add (up)
sumergible waterproof
suministrar to supply
suministro *m* supply
supercarburante *m* high-
grade fuel
superficie *f* surface; top
superior superior; higher

supermercado *m*
supermarket
superpetrolero *m*
supertanker
suplente *m* substitute
suponer to suppose
supositorio *m* suppository
supuesto: por supuesto of
course
sur *m* south
surf *m* surfing; **el surf a vela**
windsurfing
surtido(a) assorted; **el
surtido** variety
surtidor de gasolina *m*
petrol pump
sus his; her; its; their; **sus
hermanas** his sisters
suspender to put off; to call
off
suspensión *f* suspension
susto *m* fright; scare
suyo(a) his; her; their; your;
el/la suyo(a) his; hers;
theirs; yours

T

tabaco *m* tobacco; **el tabaco
negro** dark tobacco; **el
tabaco de pipa** pipe
tobacco; **el tabaco rubio**
Virginia tobacco; **tabacos**
tobacconist's
taberna *f* reasonably priced
restaurant
tabique *m* partition
tabla *f* board; list; **la tabla**

de surf surf board; **la tabla de quesos** cheeseboard
tablao flamenco *m* Flamenco show
tablero *m* dashboard
tablilla *f* splint
tablón *m* board; **el tablón de anuncios** notice board
taburete *m* stool
tacaño(a) mean
taco *m* heel
tacón *m* heel
tajo redondo *m* well-done roast beef
tal such; **tal libro** such a book
taladro *m* drill
talco *m* talc(um powder)
T.A.L.G.O. *m* Intercity train
talla *f* size; **tallas sueltas** odd sizes left
tallarines *mpl* noodles
taller *m* workshop; **taller de reparaciones** garage; **el taller mecánico** garage
talón *m* heel; counterfoil; stub; **el talón de equipajes** baggage check; **el talón bancario** cheque
talonario *m* cheque book
tamaño *m* size
también as well; also; too
tambor *m* drum
tampoco neither
tampones *mpl* tampons
tan so
tanque *m* tank
tanto(a) so much; such a lot

of; **tantos(as)** so many
tapa *f* lid; top; **se ponen tapas** shoes heeled; **las tapas** appetizers
tapar to cover
tapicería *f* upholstery
tapón *m* stopper; plug; bottle top
taquilla *f* box office; ticket office; booking office
taquímetro *m* speedometer
tarde late; **la tarde** evening; afternoon; **de la tarde** p.m.
tarifa *f* tariff; rate; **la tarifa de cambio** exchange rate; **las tarifas postales** postal charges
tarjeta *f* card; **la tarjeta del banco** banker's card; **la tarjeta de crédito** credit card; **la tarjeta de cumpleaños** birthday card; **la tarjeta de embarque** boarding pass; **la tarjeta de Navidad** Christmas card; **la tarjeta postal** postcard; **la tarjeta verde** green card
tarrina *f:* **la tarrina de la casa** homemade pâté
tarro *m* jar; pot
tarta *f* cake; tart; **la tarta de almendras** almond tart; **la tarta helada** cake containing ice cream; **la tarta de manzana** apple pie; **la tarta de nueces** walnut tart; **la tarta de queso** cheesecake
tasa *f* rate; valuation

tasca f bar; economical restaurant

taxi m taxi

taxista m taxi driver

taza f cup; **la taza de picadillo** chicken soup with chopped meat and ham; **la taza de té** teacup

té m tea; **el té con limón** lemon tea

te you; yourself

teatro m theatre; **ir al teatro** to go to the theatre

techo m ceiling; roof; **el techo doble** fly sheet

tecla f key

técnico(a) technical; **el técnico** technician

teja f roof tile

tejado m roof

tejer to knit

tejidos mpl textiles

tela f material; fabric

tele f TV

telebanco m cashpoint

teleférico m cablecar

telefonear to call; to phone

Telefónica f Spanish Telephones

telefonista m/f switchboard operator; telephonist

teléfono m phone; telephone

telegrama m wire; telegram

teleobjetivo m telephoto lens

telescopio m telescope

telesilla m ski lift; chair-lift

televisión f television; **Televisión Española**

(TVE) Spanish Television

televisor m television set

temperatura f temperature; **la temperatura ambiente** room temperature

tempestad f storm

tempestuoso(a) stormy

templo m temple; church

temporada f season; **la temporada de veraneo** the holiday season; **la temporada alta** high season; **fuera de temporada** off-season

temprano(a) early; **más temprano** earlier

tenaz stubborn

tendero m grocer

tendido m row of seats

tenedor m fork

tener to have; to hold; **tengo hambre** I am hungry; **tener que** to have to

tengo I have

teñir to dye

tenis m tennis

tensión f tension; blood pressure

tenso(a) tense

tentempié m snack

tercer, tercero(a) third

tercera f third gear

terciopelo m velvet

terminal f terminal; **la terminal internacional** international terminal; **la terminal nacional** domestic flights terminal

terminar to end; to finish

término *m* term; end; **el término municipal de Sevilla** Seville district

termómetro *m* thermometer

termos *m* vacuum flask

ternera *f* veal; **la ternera fiambre** veal pâté; **la ternera al jugo** veal casserole in white wine; **la ternera a la provenzal** casseroled veal, cooked with onions, garlic and herbs; **la ternera simple** veal steak

terraza *f* terrace

terremoto *m* earthquake

terreno *m* land

terrón *m* lump of sugar

tesoro *m* treasure

testigo *m* witness

testimonio *m* evidence

tetera *f* teapot

texto *m:* **el texto del telegrama** message here

tez *f* complexion

ti you

tía *f* aunt(ie)

tibio(a) warm

tiempo *m* time; weather; **a tiempo** on time

tienda *f* store; shop; **la tienda de campaña** tent; **la tienda de deportes** sports shop; **la tienda libre de impuestos** duty-free shop; **la tienda de repuestos** car parts shop

tiene he/she has; you have

tienes you have

tierno(a) tender

tierra *f* earth; land

tiesto *m* pot

tijeras *fpl* scissors; pair of scissors

tila *f* lime-flower tea

timbre *m* doorbell; official stamp; **el timbre de alarma** communication cord

tímido(a) shy

timón *m* rudder

tímpano *m* eardrum

tinta *f* ink

tinte *m* dye

tinto(a) red

tintorería *f* dry-cleaner's

tío *m* uncle; bloke

tiovivo *m* merry-go-round

típico(a) typical

tiple *f* soprano

tipo *m* sort; type; fellow; **el tipo de cambio** rate of exchange

tíquet *m* ticket

tirador *m* handle

tirantes *mpl* braces

tirar to throw; to throw away; to pull; **para tirar** disposable; **tire** pull

tiritas *fpl* elastoplast

tiro *m* shot; shooting; throw

títere *m* puppet

titular *m* headline

título *m* university degree; title

toalla *f* towel

toallitas *fpl:* **las toallitas**

limpiadoras para bebés baby wipes

tobillo *m* ankle

tobogán *m* slide

tocadiscos *m* record-player

tocador *m* dressing table; powder room

tocar to touch; to ring the (door-)bell; to handle; to play; **tocar el claxon** to sound one's horn

tocinito *m:* **los tocinitos con nata** caramel cream with whipped cream

tocino *m* bacon; **el tocino de cielo** rich caramel cream

todavía yet; still

todo(a) all; **todo** everything; **todo el mundo** everybody; everyone; **todo incluido** all inclusive

toldo *m* awning

toma *f* tap; socket; lead

tomar to take; **¿quiere tomar algo?** would you like a drink?; **tomar el sol** to sunbathe; **tomar una copa** to have a drink

tomate *m* tomato

tomillo *m* thyme

tomo *m* volume

tonel *m* barrel

tonelada *f* ton

tónica *f* tonic water

tono *m* tone; **el tono de marcar** dial(ling) tone

tonterías *fpl* nonsense

tonto(a) stupid

toquen: no toquen please do not touch

torcedura *f* sprain

torcer to twist; to bend; **torcer a la izquierda** to turn left

torcerse to strain; **torcerse el tobillo** to sprain one's ankle

torero *m* bullfighter

tormenta *f* thunderstorm; **la tormenta de nieve** blizzard

tornasol *m* sunflower

tornillo *m* screw

torno *m* dentist's drill

tornos *mpl* turnstiles

toro *m* bull

torpe clumsy

torre *f* tower; **la torre de control** control tower

torrijas *fpl* slices of bread dipped in milk and beaten egg and fried

torta *f* cake

tortilla *f* omelette; **la tortilla a la española** Spanish omelette made with potato, onion, garlic, tomato, peppers and seasoning; **la tortilla francesa** plain omelette; **la tortilla de legumbres** vegetable omelette; **la tortilla a la paisana** sausage and vegetable omelette; **la tortilla de patatas** potato and onion omelette; **la tortilla al rón** sweet rum omelette; **la tortilla Sacromonte** omelette of brains fried in breadcrumbs, with potatoes, peas and peppers; **la tortilla soufflé** sweet omelette soufflé

tos f cough; **la tos ferina** whooping cough

toser to cough

tostada f toast

tostador m toaster

total total; **en total** in all

tournedós m thick slice of beef fillet; **tournedós Rossini** beef fillet with foie gras and truffles, in a sherry sauce

trabajar to work

trabajo m work; job

tracción f: **la tracción delantera** front-wheel drive; **la tracción trasera** rear-wheel drive

traducción f translation; **se hacen traducciones** translations done

traducir to translate

traer to fetch; to bring

tráfico m traffic

tragaperras m slot machine

tragar to swallow

trago m a drink

traje m suit; outfit; **el traje de baño** bathing suit; **el traje de esquí** ski outfit; **el traje de etiqueta** evening dress (man's); **el traje de noche** evening dress

(woman's); **se hacen trajes a medida** suits made to measure

trámite m procedure; formality

trampolín m diving board

tranquilizante m tranquillizer

tranquilo(a) quiet; calm; peaceful

transatlántico m liner

transbordador m car-ferry

transbordo m transfer; **hay que hacer transbordo en Madrid** you have to change trains in Madrid

transeunte m/f passer-by

transferencia f transfer(ral); **hacer una transferencia** to transfer some money

transferir to transfer

tránsito m traffic; **en tránsito** in transit

transmisión f transmission; **la transmisión automática** automatic transmission

transmisor m transmitter

transpirar to perspire

transportar to carry; to transport

transporte m transport; **transporte escolar** school bus; **transportes** transport company; removers

tranvía m tram(car); short-distance train

trapo m rag
tras after; behind
trasero(a) rear
trasladar to transfer; to move
traslado m treatment; course of treatment
tratamiento m treatment; course of treatment
tratar to treat; **tratar/ trátese con cuidado** handle with care
través: a través de through; across
travesero m bolster
travesía f crossing; **Travesía Libertad** Avenue "Libertad"
trece thirteen
treinta thirty
tren m train; **el tren directo** through train; **el tren de largo recorrido** Intercity train; **el tren de mercancías** freight train; **el tren ómnibus** stopping train
tres three
triángulo m triangle; **el triángulo de avería** warning triangle
tribuna f stand
tribunal m law court
trigo m wheat
trimestre m term
trineo m sleigh; sledge
trípode m tripod
tripulación f crew
triste sad
trompeta f trumpet
tronco m trunk

tropezar to slip; to trip
trópicos mpl tropics
trozo m bit; piece
trucha f trout; **la trucha a la navarra** trout baked with ham; **las truchas a la molinera** trout cooked in butter and served with lemon
trucos mpl pool
trueno m thunder
trufa f truffle
tu your
tú you; **tú mismo(a)** you yourself
tubería f pipes; piping
tubo m pipe; tube; **el tubo de desagüe** drainpipe; **el tubo de escape** exhaust pipe; **el tubo de respiración** snorkel
tuerca f nut
tulipán m tulip
tumba f tomb
tumbona f deckchair
tumor m growth
túnel m tunnel; **túneles en 2 km** tunnels two kilometres ahead
turismo m tourism; sightseeing
turista m/f tourist; **la clase turista** tourist class
turístico(a) tourist
turno m turn; **por turno** in turn
turquesa turquoise
turrón m nougat
tus your

tuve I had
tuviste you had
tuvo he/she had
tuyo(a) yours; **el/la tuyo(a)**
  yours
TVE *see* **televisión**

U

Ud(s) *see* **Usted**
úlcera *f* ulcer
últimamente lately
último(a) last
ultramar: de ultramar
  overseas
ultramarinos *m* grocery
  shop
un(a) a; an
uña *f* nail (*human*)
undécimo(a) eleventh
ungüento *m* ointment
único(a) unique; single
unidad *f* unit; **Unidad de
  Vigilancia Intensiva
  (U.V.I.)** intensive care unit
unir to join; to unite
universidad *f* university
universo *m* universe
uno(a) one; oneself
unos(as) some
untar to spread
urbanización *f* housing
  estate
urbano(a) city
urge it is urgent; **urge
  vender** for quick sale
urgencias *fpl* casualty
  department; **urgencias
  infantil** children's casualty

ward
urgente urgent; express
urinarios *mpl* toilets
usar to use
uso *m* use; custom; **uso
  externo/tópico** for external
  use only
Usted you; **Usted
  mismo(a)** you yourself;
  Ustedes you (*plural form*);
  Ustedes mismos you
  yourselves
útil useful
utilizar to use; **utilice
  monedas de … pesetas** use
  … peseta coins
uva *f* grape; **la uva moscatel**
  muscatel grape; **la uva pasa**
  raisin
U.V.I. *see* **unidad**

V

va he/she/it goes; you go
vaca *f* cow
vacaciones *fpl* holiday; **de
  vacaciones** on holiday
vaciado *m* plaster (*for limb*)
vaciar to empty
vacilar to hesitate
vacío(a) empty
vacuna *f* vaccine
vacunación *f* vaccination
vado *m*: **vado permanente**
  no parking at any time
vagón *m* railway carriage; **el
  vagón de fumadores**
  smoker
vagón-restaurante *m*

restaurant car

vainilla f vanilla

vajilla f crockery

Valdepeñas m light red or white wine

vale m token; voucher

valer to be worth; **vale** O.K.; **vale la pena** it's worth it

válido(a) valid; **válido hasta...** valid until...

valiente brave

valija f suitcase

valla f fence

valle m valley

valor m value

válvula f valve

vapor m steam; steamer (ship); **al vapor** steamed

vaporizador m spray

vaquero m cowboy

vaqueros mpl jeans

variante f bypass

varicela f chickenpox

variedad f variety

varilla graduada f dipstick

varios(as) several

vas you go

vasco(a) Basque

vaselina f vaseline; petroleum jelly

vaso m glass

vatio m watt

veces fpl times; **¿cuántas veces?** how many times?

vecindad f neighbourhood

vecino(a) m/f neighbour

vegetariano(a) vegetarian

vehículo m vehicle; **el**

vehículo en carga loading vehicle; **el vehículo largo** long vehicle; **vehículos pesados** heavy lorries crossing

veinte twenty

veintiuno twenty-one

vejiga f bladder

vela f candle; sail; sailing; **hacer vela** to go yachting; to sail

velero m sail(ing) boat

velocidad f speed; **segunda/ tercera velocidad** 2nd/3rd gear; **cuarta/primera velocidad** top/bottom gear; **a gran velocidad** at high speed; **velocidad controlada por radar** speed checks in operation; **velocidad limitada** speed limit

velocímetro m speedometer

velódromo m cycle track

veloz fast

vena f vein

vencer to defeat

vencimiento m expiry date

venda f bandage

vendaval m gale

vendedor m vendor; **el vendedor de periódicos** newsagent

vender to sell; **se vende/ véndese** for sale

vendimia f harvest

veneno m poison

venenoso(a) poisonous

venir to come

venta f sale; country inn; **en venta** for sale; **venta anticipada de localidades** tickets on sale in advance; **la venta de billetes** ticket office; **venta de localidades con 5 días de antelación** tickets on sale five days before performance; **venta al por mayor** wholesaler's; **venta al por menor/al detalle** retailer's; **venta de parcelas** plots for sale; **venta de pisos** flats for sale; **venta de sellos** stamps sold here

ventaja m advantage

ventana f window

ventanilla f window (*in car, train*); serving hatch

ventilador m fan; ventilator

ventoso(a) windy

ver to see; to watch

veraneante m/f holiday-maker

verano m summer

verbena f street party

verdad f truth; **de verdad** true; **¿verdad?** don't you? etc; didn't he? etc; do you? etc; did he? etc

verdadero(a) true; genuine

verde green; unripe

verdulero m greengrocer

verduras fpl vegetables; **las verduras estofadas** vegetable stew with broad beans, onions, green beans, peas, lettuce and garlic

vergüenza f shame

verificar to check

verja f railings

vermut m vermouth

verruga f wart

versión f: **la versión íntegra** uncut version; **la versión original con subtítulos** original version with subtitles

verter to pour; **prohibido verter basuras/escombros** no dumping

vesícula f blister

vestíbulo m hall; lobby

vestido m dress

vestirse to dress oneself

veterinario m vet(erinary surgeon)

vez f time; **una vez más** once more; **en vez de** instead of

vía f track; rails; platform; **la vía de acceso** slip-road; **por vía oral/bucal** orally

viajar to travel; **viajar en avión** to fly; **viajar en primera clase** to travel first class

viaje m journey; trip; **el viaje de ida y vuelta** round trip; **el viaje de negocios** business trip; **el viaje organizado** package holiday

viajero m traveller

víbora f snake

vichyssoise f cold soup made from leeks, potatoes, onions and cream

víctima f victim

vida f life

vidrio m glass

vieira f scallop

viejo(a) old

viento m wind; **hace mucho viento** it's very windy; **sin viento** calm; **viento lateral** crosswinds

vientre m belly

viernes m Friday; **viernes santo** Good Friday

viga f beam (of wood)

vigilante m lifeguard

vigilar to guard

viña f vineyard

vinagre m vinegar

vinagreta f salad dressing; vinaigrette sauce

vino m wine; **el vino blanco** white wine; **el vino de la casa** house wine; **el vino clarete** light red wine; **el vino común** ordinary wine; **el vino dulce** sweet wine; **el vino espumoso** sparkling wine; **el vino de mesa** table wine; **el vino del país** local wine; **el vino rosado** rosé wine; **el vino seco** dry wine; **el vino tinto** red wine

violento(a) rough

violín m violin

violoncelo m cello

viraje m turn; swerve; **el viraje en U** U-turn

virar to tack (sailing)

viruela f smallpox

visado m visa

visibilidad f visibility

visita f visit; visitor; **la visita con guía** guided tour

visitar to visit; **visite piso piloto** visit our show flat

visor m viewfinder

víspera f eve

vista f view; eyesight

vitrina f shop window

viuda f widow

viudo m widower

víveres mpl groceries

vivienda f housing

vivir to live

vivo(a) live; alive; bright

vodka f vodka

volante m steering wheel

volar to fly

volcán m volcano

volován m vol-au-vent

voltaje m voltage

voltio m volt

volumen m volume (sound, capacity)

voluntad f will; intention

volver to come back; to go back; to return; **volver en sí** to come round; to revive; **volver algo** to turn something round

vomitar to be sick

vomitorio m exit (stadium)

vosotros(as) you (plural)

voy I go

voz *f* voice; **en voz alta** aloud
vuelco *m* spill; **dar un vuelco** to overturn
vuelo *m* flight; **el vuelo charter** charter flight; **el vuelo nocturno** night flight; **el vuelo regular** scheduled flight
vuelta *f* turn; return; change; **dar vueltas** to twist (*road*); **dar una vuelta** to take a walk
vuestro(a) your; **el/la vuestro(a)** yours

WYZ

wáter *m* lavatory; toilet
whisky *m* whisky
y and
ya already
yate *m* yacht; **el yate de motor** cabin cruiser
yema *f* egg yolk; egg dessert with brandy; **las yemas de coco** coconut sweets eaten as a dessert
yerno *m* son-in-law
yeso *m* plaster (*for wall*)
yo I
yodo *m* iodine
yogur *m* yoghurt; **el yogur natural** plain yoghurt
yugular jugular
zambullirse to dive
zanahoria *f* carrot
zancudo *m* mosquito
zapata *f* brake shoe

zapatería *f* shoeshop
zapatero *m* shoemaker; cobbler; shoe repairs
zapatilla *f* slipper; **la zapatilla de tenis** tennis shoe
zapato *m* shoe; **los zapatos de medio tacón** low-heeled shoes; **los zapatos de tacón** high-heeled shoes
zarzamora *f* blackberry
zarzuela[1] *f* Spanish light opera
zarzuela[2] *f*: **la zarzuela de mariscos** seafood casserole; **la zarzuela de pescado** fish in a spicy sauce; **la zarzuela de pescado a la levantina** casserole of assorted fish and seafood with paprika and saffron
zona *f* zone; **la zona azul/de estacionamiento limitado y vigilado** controlled parking area; **la zona recreativa** recreation area; **la zona reservada para peatones** pedestrian precinct; **la zona restringida** restricted area; **las zonas de tarificación** charge bands
zorro *m* fox
zumo *m* juice; **el zumo de limón** lemon juice; **el zumo de naranja** orange juice
zurcir to darn
zurdo(a) left-handed

ENGLISH - SPANISH

A

A negative/positive el A negativo/positivo *a negateebo/posee-teebo*

a un(a) *oon(oo-na)*

abbey la abadía *aba-dee-a*

about (*relating to*) acerca de *a-therka de*; (*approximately*) más o menos *mas o menos*

above arriba *a-rreeba*; **above the house** encima de la casa *en-theema de la kasa*

abroad en el extranjero *en el extran-khero*

abscess el absceso *abs-theso*

accelerator el acelerador *a-the-lera-dor*

accident el accidente *aktheeden-te*

accommodation el alojamiento *alo-khamyen-to*

account la cuenta *kwenta*; **Giro account** la cuenta de Giro Bank *kwenta de giro bank*

accountant el contable *konta-ble*

ache el dolor *dolor*

acid el ácido *a-theedo*

across (*on the other side of*) al otro lado de *al otro lado de*

acrylic el acrílico *a-kreelee-ko*

act actuar *aktoo-ar*

activities las actividades *aktee-beeda-des*

actor el actor *aktor*

actress la actriz *aktreeth*

adaptor (*electrical*) el enchufe múltiple *enchoo-fe mooltee-ple*

add añadir *anya-deer*; (*figures*) sumar *soomar*

address la dirección *deerek-thyon*

adhesive tape la cinta adhesiva *theenta a-de-seeba*

adjust ajustar *akhoos-tar*

admission la entrada *en-trada*; **admission charge** el precio de entrada *prethyo de en-trada*

adopted (*child*) adoptivo(a) *adop-teebo(a)*

adult el/la adulto(a) *a-doolto(a)*

advance: in advance por adelantado *por a-delan-tado*

advertisement el anuncio *a-noonthyo*

aerial la antena *an-tena*

afford: I can't afford it no tengo suficiente dinero *no tengo soofee-thyen-te dee-nero*

afraid: I'm afraid tengo miedo *tengo myedo*

African africano(a) *afree-kano(a)*

after después *des-pwes*; **after lunch** después del almuerzo *des-pwes del al-mwertho*

afternoon la tarde *tar-de*

aftershave la loción para después del afeitado *lothyon para despwes del afey-tado*

again otra vez *otra beth*

against contra *kontra*

age la edad *e-dad*

agent el agente *a-khen-te*

ago: long ago hace mucho tiempo *a-the moocho tyempo*

agree estar de acuerdo *estar de a-kwerdo*

air el aire *a-ee-re*

air-conditioning el aire acondicionado *a-ee-re a-kondee-thyo-nado*

aircraft el avión *a-byon*

air filter el filtro de aire *feeltro de a-ee-re*

air hostess la azafata *a-thafa-ta*

airline la línea aérea *lee-ne-a a-e-rea*

air mail el correo aéreo *ko-rre-o a-e-reo*

air-mattress el colchón neumático *kolchon ne-ooma-teeko*

airport el aeropuerto *a-ero-pwerto*

aisle (*in theatre*) el pasillo *pa-seelyo*; (*in church*) la nave *na-be*

à la carte a la carta *a la karta*

alarm la alarma *a-larma*

alarm clock el despertador *desper-tador*

album (*record*) el elepé *e-le-pe*; (*for photos*) el álbum *alboom*

alcohol el alcohol *alkol*

alcoholic alcohólico(a) *alko-leeko(a)*

alive vivo(a) *beebo(a)*

all todo(a), todos(as) *todo(a), todos(as)*

allergic: to be allergic to tener alergia a *tener aler-khee-a a*

allow permitir *permee-teer*

all right (*agreed*) de acuerdo *de a-kwerdo*; **are you all right?** ¿está bien? *esta byen*

almond la almendra *al-mendra*

almost casi *kasee*

alone solo(a) *solo(a)*

along por *por*; **along the coast** a lo largo de la costa *a lo largo de la kosta*

already ya *ya*

also también *tam-byen*

altar el altar *altar*

alternator el alternador *al-terna-dor*

although aunque *a-oon-ke*
altitude la altitud *altee-tood*
always siempre *syem-pre*
am: I am English soy inglés
soy een-gles; **I'm here/
tired** estoy aquí/cansado *estoy a-kee/kan-sado*
ambassador el embajador
emba-khador
ambulance la ambulancia
amboo-lanthya
America la América del
Norte *a-meree-ka del nor-te*
American
norteamericano(a) *nor-te-a-
meree-kano(a)*
among entre *en-tre*
amount la cantidad *kantee-
dad*; *(of bill)* la suma *sooma*
amusement park el parque
de atracciones *par-ke de
atrak-thyo-nes*
an un(a) *oon(oo-na)*
anaesthetic el anestésico *a-
nes-tesee-ko*
anchor el ancla *ankla*
and y *ee*; *(before i-, hi-)* e *e*
angel el ángel *an-khel*
angry enfadado(a) *enfa-
dado(a)*
animal el animal *a-neemal*
ankle el tobillo *tobee-lyo*
anniversary el aniversario *a-
neeber-saree-o*
annoyed molesto(a) *mo-
lesto(a)*
anorak el anorak *a-norak*
another *(additional)* otro(a)
o-tro(a); *(different)*

distinto(a) *deesteen-to(a)*
answer[1] *n* la respuesta *res-
pwesta*
answer[2] *vb* contestar *kon-
testar*
antibiotic el antibiótico
antee-bee-o-teeko
antifreeze el anticongelante
antee-kon-khelan-te
antique la antigüedad *antee-
gwedad*
antiseptic el antiséptico
antee-septee-ko
any alguno(a) *al-goono(a)*;
have you any apples?
¿tiene manzanas? *tye-ne
man-thanas*; **I haven't any
ties** no tengo ninguna
corbata *no tengo neen-goo*na
kor-bata
anybody cualquiera *kwal-
kyera*; *(in questions)* alguien
al-gyen; **I can't see
anybody** no veo a nadie *no
be-o a na-dye*
anything cualquier cosa
kwal-kyer kosa; *(in questions)*
algo *algo*; **anything else?**
¿algo más? *algo mas*
anyway de todas formas *de
todas formas*
anywhere en cualquier parte
en kwal-kyer par-te; **I can't
find it anywhere** no lo
encuentro en ninguna parte
*no lo en-kwentro en neen-
goo*na *par-te*
apartment el apartamento *a-
parta-mento*

aperitif el aperitivo *a-peree-teebo*

appendicitis la apendicitis *a-pendee-theetees*

apple la manzana *man-thana*

appointment la cita *theeta*

apricot el albaricoque *alba-reeko-ke*

April abril (*m*) *a-breel*

arch el arco *arko*

archeology la arqueología *ar-ke-olo-khee-a*

architect el arquitecto *arkee-tekto*

architecture la arquitectura *arkee-tektoo-ra*

are: we are from London somos de Londres *somos de lon-dres*; **we are pleased** estamos contentos *es-tamos kon-tentos*; **are you Spanish?** ¿usted es español? *oos-ted es espa-nyol*; **are you married?** ¿está casado usted? *esta ka-sado oos-ted*; **they are new** son nuevos *son nwebos*; **they are there** están ahí *estan a-ee*

area el área *a-re-a*

arm el brazo *bratho*

armbands (*swimming*) los flotadores *flota-do-res*

around alrededor *al-re-dedor*

arrange organizar *orga-neethar*

arrival la llegada *lye-gada*

arrive llegar *lyegar*

art gallery la galería de arte *ga-leree-a de ar-te*

arthritis la artritis *ar-treetees*

artichoke la alcachofa *alka-chofa*

artificial artificial *artee-feethyal*

artist el/la artista *ar-teesta*

as como *komo*

ash (*from burning*) la ceniza *the-neetha*

ashore en tierra *en tyerra*

ashtray el cenicero *thenee-thero*

ask preguntar *pregoon-tar*; **to ask for something** pedir algo *pedeer al-go*; **to ask someone to do...** pedir a alguien que... *pedeer a al-gyen ke*

asleep dormido(a) *dor-meedo(a)*

asparagus los espárragos *espa-rragos*

aspirin la aspirina *aspee-reena*

assistant el/la ayudante *a-yoodan-te*

asthma el asma *asma*

at a *a*

athletics el atletismo *at-letees-mo*

attendant el empleado *em-ple-a-do*

aubergine la berenjena *beren-khena*

auction la subasta *soo-basta*

August agosto (*m*) *a-gosto*

aunt la tía *tee-a*

au pair la au pair *au pair*

Australia la Australia *owstra-lya*

Australian australiano(a) *owstra-lyano(a)*

author el autor *owtor*

automatic la transmisión automática *transmee-syon owto-matee-ka*

autumn el otoño *o-tonyo*

avocado el aguacate *agwaka-te*

avoid (*obstacle*) evitar *e-beetar;* (*person*) esquivar *eskee-bar*

awake despierto(a) *despyerto(a)*

away: he's away no está *no esta;* **10 kilometres away** a 10 kilómetros *a dyeth keelo-metros*

awful espantoso(a) *espantoso(a)*

awkward difícil *dee-feetheel*

axe el hacha *a-cha*

axle el eje *e-khe*

B

B positive/negative B positivo/negativo *be poseeteebo/nega-teebo*

baby el/la bebé *be-be*

baby food la comida para niños *ko-meeda para neenyos*

babysitter el canguro *kangooro*

babysitting service el servicio para cuidar a los niños *ser-beethyo para kweedar a los neenyos*

baby wipes las toallitas limpiadoras *toa-lyee-tas leempya-doras*

back[1] *adj* (*rear*) de atrás *de a-tras*

back[2] *n* (*of body*) la espalda *es-palda;* (*of cheque*) el dorso *dorso;* (*of hand, head*) el revés *re-bes*

backpack la mochila *mocheela*

backwards hacia atrás *a-thya a-tras*

bacon el beicon *beykon*

bad malo(a) *malo(a);* (*food*) podrido(a) *po-dreedo(a)*

badge la placa *plaka*

bag la bolsa *bolsa;* (*suitcase*) la maleta *ma-leta;* (*handbag*) el bolso *bolso*

baggage reclaim la entrega de equipajes *en-trega de ekee-pa-khes*

baker's la panadería *panaderee-a*

balcony el balcón *balkon*

bald (*person*) calvo(a) *kalbo(a);* (*tyre*) liso(a) *leeso(a)*

ball la pelota *pe-lota;* (*dance*) el baile *ba-ee-le;* (*football*) el balón *balon*

ballet el ballet *ba-le*

ballpoint el bolígrafo *boleegrafo*

banana el plátano *pla-tano*

band (*music*) la banda *banda*

bandage la venda *benda*

bank el banco *banko*

bank holiday el día festivo *dee-a festeebo*

baptism el bautismo *bowteesmo*

bar el bar *bar*

barber's la peluquería *pelookeree-a*

bargain (*agreement*) el pacto *pakto;* (*cheap buy*) la ganga *ganga*

barmaid la camarera *kamarera*

barman el camarero *kamarero*

basket la cesta *thesta*

bathe bañarse *banyar-se*

bathing cap el gorro de baño *gorro de banyo*

bathroom el cuarto de baño *kwarto de banyo*

battery la pila *peela;* (*in car*) la batería *ba-teree-a*

bay la bahía *ba-ee-a*

be: to be English/a doctor ser inglés/médico *ser eengles/medee-ko;* **to be in Madrid/pleased** estar en Madrid/contento *estar en madreed/kon-tento*

beach la playa *playa*

bean la judía *khoodee-a*

beautiful hermoso(a) *ermoso(a)*

because porque *por-ke*

bed la cama *kama*

bedding la ropa de cama *ropa de kama*

bedroom el dormitorio *dormee-toryo*

bee la abeja *a-bekha*

beef la carne de vaca *kar-ne de baka*

beer la cerveza *ther-betha*

beetle el escarabajo *eskaraba-kho*

beetroot la remolacha *remolacha*

before (*in time*) antes de *antes de;* (*in place*) delante de *delan-te de*

begin empezar *em-pethar*

behind detrás *detras;* **behind the house** detrás de la casa *detras de la kasa*

beige beige *be-ees*

believe creer *kre-er*

bell la campana *kam-pana;* (*doorbell*) el timbre *teem-bre*

belong: to belong to pertenecer a *per-te-ne-ther a*

below abajo *a-bakho;* **below the hotel** por debajo del hotel *por de-bakho del o-tel*

belt el cinturón *theentoo-ron*

bend la curva *koorba*

bent torcido(a) *tor-theedo(a)*

berry la baya *baya*

berth la litera *lee-tera*

beside al lado de *al lado de*

best el/la mejor *mekhor;* **best wishes!** ¡felicidades! *feleetheeda-des*

better mejor *mekhor*

between entre *en-tre*

beyond (*further than*) más allá de *mas a-lya de;* (*on the other side of*) del otro lado de

del o-tro lado de
Bible la Biblia *beeblee-a*
bicycle la bicicleta *beethee-kleta*
big grande *gran-de*; **bigger** más grande *mas gran-de*
bikini el bikini *bee-keenee*
bill la cuenta *kwenta*
bin el cubo *koobo*
binoculars los prismáticos *preesma-teekos*
bird el pájaro *pa-kharo*
biro el bolígrafo *bolee-grafo*
birthday el cumpleaños *koom-ple-a-nyos*
birthday card la tarjeta de cumpleaños *tar-kheta de koom-ple-a-nyos*
bit el pedazo *pe-datho*; **a bit (of)** un poco (de) *oon poko (de)*
bite (*animal*) morder *mor-der*; (*insect*) picar *peekar*
bitter amargo(a) *a-margo(a)*
black negro(a) *negro(a)*
black coffee el café solo *ka-fe solo*
blackcurrant la grosella negra *gro-selya negra*
bladder la vejiga *be-kheega*
blanket la manta *manta*
bleach la lejía *lekhee-a*
bleeding sangrante *sangran-te*
blind ciego(a) *thyego(a)*
blister la ampolla *am-polya*
blocked (*road*) cerrado(a) *the-rrado(a)*; (*pipe*) obstruido(a) *obstroo-eedo(a)*

blood la sangre *san-gre*
blood group el grupo sanguíneo *groopo sangee-ne-o*
blouse la blusa *bloosa*
blow soplar *soplar*
blow-dry el secado a mano *se-kado a mano*
blue azul *a-thool*
blusher el colorete *kolo-re-te*
board (*ship, plane*) embarcarse en *em-barkar-se en*
boarding card la tarjeta de embarque *tar-kheta de embar-ke*
boarding house la pensión *pensyon*
boat el barco *barko*; **boat trip** la excursión en barco *exkoor-syon en barko*
body el cuerpo *kwerpo*
boil hervir *erbeer*
boiled egg el huevo cocido *webo ko-theedo*
bomb la bomba *bomba*
bone el hueso *weso*
bonnet (*of car*) el capó *kapo*
book[1] *n* el libro *leebro*; **book of tickets** el talonario *talo-naryo*
book[2] *vb* reservar *re-serbar*
booking la reserva *re-serba*
booking office el despacho de billetes *des-pacho de bee-lye-tes*
book shop la librería *lee-breree-a*
boom (*sailing*) la botavara

bota-*bara*

boot (*of car*) el maletero *ma-le-tero*; (*to wear*) la bota *bota*

border (*frontier*) la frontera *fron-tera*; (*edge*) el borde *bor-de*

bored aburrido(a) *aboo-rreedo(a)*

born nacido(a) *na-theedo(a)*

both ambos(as) *ambos(as)*

bottle la botella *bo-telya*; (*empty*) el envase *enba-se*

bottle opener el abrebotellas *a-brebo-telyas*

bottom el fondo *fondo*; (*of person*) el trasero *tra-sero*

bow[1] *n* (*of ship*) la proa *pro-a*

bow[2] *n* (*knot*) el lazo *latho*

bowels los intestinos *een-testee-nos*

bowl el tazón *tathon*

box (*container*) la caja *kakha*; (*in theatre*) el palco *palko*

box office la taquilla *ta-keelya*

boy el chico *cheeko*

boyfriend el novio *nobyo*

bra el sostén *sos-ten*

bracelet la pulsera *pool-sera*

braces los tirantes *teeran-tes*

brake el freno *freno*; **to put the brakes on** frenar *frenar*

brake fluid el líquido de frenos *lee-keedo de frenos*

branch (*of tree*) la rama *rama*; (*of bank etc*) la sucursal *sookoor-sal*

brand la marca *marka*

brandy el coñac *konyak*

brass el latón *laton*

brave valiente *balyen-te*

bread el pan *pan*

break romper *rom-per*

breakable quebradizo(a) *kebra-deetho(a)*

breakdown van la grúa *groo-a*

breakfast el desayuno *desa-yoono*

breast el seno *seno*

breathe respirar *respee-rar*

breeze la brisa *breesa*

bride la novia *nobya*

bridegroom el novio *nobyo*

bridge el puente *pwen-te*

briefcase la cartera *kar-tera*

briefs (*man's*) los calzoncillos *kalthon-theelyos*; (*woman's*) las bragas *bragas*

bright (*light, sun*) fuerte *fwerte*; (*colour*) vivo(a) *beebo(a)*

bring traer *tra-er*

Britain la Gran Bretaña *gran bre-tanya*

British británico(a) *breeta-neeko(a)*

broad ancho(a) *ancho(a)*

brochure el folleto *fo-lyeto*

broken (*object, bone*) roto(a) *roto(a)*; **broken down** averiado(a) *a-beree-a-do(a)*

bronchitis la bronquitis *bron-keetees*

bronze el bronce *bron-the*

brooch el broche *bro-che*

broom la escoba *es-koba*

brother el hermano *er-mano*

brown marrón *marron*; (*hair*) castaño(a) *kastanyo(a)*; **brown paper** el papel de estraza *pa-pel de estratha*; **brown sugar** el azúcar terciado *a-thookar terthyado*

bruise el cardenal *kar-denal*

brush el cepillo *the-peelyo*

Brussels sprouts las coles de Bruselas *ko-les de brooselas*

bucket el cubo *koobo*

buffet la cafetería *ka-fe-tereea*

buffet car el coche-comedor *ko-che-ko-medor*

build construir *konstroo-eer*

building el edificio *edeefeethyo*

bulb (*electric*) la bombilla *bombee-lya*

bull el toro *toro*

bullet la bala *bala*

bumper el parachoques *paracho-kes*

bun el bollo *bolyo*

bureau de change el cambio *kambyo*

burn[1] *vb* quemar *kemar*

burn[2] *n* la quemadura *kemadoora*

burst: a burst tyre un neumático pinchado *oon ne-oo-matee-ko peen-chado*

bus el autobús *owto-boos*

bus depot la estación de autobuses *esta-thyon de owto-boo-ses*

bush el arbusto *ar-boosto*

business los negocios *negothyos*; **business card** la tarjeta de visita *tar-kheta de bee-seeta*; **business trip** el viaje de negocios *bya-khe de ne-gothyos*

bus station la terminal de autobuses *termee-nal de owto-boo-ses*

bus stop la parada de autobús *pa-rada de owto-boos*

bus tour la excursión en autobús *exkoor-syon en owto-boos*

busy ocupado(a) *okoopado(a)*

but pero *pero*

butcher's la carnicería *karnee-theree-a*

butter la mantequilla *mantekee-lya*

butterfly la mariposa *maree-posa*

button el botón *boton*

buy comprar *komprar*

by *prep* (*beside*) al lado de *al lado de*; (*via*) por *por*

bypass la carretera de circunvalación *ka-rre-tera de theerkoon-bala-thyon*

C

cabaret el cabaret *kaba-re*

cabbage la col *kol*

cabin la cabina *ka-beena*

cablecar el teleférico *te-le-fe-reeko*

café el café *ka-fe*
cagoule el anorak *ano-rak*
cake el pastel *pas-tel*
calculator la calculadora *kalkoo-lado-ra*
call vb (*shout*) llamar *lyamar*; (*on telephone*) llamar por teléfono *lyamar por te-lefo-no*
call box la cabina telefónica *ka-beena te-lefo-neeka*
calm tranquilo(a) *tran-keelo(a)*
camera la máquina de fotos *ma-keena de fotos*
camp acampar *akam-par*
camp bed la cama de camping *kama de kampeen*
camp site el camping *kampeen*
can[1] n el bote *bo-te*
can[2] vb: **I can** puedo *pwedo*; **you can** usted puede *oos-ted pwe-de*; **he can** puede *pwe-de*; **they can** pueden *pwe-den*
Canada el Canadá *kana-da*
Canadian canadiense *kana-dyen-se*
cancel cancelar *kan-thelar*
cancer el cáncer *kan-ther*
candle la vela *bela*
canoe la canoa *kano-a*
can opener el abrelatas *a-brela-tas*
capital (*of a country*) la capital *kapee-tal*
captain el capitán *kapee-tan*
car el coche *ko-che*; **car documents** los documentos del coche *dokoo-mentos del ko-che*; **car ferry** el transbordador *transbor-dador*; **car key** la llave del coche *lya-be del ko-che*; **car number** la matrícula *matree-koola*; **car park** el aparcamiento *apar-kamyen-to*; **car wash** el lavado automático *la-bado owto-matee-ko*
carafe la garrafa *ga-rrafa*
caravan la caravana *kara-bana*
caravan site el camping *kampeen*
carburettor el carburador *karboo-rador*
card (*greetings*) la tarjeta *tar-kheta*; (*playing*) el naipe *na-ee-pe*
cardigan la rebeca *re-beka*
care: **take care** tenga cuidado *tenga kwee-dado*; **I don't care** no me importa *no me eem-porta*
careful cuidadoso(a) *kweeda-doso(a)*
careless descuidado(a) *deskwee-dado(a)*
carpet la alfombra *al-fombra*
carriage el vagón *bagon*
carrier bag (*plastic*) la bolsa de plástico *bolsa de plas-teeko*
carrot la zanahoria *thana-o-rya*
carry llevar *lyebar*
cartridge el cartucho *kar-*

toocho

case (*suitcase*) la maleta *maleta;* (*medical*) el caso *kaso*

cash[1] *n* el dinero en efectivo *dee-nero en efek-teebo*

cash[2] *vb* (*cheque*) cobrar *kobrar*

cash advance el adelanto en efectivo *a-de-lanto en efek-teebo*

cash desk la caja *kakha*

cashier el/la cajero(a) *ka-khero(a)*

casino el casino *ka-seeno*

cassette la casete *kaset*

castle el castillo *kas-teelyo*

cat el gato *gato*

catalogue el catálogo *kata-logo*

catch coger *ko-kher*

cathedral la catedral *ka-tedral*

Catholic católico(a) *kato-leeko(a)*

cauliflower la coliflor *kolee-flor*

cause causar *kowsar*

cave la cueva *kweba*

ceiling el techo *techo*

celeriac el apio-nabo *apyo-nabo*

celery el apio *a-pyo*

cellar (*of house*) el sótano *sotano;* (*for wine*) la bodega *bo-dega*

cemetery el cementerio *cemen-teryo*

centigrade centigrado(a) *thentee-grado(a)*

centimetre el centímetro *thentee-metro*

central central *thentral*

central heating la calefacción central *ka-lefak-thyon thentral*

centre el centro *thentro*

cereal (*breakfast*) los cereales *the-re-a-les*

certain (*sure*) seguro(a) *se-gooro(a)*

certificate el certificado *thertee-feeka-do*

chain la cadena *ka-dena*

chair la silla *seelya*

chairlift el telesilla *te-le-seelya*

chalet el chalet *cha-le*

champagne el champán *champan*

change[1] *n* el cambio *kambyo;* (*small coins*) el suelto *swelto;* (*money returned*) la vuelta *bwelta*

change[2] *vb* cambiar *kambyar;* **to change clothes** cambiarse *kambyar-se;* **to change trains** hacer transbordo *ather trans-bordo*

changing room el probador *proba-dor*

chapel la capilla *ka-peelya*

charge el precio *prethyo*

chart la carta *karta*

charter flight el vuelo chárter *bwelo charter*

chassis el chasis *chasees*

chauffeur el chófer *cho-fer*

cheap barato(a) *ba-rato(a);*

cheaper más barato(a) *mas ba-rato(a)*

check controlar *kontro-lar*; **to check in** (*at airport*) presentarse *pre-sentar-se*; (*at hotel*) registrarse *re-kheestrar-se*

check-in desk el mostrador de facturación *mostra-dor de faktoo-rathyon*

cheek la mejilla *me-kheelya*

cheeky descarado(a) *deska-rado(a)*

cheers! ¡salud! *salood*

cheese el queso *keso*

cheesecake la tarta de queso *tarta de keso*

chef el cocinero *kothee-nero*

chemist's la farmacia *far-mathya*

cheque el cheque *che-ke*

cheque book el talonario *talo-naryo*

cheque card la tarjeta de identidad bancaria *tar-kheta de eeden-teedad ban-karya*

cherry la cereza *the-retha*

chess el ajedrez *a-khe-dreth*

chest el pecho *pecho*

chestnut (*fruit*) la castaña *kas-tanya*

chewing gum el chicle *chee-kle*

chicken el pollo *polyo*

chickenpox la varicela *baree-thela*

chilblain el sabañón *saba-nyon*

child (*boy*) el niño *neenyo*;

(*girl*) la niña *neenya*;

children los niños *neenyos*;

children's pool la piscina para niños *pees-theena para neenyos*

chill (*wine*) enfriar *enfree-ar*

chilli el chile *chee-le*

chimney la chimenea *chee-me-ne-a*

chin la barbilla *bar-beelya*

china la porcelana *por-thela-na*

chips las patatas fritas *pa-tatas freetas*

chocolate el chocolate *choko-la-te*; **chocolates** los bombones *bombo-nes*

choke el stárter *star-ter*

choose elegir *e-lekheer*

chop (*meat*) la chuleta *choo-leta*

Christian name el nombre de pila *nom-bre de pee-la*

Christmas la Navidad *nabee-dad*

church la iglesia *ee-glesya*

churchyard el cementerio *themen-teryo*

cider la sidra *seedra*

cigar el puro *pooro*

cigarette el cigarrillo *theega-reelyo*; **cigarette papers** los papeles de fumar *pa-pe-les de foomar*

cine camera la cámara cinematográfica *ka-mara thee-nema-togra-feeka*

cinema el cine *thee-ne*

cinnamon la canela *ka-nela*

circle el círculo *theer-koolo*; (*in theatre*) el anfiteatro *anfee-te-a-tro*

circus el circo *theerko*

city la ciudad *thyoodad*

claim (*expenses, damages*) reclamar *rekla-mar*

clam la almeja *al-mekha*

class la clase *kla-se*

clean[1] *adj* limpio(a) *leempyo(a)*

clean[2] *vb* limpiar *leempyar*

cleaner (*person*) el/la asistente(a) *asees-ten-te(a)*

cleansing cream la crema limpiadora *krema leempya-dora*

clear claro(a) *klaro(a)*; (*obvious*) evidente *ebee-den-te*; (*transparent*) transparente *transpa-ren-te*

clerk el empleado *em-ple-a-do*

clever inteligente *een-telee-khen-te*

client el cliente *klee-en-te*

cliff el acantilado *akan-teela-do*

climate el clima *kleema*

climber el alpinista *alpee-neesta*

climbing el alpinismo *alpee-neesmo*

cloakroom el guardarropa *gwarda-rropa*

clock el reloj *relo*

close[1] *adj* (*near*) cercano(a) *ther-kano(a)*; (*weather*) pesado(a) *pe-sado(a)*

close[2] *vb* cerrar *therrar*

closed cerrado(a) *the-rrado(a)*

cloth el trapo *trapo*

clothes la ropa *ropa*

clothes peg la pinza *peentha*

cloud la nube *noo-be*

cloudy nublado(a) *noo-blado(a)*

clove el clavo *klabo*

club el club *kloob*; (*golf implement*) el palo *palo*

clumsy torpe *tor-pe*

clutch (*in car*) el embrague *embra-ge*

coach (*bus*) el autocar *owto-kar*; (*train*) el vagón *bagon*; (*instructor*) el entrenador *entre-nador*; **coach trip** la excursión en autocar *exkoor-syon en owto-kar*

coal el carbón *karbon*

coarse burdo(a) *boordo(a)*

coast la costa *kosta*

coastguard el guardacostas *gwarda-kostas*

coat el abrigo *a-breego*

coat-hanger la percha *percha*

cock el gallo *galyo*

cockle el berberecho *ber-be-recho*

cocktail el cóctel *koktel*

cocoa el cacao *kaka-o*; (*drink*) el chocolate *cho-kola-te*

coconut el coco *koko*

cod el bacalao *ba-kala-o*

coffee el café *ka-fe*

coin la moneda *mo-neda*

coke la coca *koka* **kola**

colander el colador *kola-dor*

cold[1] *n* el resfriado *resfree-a-do*

cold[2] *adj* frio(a) *free-o(a)*

collar el cuello *kwelyo*

colleague el/la colega *ko-lega*

collect (*assemble*) reunir *re-oo-neer*; (*stamps*) coleccionar *kolek-thyonar*; **I'll collect you** te recojo *te re-kokho*

collection (*of stamps*) la colección *kolek-thyon*

college el colegio *ko-lekhee-o*

colour el color *kolor*; **colour-blind** daltoniano(a) *dalto-nyano(a)*; **colour print film** la película en color *pelee-koola en kolor*; **colour slide film** la película de diapositivas en color *pelee-koola de dee-apo-seetee-bas en kolor*

comb el peine *pe-ee-ne*

come venir *beneer*; **to come off** (*button*) desprenderse *despren-der-se*; **to come out** salir *saleer*; (*stain*) quitarse *keetar-se*; **to come to** (*after faint*) recobrar el conocimiento *reko-brar el kono-theemyen-to*

comfortable cómodo(a) *ko-modo(a)*

comic (*paper*) el tebeo *te-be-o*

commentary el comentario *komen-taryo*

commercial comercial *comer-thyal*

common común *komoon*

communication cord el timbre de alarma *teem-bre de a-larma*

communion la comunión *komoo-nyon*

company la compañía *kompa-nyee-a*

compare comparar *kompa-rar*

compartment el compartimento *kompar-teemen-to*

compass la brújula *broo-khoola*

competition el concurso *kon-koorso*

complain quejarse *kekhar-se*; (*in shop*) reclamar *rekla-mar*

complaint la queja *kekha*; (*in shop*) la reclamación *rekla-mathyon*

completely completamente *kom-ple-tamen-te*

complicated complicado(a) *komplee-kado(a)*

comprehensive (*insurance*) a todo riesgo *a todo ryesgo*

compulsory obligatorio(a) *oblee-gato-ryo(a)*

computer el computador *kompoo-tador*

concert el concierto *kon-thyerto*

concussion la conmoción cerebral *kon-mothyon the-*

rebral

condensed milk la leche condensada *le-che kondensada*

condition la condición *kondee-thyon*

conditioner (*for hair*) el condicionador *kondeethyona-dor*

conductor (*on bus*) el cobrador *kobra-dor*

conference la conferencia *kon-feren-thya*

confession la confesión *konfesyon*

confidential confidencial *konfee-denthyal*

confirm confirmar *konfeermar*

congratulations ¡felicitaciones! *felee-theetathyo-nes*

conjunctivitis la conjuntivitis *konkhoonteebee-tees*

connect conectar *konek-tar*

conscious consciente *konsthyen-te*

constipated estreñido(a) *estrenyee-do(a)*

consul el cónsul *konsool*

consulate el consulado *konsoo-lado*

contact comunicarse con *komoo-neekar-se kon*

contact lenses los lentes de contacto *len-tes de kon-takto*; **contact lens cleaner** la solución limpiadora para lentes de contacto *soloo-thyon leempya-dora para lentes de kon-takto*

Continental europeo(a) *e-ooro-pe-o(a)*

contraceptive el anticonceptivo *antee-konthepteebo*

contract el contrato *kontrato*

controls los mandos *mandos*

convenient práctico(a) *prak-teeko(a)*

convent el convento *konbento*

cook[1] *vb* cocinar *kothee-nar*

cook[2] *n* el/la cocinero(a) *kothee-nero(a)*

cooker la cocina *ko-theena*

cool fresco(a) *fresko(a)*

cooling system el sistema de refrigeración *sees-tema de refree-khera-thyon*

copper el cobre *ko-bre*

copy[1] *n* la copia *kopya*; (*of book*) el ejemplar *e-khemplar*

copy[2] *vb* copiar *kopyar*

corduroy la pana *pana*

cork el corcho *korcho*

corkscrew el sacacorchos *saka-korchos*

corn (*sweet corn*) el maiz tierno *ma-eeth tyerno*; (*on foot*) el callo *kalyo*; **corn on the cob** el maiz en la mazorca *ma-eeth en la mathorka*

corner la esquina *es-keena*; (*of room*) el rincón *reenkon*

cornflakes los copos de maíz *kopos de ma-eeth*

cornflour la harina de maíz *a-reena de ma-eeth*

correct correcto(a) *korrekto(a)*

corridor el pasillo *pa-seelyo*

cortisone la cortisona *korteesona*

cosmetics los cosméticos *kos-metee-kos*

cost[1] *vb* costar *kostar*; **how much does it cost?** ¿cuánto cuesta? *kwanto kwesta*

cost[2] *n* el precio *prethyo*

cot la cuna *koona*

cottage la casita de campo *kaseeta de kampo*

cottage cheese el requesón *re-keson*

cotton el algodón *algo-don*; **cotton wool** el algodón hidrófilo *algo-don eedrofeelo*

couch el sofá *sofa*

couchette la litera *lee-tera*

cough la tos *tos*

cough medicine el jarabe para la tos *kha-rabe para la tos*

count contar *kontar*

counter (*in bank, post office*) la ventanilla *benta-neelya*

country el país *pa-ees*; (*not town*) el campo *kampo*

couple (*people*) la pareja *parekha*

courgettes los calabacines *kala-bathee-nes*

courier (*for tourists*) el guía de turismo *gee-a de too-reesmo*

course el plato *plato*

courtyard el patio *patyo*

cousin el/la primo(a) *preemo(a)*

cover[1] *n* la cubierta *koobyerta*

cover[2] *vb* cubrir *koobreer*

cover charge el precio del cubierto *prethyo del koobyerto*

cow la vaca *baka*

crab el cangrejo *kan-grekho*

crack[1] *vb* quebrar *kebrar*

crack[2] *n* la grieta *gree-e-ta*

crash helmet el casco protector *kasko protek-tor*

cream (*on milk*) la nata *nata*; (*lotion*) la crema *krema*

crèche la guardería *gwarderee-a*

credit card la tarjeta de crédito *tar-kheta de kre-deeto*

cress el berro *berro*

crew la tripulación *treepoo-lathyon*

crimson carmesí *kar-mesee*

crisp fresco(a) *fresko(a)*

crisps las patatas fritas *patatas freetas*

crochet hacer en croché *a-ther en kro-che*

crooked torcido(a) *tor-theedo(a)*

croquette la croqueta *kroketa*

cross[1] *n* la cruz *krooth*

cross[2] *vb* (*a road*) atravesar

atra-besar; (a cheque) cruzar kroothar; **a crossed line** un cruce de línea *oon kroo-the de lee-ne-a*

crossing *(by sea)* la travesía *tra-besee-a; (road junction)* el cruce *kroo-the; (trains)* el paso a nivel *paso a nee-bel*

crossroads el cruce *kroo-the*

crossword el crucigrama *kroothee-grama*

crowded atestado(a) *a-testado(a)*

crown la corona *ko-rona*

crucifix el crucifijo *kroothee-feekho*

cruel cruel *kroo-el*

cruise el crucero *kroo-thero*

crush aplastar *aplas-tar*

crust la corteza *kor-tetha*

crutch la muleta *moo-leta*

cry llorar *lyorar*

crystal el cristal *kreestal*

cube el cubo *koobo*

cucumber el pepino *pe-peeno*

cuddle abrazar *abra-thar*

cuff el puño *poonyo*

cup la taza *tatha*

cupboard el armario *ar-maryo*

cure[1] *vb* curar *koorar*

cure[2] *n* el remedio *re-medyo*

curl rizar *reethar*

curly rizado(a) *ree-thado(a)*

currant la pasa *pasa*

currency la moneda *mo-neda*

current la corriente *korryen-te*

curry el curry *koo-rre*

curtain la cortina *kor-teena*

curve la curva *koorba*

cushion el cojín *kokheen*

custard las natillas *na-teelyas*

customs la aduana *a-dwana*

customs officer el aduanero *adwa-nero*

cut[1] *vb* cortar *kortar;* **to cut off** cortar *kortar*

cut[2] *n* el corte *kor-te*

cutlery los cubiertos *koo-byertos*

cycling el ciclismo *thee-kleesmo*

cyclist el/la ciclista *thee-kleesta*

D

daily: daily rate la tarifa por día *ta-reefa por dee-a*

damage[1] *n* los desperfectos *desper-fektos*

damage[2] *vb* dañar *danyar*

damp húmedo(a) *oo-medo(a)*

damson la ciruela damascena *thee-rwela damas-thena*

dance bailar *ba-eelar*

dangerous peligroso(a) *pelee-groso(a)*

dark oscuro(a) *oskoo-ro(a)*

darling querido(a) *ke-reedo(a)*

darn zurcir *thoortheer*

darts los dardos *dardos*

dashboard el salpicadero *sal-peeka-dero*

data los datos *datos*

date of birth la fecha de nacimiento *fecha de natheemyento*

daughter la hija *eekha*

day el día *dee-a*

dead muerto(a) *mwerto(a)*

deaf sordo(a) *sordo(a)*

dealer el comerciante *komerthyan-te*

dear querido(a) *ke-reedo(a)*; (*expensive*) caro(a) *karo(a)*;
Dear Mary querida Mary *ke-reeda Mary*; **Dear Sir** muy señor mío *mooy senyor mee-o*

debt la deuda *de-oo-da*

decaffeinated:
decaffeinated coffee el café descafeinado *ka-fe deska-fe-ee-nado*

December diciembre (*m*) *deethyem-bre*

decide decidir *dethee-deer*

decimal decimal *dethee-mal*

deck la cubierta *koo-byerta*

deck chair la tumbona *toom-bona*

declare declarar *dekla-rar*

deep profundo(a) *profoondo(a)*

deep freeze el congelador *kon-khela-dor*

deer el ciervo *thyerbo*

defrost (*frozen food*) deshelar *des-e-lar*

degree (*on scale*) el grado *grado*; (*university*) el título *tee-toolo*

de-ice deshelar *des-e-lar*

delay[1] *n* la demora *de-mora*

delay[2] *vb* demorar *de-morar*

delicate delicado(a) *delee-kado(a)*

delicious delicioso(a) *de-lee-thyoso(a)*

demonstration (*showing*) la demostración *demostrathyon*; (*political*) la manifestación *manee-festathyon*

denim la mezclilla *meth-kleelya*

dent *vb* abollar *abo-lyar*

dented abollado(a) *abolyado(a)*

dentist el dentista *den-teesta*

dentures la dentadura postiza *denta-doora pos-teetha*

deodorant el desodorante *deso-doran-te*

department el departamento *depar-tamen-to*

department stores los grandes almacenes *gran-des alma-the-nes*

departure la salida *sa-leeda*

departure lounge la sala de embarque *sala de embar-ke*

deposit el depósito *depo-seeto*

describe describir *deskree-beer*

description la descripción *deskreep-thyon*

design[1] *n* (*pattern*) el diseño *dee-senyo*

design[2] *vb* diseñar *dee-senyar*

desk (in hotel) la recepción *re-thepthyon*; (in office) el escritorio *eskree-toryo*
dessert el postre *pos-tre*
dessertspoon la cuchara de mesa *koo-chara de mesa*
details los detalles *deta-lyes*
detective el detective *detek-tee-be*
detergent el detergente *deter-khen-te*
detour la desviación *desbee-a-thyon*
develop desarrollar *desa-rrolyar*
diabetic diabético(a) *dee-a-betee-ko(a)*
dial: to dial a number marcar un número *markar oon noo-mero*
dialling code el prefijo *pre-feekho*
dialling tone el tono de marcar *tono de markar*
diamond el diamante *dee-a-man-te*
diarrhoea la diarrea *dee-a-rre-a*
diary la agenda *a-khenda*
dice los dados *dados*
dictionary el diccionario *deek-thyo-naryo*
did: I did it lo he hecho yo *lo e echo yo*; **did he go?** ¿fue? *fwe*
didn't: I didn't do it no lo he hecho yo *no lo e-cho yo*
die morir *moreer*
diesel el gasoil *gaso-eel*

diet el régimen *re-kheemen*; **I'm on a diet** estoy a régimen *estoy a re-kheemen*
different distinto(a) *dees-teento(a)*
difficult difícil *dee-feetheel*
dinghy el barco a vela *barko a bela*
dining room el comedor *ko-medor*
dinner la cena *thena*; **dinner jacket** el smóking *smoking*
dip: to dip one's headlights bajar los faros *bakhar los faros*
diplomat el diplomático *deeplo-matee-ko*
direct directo(a) *dee-rekto(a)*
directory la guía telefónica *gee-a te-le-fonee-ka*
dirty sucio(a) *soothyo(a)*
disabled minusválido(a) *meenoos-balee-do(a)*
disappointed decepcionado(a) *dethep-thyona-do(a)*
disappointing decepcionante *dethep-thyonan-te*
disco la discoteca *deesko-teka*
discount el descuento *des-kwento*
dish el plato *plato*
dishcloth la bayeta *ba-yeta*
dishrack el escurreplatos *eskoo-rre-platos*
dishtowel el trapo *trapo*
dishwasher el lavaplatos *laba-platos*

disinfectant el desinfectante *deseen-fektan-te*

dislocate dislocarse *deeslo-kar-se*

disposable nappies los braga-pañales *braga-panya-les*

distance la distancia *dees-tan-thya*

distilled water el agua destilada *a-gwa destee-lada*

distributor el distribuidor *deestree-bweedor*

district la zona *thona*

disturb molestar *molestar*

dive: to dive into the water saltar al agua *saltar al a-gwa*

diver el saltador *salta-dor*

divorced divorciado(a) *deebor-thyado(a)*

dizzy mareado(a) *ma-re-a-do(a)*

do hacer *a-ther*; **I do** hago *a-go*; **you do** usted hace *oos-ted a-the*

doctor el médico *me-deeko*

documents los documentos *dokoo-mentos*

does: he does hace *a-the*

dog el perro *perro*

doll la muñeca *moo-nyeka*

dollar el dólar *dolar*

dome la cúpula *koo-poola*

dominoes el dominó *domee-no*

donkey el burro *boorro*

door la puerta *pwerta*

double doble *do-ble*; **double**

bed la cama de matrimonio *kama de matree-monyo*;

double room la habitación doble *abee-tathyon do-ble*;

double whisky el whisky doble *weeskee do-ble*

dough la masa *masa*

doughnut el churro *choorro*

down abajo *a-bakho*; **to go down** bajar *bakhar*; **down the street** calle abajo *ka-lye a-bakho*

downstairs abajo *a-bakho*

drain[1] *n* el desaguadero *desagwa-dero*

drain[2] *vb* (*vegetables*) escurrir *eskoo-rrer*; (*tank*) vaciar *bathyar*

draught (*of air*) la corriente *korryen-te*

draughts el juego de damas *khwego de damas*

draw (*picture*) dibujar *deeboo-khar*; (*money*) retirar *re-teerar*

drawer el cajón *kakhon*

drawing book el libro de dibujos *leebro de dee-bookhos*

dreadful espantoso(a) *espan-toso(a)*

dress[1] *n* el vestido *bes-teedo*

dress[2] *vb*: **to get dressed** vestirse *besteer-se*

dressing (*for salad*) el aliño *a-leenyo*

drier (*for hair*) el secador *seka-dor*; (*for clothes*) la secadora *seka-dora*

drink[1] *n* la bebida *be-beeda*; **let's have a drink** vamos a tomar una copa *bamos a tomar oona kopa*

drink[2] *vb* beber *beber*

drinking chocolate el chocolate caliente *choko-la-te ka-lyen-te*

drinking water el agua potable *a-gwa pota-ble*

drip gotear *go-tear*

drive conducir *kondoo-theer*

driver el conductor/la conductora *kondook-tor/ kondook-tora*

driving el conducir *kondoo-theer*

driving licence el carné de conducir *kar-ne de kondoo-theer*

drown ahogarse *a-o-gar-se*

drug la droga *droga*

drum el tambor *tambor*

drunk borracho(a) *bo-rracho(a)*

dry[1] *adj* seco(a) *seko(a)*

dry[2] *vb* secar *sekar*

dry cleaner's la tintorería *teento-reree-a*

dual carriageway la carretera de doble calzada *ka-rre-tera de do-ble kal-thada*

duck el pato *pato*

due: when is the train due? ¿cuándo debe llegar el tren? *kwando de-be lyegar el tren*

dull (*weather*) gris *grees*

dumb mudo(a) *moodo(a)*

dummy el chupete *choo-pe-te*

dune la duna *doona*

during durante *dooran-te*

dust el polvo *polbo*

dusty polvoriento(a) *polbo-ryento(a)*

duty (*tax*) los derechos *de-rechos*

duty-free libre de derechos de aduana *lee-bre de de-rechos de a-dwana*; **duty-free shop** la tienda 'duty free' *tyenda duty-free*

duvet el edredón *e-dredon*

dye[1] *n* el tinte *teen-te*

dye[2] *vb* teñir *tenyeer*

dynamo la dinamo *dee-namo*

E

each cada *kada*

eagle la águila *a-geela*

ear la oreja *o-rekha*

earache: I have earache me duele el oído *me dwe-le el o-ee-do*

early temprano *tem-prano*

earn ganar *ganar*

earphones los auriculares *owree-koola-res*

earplugs los tapones para los oídos *tapo-nes para los o-eedos*

earrings los pendientes *pendyen-tes*

earth la tierra *tyerra*

earthquake el terremoto *te-rremo-to*

east el este *es-te*
Easter la Pascua *paskwa*
easy fácil *fatheel*
eat comer *komer*
economical económico(a)
eko-nomee-ko(a)
eczema el eczema *ek-thema*
edge (*of cliff, wood*) el borde
bor-de; (*of lake*) la orilla *o-reelya*
eel la anguila *an-geela*
efficient eficaz *efee-kath*
egg el huevo *webo*
eggcup la huevera *we-bera*
eight ocho *o-cho*
eighteen dieciocho *dyethee-o-cho*
eighty ochenta *o-chenta*
either cualquiera de los dos
kwal-kyera de los dos
elastic band la goma *goma*
elbow el codo *kodo*
election la elección *elek-thyon*
electric blanket la manta
eléctrica *manta e-lektree-ka*
electric fire la estufa
eléctrica *es-toofa e-lektree-ka*
electrician el electricista
elek-treethees-ta
electricity la electricidad
elek-treethee-dad
electricity meter el
contador de la luz *konta-dor de la looth*
electric razor la máquina de
afeitar eléctrica *ma-keena de
a-fe-eetar e-lektree-ka*
electrics el sistema eléctrico

sees-tema e-lektree-ko
electronic electrónico(a)
elek-tronee-ko(a)
element el elemento *e-lemen-to*
elephant el elefante *e-lefan-te*
eleven once *on-the*
eleventh undécimo *oon-dethee-mo*
embarrass avergonzar *aber-gonthar*
embarrassing
embarazoso(a) *emba-ratho-so(a)*
embassy la embajada *emba-khada*
embroidery el bordado *bor-dado*
emerald la esmeralda *es-meral-da*
emergency la emergencia
emer-khenthya; **emergency
windscreen** el parabrisas de
repuesto *para-breesas de re-pwesto*
emery boards las limas de
uñas *leemas de oo-nyas*
empty[1] *adj* vacío(a) *bathee-o(a)*; (*house, room*)
desocupado(a) *des-okoo-pado(a)*
empty[2] *vb* vaciar *bathyar*
enamel el esmalte *esmal-te*
encyclopedia la enciclopedia
en-theeklo-pedya
end el fin *feen*
endive la endibia *en-deebya*
energetic enérgico(a) *e-*

nerkhee-ko(a)
engaged (*to be married*)
prometido(a) *pro-
meteedo(a);* (*toilet*)
ocupado(a) *okoo-pado(a);*
the number is engaged
están comunicando *estan
komoo-neekan-do*
engine el motor *motor*
engineer el ingeniero *een-
khenye-ro*
England la Inglaterra *eengla-
terra*
English inglés/inglesa *een-
gles/een-glesa;* **do you
speak English?** ¿habla
usted inglés? *a-bla oosted
een-gles*
enjoy gozar de *gothar de;* **to
enjoy oneself** divertirse *dee-
berteer-se*
enough bastante *bastan-te*
enquiry desk la mesa de
informes *mesa de een-formes*
entertainments las
diversiones *dee-bersyo-nes*
enthusiastic entusiasta
entoo-syasta
entrance la entrada *en-trada*
entry visa la visa de entrada
beesa de en-trada
envelope el sobre *so-bre*
epilepsy la epilepsia *epee-
lepsya*
equal igual *ee-gwal*
equipment el equipo *e-
keepo*
escalator la escalera
mecánica *eska-lera meka-*

neeka
especially especialmente *es-
pethyal-men-te*
essential imprescindible
eempres-theendee-ble
estate (*land*) la finca *feenka;*
(*housing*) la urbanización
oorba-neetha-thyon
estate agent el agente
inmobiliario *a-khen-te
eenmo-beelya-ryo*
Europe la Europa *e-ooro-pa*
European europeo(a) *e-
ooro-pe-o(a)*
evaporated milk la leche
evaporada *le-che eba-pora-da*
even (*numbers*) par *par;* **even
on Sundays** hasta los
domingos *asta los do-
meengos*
evening la tarde *tar-de;*
evening dress (*woman's*) el
traje de noche *tra-khe de noche;* **evening meal** la cena
thena
every (*each*) cada *kada;* (*all*)
todo(a) *todo(a)*
everyone todo el mundo
todo el moondo
everything todo *todo*
everywhere en todas partes
en todas par-tes
evidence la prueba *prweba*
examination (*medical*) el
reconocimiento *reko-nothee-
myento;* (*school etc*) el
examen *ek-samen*
example el ejemplo *e-
khemplo*

excellent excelente *ex-thelen-te*

except salvo *salbo*

excess luggage el exceso de equipaje *ex-theso de ekeepa-khe*

exchange cambiar *kambyar*

exchange rate el tipo de cambio *teepo de kambyo*

excited excitado(a) *extheeta-do(a)*

exciting emocionante *emothyonan-te*

excursion la excursión *exkoor-syon*

excuse perdonar *perdo-nar*; **excuse me** (*sorry*) ¡perdón! *perdon*

exercise el ejercicio *ekhertheethyo*

exhaust pipe el tubo de escape *toobo de eska-pe*

exhibition la exposición *expo-seethyon*

exit la salida *sa-leeda*

expect esperar *es-perar*

expensive caro(a) *karo(a)*

expert el experto *ex-perto*

expire caducar *kadoo-kar*

explain explicar *explee-kar*

explosion la explosión *explo-syon*

export[1] *n* la exportación *expor-tathyon*

export[2] *vb* exportar *expor-tar*

exposure meter el fotómetro *foto-metro*

express[1] *n* (*train*) el rápido *ra-peedo*

express[2] *adj*: **to send a letter express** enviar una carta por correo urgente *enbyar oona karta por ko-rre-o oorkhen-te*

extension la extensión *exten-syon*

extra: **wine is extra** el vino es aparte *el beeno es a-par-te*; **extra time** más tiempo *mas tyempo*

eye el ojo *o-kho*

eye bath la ojera *o-khera*

eyebrow la ceja *thekha*

eyebrow pencil el lápiz de cejas *lapeeth de thekhas*

eyelash la pestaña *pes-tanya*

eye liner el rímel *reemel*

eye shadow la sombra de ojos *sombra de o-khos*

F

fabric el tejido *te-kheedo*

face la cara *kara*; **face cloth** la manopla *ma-nopla*; **face cream** la crema de belleza *krema de bel-yetha*; **face powder** los polvos (de tocador) *polbos (de toka-dor)*

facilities las facilidades *fathee-leeda-des*

fact el hecho *e-cho*

factory la fábrica *fa-bree-ka*

failure el fracaso *fra-kaso*

faint desmayarse *desma-yar-se*

fair[1] *adj* (*hair*) rubio(a) *roobyo(a)*

fair² *n* (*trade fair*) la feria de muestras *ferya de mwestras;* (*funfair*) el parque de atracciones *par-ke de atrak-thyo-nes*

faithfully: Yours faithfully le saluda atentamente *le sa-loo-da aten-ta-men-te*

fake falso(a) *falso(a)*

fall caer *ka-er*

false teeth la dentadura postiza *denta-doora pos-teetha*

family la familia *famee-lya*

famous famoso(a) *fa-moso(a)*

fan (*electric*) el ventilador eléctrico *bentee-lador e-lektree-ko;* (*paper*) el abanico *aba-neeko;* (*supporter*) el hincha *een-cha*

fan belt la correa del ventilador *ko-rre-a del bentee-lador*

fancy dress el disfraz *dees-frath*

far lejos *lekhos;* **is it far?** ¿está lejos? *esta lekhos*

fare el precio del billete *prethyo del bee-lye-te*

farm la granja *grankha*

farmer el granjero *gran-khero*

farmhouse la granja *grankha*

farther más lejos *mas lekhos*

fast rápido(a) *ra-peedo(a)*

fasten sujetar *soo-khetar*

fat¹ *adj* gordo(a) *gordo(a)*

fat² *n* la grasa *grasa*

fatal fatal *fatal*

father el padre *pa-dre*

father-in-law el suegro *swegro*

fault la culpa *koolpa*

favourite favorito(a) *fabo-reeto(a)*

fawn (*colour*) de un pardo claro *de oon pardo klaro*

feather la pluma *plooma*

February febrero (*m*) *fe-brero*

fed-up harto(a) *arto(a)*

fee los honorarios *ono-raryos*

feed dar de comer a *dar de komer a;* (*baby*) dar el pecho a *dar el pecho a*

feel sentir *senteer;* **I feel sick** siento náuseas *syento nowseas*

felt-tip pen el rotulador *rotoo-lador*

female femenino(a) *fe-me-neeno(a)*

fence la cerca *therka*

fern el helecho *e-lecho*

ferry el transbordador *transbor-dador*

festival la fiesta *fyesta*

fetch (*thing*) traer *tra-er;* (*person*) ir a buscar *eer a booskar*

fever la fiebre *fye-bre*

few pocos(as) *pokos(as);* **a few** algunos(as) *al-goonos(as);* **a few books** algunos libros *al-goonos leebros*

fiancé(e) el/la novio(a) *nobyo(a)*

fibreglass la fibra de vidrio *feebra de bee-dryo*

field el campo *kampo*

fifteen quince *keen-the*

fifth quinto(a) *keento(a)*

fifty cincuenta *theen-kwenta*

fight[1] *vb* pelear *pe-lear*

fight[2] *n* la pelea *pe-le-a*

fifty cincuenta *theen-kwenta*

fill llenar *lyenar*; **to fill in** (*form*) rellenar *re-lyenar*; **to fill up** (*container*) llenar *lyenar*

fillet el filete *fee-le-te*

filling (*in tooth*) el empaste *empas-te*; (*in food*) el relleno *re-lyeno*

film (*at cinema*) la película *pelee-koola*; (*for camera*) el carrete *ka-rre-te*; **film show** la sesión de cine *sesyon de thee-ne*

filter-tipped con filtro *kon feeltro*

fine[1] *adj* (*weather*) bueno(a) *bweno(a)*; **fine!** vale! *ba-le*

fine[2] *n* la multa *moolta*

finger el dedo *dedo*

finish acabar *aka-bar*

fire el fuego *fwego*; **fire!** ¡fuego! *fwego*; **fire brigade** los bomberos *bom-beros*; **fire extinguisher** el extintor *eksteen-tor*

fireworks los fuegos artificiales *fwegos artee-fee-thya-les*

first primero(a) *pree-*
mero(a); **first class** de primera clase *de pree-mera kla-se*; **first floor** el primer piso *pree-mer peeso*; **first name** el nombre de pila *nom-bre de peela*

first aid los primeros auxilios *pree-meros owk-seelyos*

fish[1] *n* el pescado *pes-kado*

fish[2] *vb* pescar *pes-kar*

fishing la pesca *peska*

fishing rod la caña de pescar *kanya de peskar*

fit[1] *adj* (*healthy*) en forma *en forma*

fit[2] *vb* (*clothes*) sentar *sentar*; (*go in*) entrar *entrar*

five cinco *theenko*

fix fijar *feekhar*

fizzy gaseoso(a) *ga-se-o-so(a)*

flag la bandera *ban-dera*

flannel (*facecloth*) el paño *panyo*

flash el flash *flash*; **flash bulb** la bombilla de flash *bom-beelya de flash*; **flash cube** el cubo de flash *koobo de flash*

flask el frasco *frasko*

flat[1] *adj* llano(a) *lya-no(a)*; (*battery*) descargado(a) *deskar-gado(a)*; **flat tyre** la rueda pinchada *rweda peen-chada*

flat[2] *n* el apartamento *apar-tamen-to*

flavour el sabor *sabor*

flaw el defecto *de-fekto*

flea la pulga *poolga*

flight el vuelo *bwelo*

flight bag la bolsa de viaje *bolsa de bya-khe*

flippers las aletas *a-letas*

float flotar *flotar*

flood la inundación *eenoondathyon*

floodlight el foco *foko*; **floodlit** iluminado(a) con focos *ee-loomee-nado(a) kon fokos*

floor el piso *peeso*

flour la harina *a-reena*

flow correr *ko-rrer*

flower la flor *flor*

flu la gripe *gree-pe*

fluent: he is fluent in Spanish domina el español *do-meena el espa-nyol*

flush: to flush the toilet hacer funcionar la cisterna del váter *a-ther foonthyo-nar la thees-terna del ba-ter*

fly[1] *vb* volar *bolar*

fly[2] *n* la mosca *moska*

fly sheet el doble techo *doble techo*

fog la niebla *nyebla*

foggy nebuloso(a) *nebooloso(a)*

foil el papel de estaño *pa-pel de es-tanyo*

fold[1] *vb* doblar *doblar*

fold[2] *n* el pliegue *plee-e-ge*

follow seguir *segeer*

food el alimento *alee-mento*; **food poisoning** la intoxicación por alimentos *eentok-seeka-thyon por alee-mentos*

foot el pie *pye;* (*measure*) = 30.48 cm

football el fútbol *footbol*

for para *para;* **for 100 pesetas** por cien pesetas *por thyen pesetas;* **for you** para usted *para oos-ted*

forbidden prohibido(a) *proee-beedo(a)*

foreign extranjero(a) *ekstran-khero(a)*

foreigner el extranjero *ekstran-khero*

forest el bosque *bos-ke*

forget olvidar *olbee-dar*

forgive perdonar *perdo-nar*

fork el tenedor *te-nedor*

form (*document*) el formulario *for-moo-laryo*

fortnight quince días *keen-the dee-as*

forty cuarenta *kwa-renta*

foundation cream la crema base *krema ba-se*

fountain la fuente *fwen-te*

four cuatro *kwatro*

fourteen catorce *kator-the*

fourth cuarto(a) *kwarto(a)*

France la Francia *franthya*

free (*not occupied*) libre *leebre;* (*costing nothing*) gratis *gratees*

freezer el congelador *konkhela-dor*

French francés/francesa *franthes/fran-thesa*

french beans las judías verdes *khoodee-as ber-des*

frequent frecuente *frekwen-te*

fresh (*food*) fresco(a) *fresko(a)*

Friday el viernes *byer-nes*; **Good Friday** el Viernes Santo *byer-nes santo*

fridge el frigorífico *freego-reefee-ko*

fried frito(a) *freeto(a)*

friend el/la amigo(a) *a-meego(a)*

frill el volante *bolan-te*

fringe el flequillo *fle-kee-lyo*

frog la rana *rana*

from de *de*

front la parte delantera *par-te delan-tera*; **front door** la puerta principal *pwerta preenthee-pal*; **in front** adelante *a-de-lan-te*

frost la helada *e-lada*

frostbite la congelación *kon-khela-thyon*

frozen congelado(a) *kon-khela-do(a)*

fruit la fruta *froota*

fruit juice el zumo *thoomo*

fruit salad la ensalada de frutas *ensa-lada de frootas*

frying pan el sartén *sar-ten*

fuel el carburante *karboo-ran-te*

fuel gauge el indicador del nivel de gasolina *eendee-kador del neebel de gaso-leena*

fuel pump el surtidor de gasolina *soortee-dor de gaso-*

leena

full lleno(a) *lyeno(a)*

full board la pensión completa *pensyon kom-pleta*

fumes el humo *oomo*

fun: to have fun divertirse *dee-berteer-se*

funeral el entierro *en-tyerro*

fun fair el parque de atracciones *par-ke de atrak-thyo-nes*

funny divertido(a) *deeber-teedo(a)*

fur la piel *pyel*

furniture los muebles *mwe-bles*

fuse el fusible *foosee-ble*

G

gale el vendaval *benda-bal*

gallery (*art gallery*) la galería *ga-leree-a*; (*in theatre*) el paraíso *pa-ra-eeso*

gallon el galón *galon*

gallstone el cálculo biliario *kal-koolo bee-lyaryo*

gambling el juego *khwego*

game el juego *khwego*; (*match*) el partido *par-teedo*

garage el garaje *gara-khe*

garden el jardín *khardeen*

garlic el ajo *a-kho*

gas el gas *gas*; **gas cylinder** la bombona de gas *bom-bona de gas*; **gas refill** el cargador de gas *karga-dor de gas*

gasket la junta de culata *khoonta de koo-lata*

gate la puerta *pwerta*

gear: first/second gear la primera/segunda velocidad *pree-mera/se-goonda belo-theedad*

gearbox la caja de cambios *kakha de kambyos*

gear lever la palanca de cambio *pa-lanka de kambyo*

gears los cambios *kambyos*

general general *khe-neral*

generous generoso(a) *khe-ne-roso(a)*

gentle suave *swa-be*

gentleman el señor *senyor*; **Gents'** los servicios *ser-beethyos*

genuine auténtico(a) *ow-tentee-ko(a)*

germ el microbio *mee-krobyo*

German alemán(mana) *a-le-man(mana)*

Germany la Alemania *a-le-manya*

get (*obtain*) obtener *ob-tener*; (*receive*) recibir *re-theebeer*; (*fetch*) traer *tra-er*; **to get into** entrar en *entrar en*; **to get off** bajarse *bakhar-se*; **to get on** subir a *soobeer a*; **to get through** (*on phone*) conseguir comunicar *konsegeer komoo-neekar*

gherkin el pepinillo *pepee-neelyo*

Gibraltar Gibraltar *kheebral-tar*

gift el regalo *re-galo*

gift shop la tienda de regalos

tyenda de re-galos

gin: gin and tonic el gin tónic *jeen toneek*

ginger el jengibre *khenkhee-bre*

girl la chica *cheeka*

girlfriend la novia *nobya*

give dar *dar*; **to give back** devolver *debol-ber*

glad feliz *feleeth*

glass (*substance*) el vidrio *beedryo*; (*for drinking*) el vaso *baso*

glasses las gafas *gafas*

gloves los guantes *gwan-tes*

glucose la glucosa *gloo-kosa*

glue la cola *kola*

go ir *eer*; **I go/am going** voy *boy*; **you go/are going** Ud va *oos-ted ba*; **he goes/is going** va *ba*

goal (*football*) el gol *gol*

goat la cabra *kabra*

God Dios *dyos*

go down bajar *bakhar*

goggles las gafas de bucear *gafas de boo-the-ar*; (*for skiing*) las gafas de esquí *gafas de eskee*

going: I am going to do it voy a hacerlo *boy a a-therlo*

gold el oro *oro*; **a gold ring** un anillo de oro *oon a-neelyo de oro*

golf el golf *golf*

golf course el campo de golf *kampo de golf*

good bueno(a) *bweno(a)*; **good afternoon/evening!**

¡buenas tardes! *bwenas tardes*; **good morning!**
¡buenos días! *bwenos dee-as*;
good night! ¡buenas noches!
bwenas no-ches
goodbye ¡adiós! *a-dyos*
goose el ganso *ganso*
gooseberry la grosella
espinosa *gro-se-lya espee-nosa*
go out salir *saleer*
go up subir *soobeer*
gown el traje *tra-khe*
grammar la gramática
grama-teeka
gramme el gramo *gramo*;
100 grammes of cien
gramos de *thyen gramos de*
grandchildren los nietos
nyetos
granddaughter la nieta
nyeta
grandfather el abuelo *a-bwelo*
grandmother la abuela *a-bwela*
grandson el nieto *nyeto*
grape la uva *oo-ba*
grapefruit el pomelo *po-melo*
grapefruit juice el jugo de
pomelo *khoogo de po-melo*
grass la hierba *yerba*; (*lawn*)
el césped *thes-ped*
grateful agradecido(a) *agra-dethee-do(a)*
grave la tumba *toomba*
gravy la salsa de carne *salsa
de kar-ne*

greasy grasiento(a) *gra-syento(a)*
great grande *gran-de*
greedy goloso(a) *go-loso(a)*
green verde *ber-de*; **green
card** la carta verde *karta ber-de*
greetings card la tarjeta de
felicitaciones *tar-kheta de
felee-theeta-thyones*
grey gris *grees*
grilled a la parrilla *a la pa-rreelya*
grocer's la tienda de
ultramarinos *tyenda de
ooltra-maree-nos*
ground el suelo *swelo*;
ground floor la planta baja
pıanta bakha
groundsheet la tela
impermeable *tela eemper-me-a-ble*
group el grupo *groopo*
grow crecer *kre-ther*
guarantee la garantía *garan-tee-a*
guard (*railway*) el jefe de
tren *khe-fe de tren*
guess adivinar *adee-beenar*
guest el/la invitado(a)
eenbee-tado(a); (*in hotel*) el
huésped *wes-ped*
guesthouse la pensión
pensyon
guide el/la guía *gee-a*
guide book la guía turística
gee-a toorees-teeka
guided tour la visita con
guía *bee-seeta kon gee-a*

guilty culpable *koolpa-ble*
guitar la guitarra *gee-tarra*
gums las encías *enthee-as*
gun el fusil *fooseel*
guy rope el viento *byento*
gymnasium el gimnasio *kheem-nasyo*
gym shoes las zapatillas *thapa-teelyas*

H

had: I had tenía *te-nee-a*; **he had** tenía *te-nee-a*; **you had** Ud tenía *oos-ted te-nee-a*
haddock el abadejo *abadekho*
haemorrhoids las hemorroides *e-moro-ee-des*
hail el granizo *gra-neetho*
hair el pelo *pelo*
hairbrush el cepillo para el pelo *the-peelyo para el pelo*
haircut el corte de pelo *korte de pelo*
hairdresser el peluquero *peloo-kero*
hairdryer el secador de pelo *seka-dor de pelo*
hairgrip la horquilla *orkeelya*
hair spray la laca *laka*
half medio(a) *medyo(a)*; **a half bottle of...** media botella de... *medya bo-telya de...*; **half past two** las dos y media *las dos ee medya*; **half fare** el medio billete *medyo bee-lye-te*; **half-board** la

media pensión *medya pensyon*
halibut el halibut *alee-boo*
hall (*in house*) el vestíbulo *bestee-boolo;* (*for concerts etc*) la sala *sala*
ham el jamón *khamon*
hamburger la hamburguesa *amboor-gesa*
hammer el martillo *marteelyo*
hand la mano *mano*
handbag el bolso *bolso*
handbrake el freno de mano *freno de mano*
hand cream la crema de manos *krema de manos*
handicapped minusválido(a) *meenoosbalee-do(a)*
handkerchief el pañuelo *panywelo*
handle el asa *a-sa;* (*of door*) el tirador *teera-dor*
hand luggage el equipaje de mano *ekee-pa-khe de mano*
hand-made hecho(a) a mano *e-cho(a) a mano*
hang colgar *kolgar*; **to hang up** colgar *kolgar*
hangover la resaca *re-saka*
happen pasar *pasar*
happy feliz *feleeth*
harbour el puerto *pwerto*
hard duro(a) *dooro(a)*; **hard shoulder** el arcén *ar-then*
hard-boiled egg el huevo duro *webo dooro*
hare la liebre *lye-bre*

harvest la cosecha *ko-secha*
has: he has tiene *tye-ne*
hat el sombrero *som-brero*
hate odiar *o-dyar*
have tener *te-ner*; **I have**
tengo *tengo*; **you have** Ud
tiene *oos-ted tye-ne*; **they
have** tienen *tye-nen*
hay el heno *e-no*
hay fever la fiebre del heno
fye-bre del e-no
hazard lights el
intermitente de emergencia
*eenter-meeten-te de emer-
khenthya*
hazelnut la avellana *a-be-
lyana*
hazy nublado(a) *noo-
blado(a)*
he él *el*
head la cabeza *ka-betha*
headache el dolor de cabeza
dolor de ka-betha
headlights los faros *faros*
head waiter el maître *ma-
ee-tre*
heal curar *koorar*
health le salud *salood*
healthy sano(a) *sano(a)*
hear oir *o-eer*
hearing aid el audífono *ow-
dee-fono*
heart el corazón *kora-thon*;
heart attack el ataque
cardíaco *a-ta-ke kar-dee-ako*
heat el calor *kalor*
heater el calentador *kalen-
tador*
heating la calefacción *ka-
lefak-thyon*
heatstroke la insolación
eenso-lathyon
heavy pesado(a) *pe-sado(a)*;
heavy rain la lluvia fuerte
lyoobya fwer-te
hedge el seto *seto*
heel (*of person*) el talón *talon;*
(*of shoe*) el tacón *takon*
height la altura *al-toora*
helicopter el helicóptero
elee-kop-tero
hello ¡hola! *o-la;* (*on
telephone*) ¡diga! *deega*
help[1] *n* la ayuda *a-yooda*;
help! ¡socorro! *so-korro*
help[2] *vb* ayudar *ayoo-dar*;
can you help me? ¿puede
ayudarme? *pwe-de ayoo-
dar-me*
hem el dobladillo *dobla-
deelyo*
hen la gallina *ga-lyeena*
her la *la*; **I gave her a book**
le he dado un libro *le e dado
oon leebro*; **with her** con
ella *kon el-ya*; **her house/
friend** su casa/amigo *soo
kasa/a-meego*; **her things**
sus cosas *soos kosas*
herb la hierba *yerba*
here aquí *a-kee*
heroin la heroína *ero-eena*
herring el arenque *a-ren-ke*
hers: it's hers es suyo *es
sooyo*; **they're hers** son
suyos *son sooyos*
**hiccup: to have (the)
hiccups** tener hipo *te-ner*

eepo

hide esconder *eskon-der*

high alto(a) *alto(a)*; **high blood pressure** la tensión alta *tensyon alta*; **high chair** la silla alta *seelya alta*; **high season** la temporada alta *tempo-rada alta*; **high tide** la marea alta *ma-re-a alta*

higher más alto(a) *mas alto(a)*

hijack secuestrar *se-kwestrar*

hill la colina *ko-leena*

hill-walking el montañismo *monta-nyeesmo*

him le *le*; **for him** para él *para el*

hip la cadera *ka-dera*

hire alquilar *alkee-lar*

his su *soo*; **his cases** sus maletas *soos ma-letas*; **it's his** es suyo *es sooyo*; **they're his** son suyos *son sooyos*

history la historia *ees-torya*

hit (*strike*) pegar *pegar*

hitchhike hacer autostop *a-ther owto-stop*

hitchhiker el autostopista *owto-stopees-ta*

hoarse ronco(a) *ronko(a)*

hobby el pasatiempo *pasa-tyempo*

hold tener *te-ner*

hold-up el embotellamiento *embo-telya-myento*

hole el agujero *agoo-khero*

holiday las vacaciones *baka-thyo-nes;* (*public*) la fiesta

fyesta

hollow hueco(a) *weko(a)*

holy santo(a) *santo(a)*

home la casa *kasa*; **at home** en casa *en kasa*; **to go home** volver a casa *bolber a kasa*

homesick: to be homesick sentir saudade *senteer sowdade*

honey la miel *myel*

honeymoon la luna de miel *loona de myel*

honest honrado(a) *on-rado(a)*

hood (*of car*) la capota *ka-pota*

hook (*fishing*) el anzuelo *an-thwelo;* (*for coats*) el colgadero *kolga-dero*

hope esperar *es-perar*

horn la bocina *bo-theena*

horrible horrible *o-rree-ble*

hors d'oeuvre los entremeses *en-tre-me-ses*

horse el caballo *ka-balyo*

hose la manguera *man-gera*

hospital el hospital *ospee-tal*

host el anfitrión *an-fee-tryon*

hostel: youth hostel el albergue de juventud *al-ber-ge de khoo-bentood*

hostess la anfitriona *anfee-tryona*

hot caliente *kalyen-te*; **it's hot** (*weather*) hace mucho calor *a-the moocho kalor*; **I'm hot** tengo calor *tengo kalor*

hotel el hotel *o-tel*

hotplate el calientaplatos *ka-lyenta-platos*

hot-water bottle la bolsa de agua caliente *bolsa de a-gwa kalyen-te*

hour la hora *o-ra*

house la casa *kasa*

housewife el ama de casa *a-ma de kasa*

house wine el vino de la casa *beeno de la kasa*

hovercraft el aerodeslizador *a-ero-deslee-thador*

how cómo *komo*; **how are you?** ¿cómo está? *komo esta*; **how much?** ¿cuánto? *kwanto*; **how long?** ¿cuánto tiempo? *kwanto tyempo*; **how many?** ¿cuántos? *kwantos*

human humano(a) *oo-mano(a)*

hundred cien *thyen*; **a hundred and ten** ciento diez *thyento dyeth*

hungry: I'm hungry tengo hambre *tengo am-bre*

hurry: I'm in a hurry tengo prisa *tengo preesa*

hurt: my leg hurts me duele la pierna *me dwe-le la pyerna*

husband el marido *ma-reedo*

hut la cabaña *ka-banya*

hydrofoil el aerodeslizador *a-ero-deslee-thador*

I

I yo *yo*

ice el hielo *yelo*

ice cream el helado *e-lado*

ice lolly el polo *polo*

ice rink la pista de patinaje *peesta de patee-na-khe*

icing la alcorza *al-kortha*

idea la idea *ee-de-a*

if si *see*

ignition el encendido *enthen-deedo*

ignition key la llave de contacto *lya-be de kon-takto*

ill enfermo(a) *enfer-mo(a)*

illness la enfermedad *enfer-medad*

imagine imaginar *eema-kheenar*

immediately inmediatamente *een-medya-tamen-te*

immerser el calentador de inmersión *kalen-tador de eenmer-syon*

impatient impaciente *eempa-thyen-te*

important importante *eempor-tan-te*

impossible imposible *eempo-see-ble*

in en *en*; **in advance** por adelantado *por a-delan-tado*; **in 10 minutes** dentro de 10 minutos *dentro de dyeth mee-nootos*

inch la pulgada *pool-gada*

included incluido *eenkloo-ee-do*

income los ingresos *een-*

gresos
independent independiente *een-depen-dyen-te*
indicator el intermitente *eenter-meeten-te*
indigestion la indigestión *eendee-khes-tyon*
indoors dentro *dentro*
industry la industria *eendoostrya*
infection la infección *eenfekthyon*
infectious contagioso(a) *kontakh-yoso(a)*
inflamed inflamado(a) *eenfla-mado(a)*
inflatable inflable *een-flable*
informal informal *eenformal*
information la información *eenfor-mathyon*
information office la Oficina de Información Turística *ofee-theena de eenfor-mathyon toorees-teeka*
initials las iniciales *eeneethya-les*
injection la inyección *eenyek-thyon*
injured herido(a) *e-reedo(a)*
injury la herida *e-reeda*
ink la tinta *teenta*; **ink cartridge** el cartucho *kartoocho*
innocent inocente *eenothen-te*
insect el insecto *een-sekto*;

insect bite la picadura *peeka-doora*; **insect repellant** la loción contra insectos *lothyon kontra eensektos*
inside el interior *een-teryor*; **inside the car** dentro del coche *dentro del ko-che*
insist insistir *eensees-teer*
instant coffee el café instantáneo *ka-fe eenstantane-o*
instead of en lugar de *en loogar de*
instructor el instructor *eenstrook-tor*
insulin la insulina *eensooleena*
insult el insulto *een-soolto*
insurance el seguro *se-gooro*
insurance certificate el certificado de seguros *therteefeeka-do de se-gooros*
insurance company la compañia de seguros *kompanyee-a de se-gooros*
insurance policy la póliza de seguros *po-leetha de se-gooros*
insure asegurar *a-se-goorar*
intelligent inteligente *eentelee-khen-te*
interested: I'm interested in... me interesa... *me een-teresa*
interesting interesante *eente-resan-te*
international internacional *eenter-nathyo-nal*

interpreter el/la intérprete *een-ter-pre-te*
interval (*theatre, sport*) el descanso *des-kanso*
interview la entrevista *en-tre-beesta*
into en *en*
introduce presentar *pre-sentar*
invalid el minusválido *meenoos-ba-leedo*
invitation la invitación *eenbee-tathyon*
invite invitar *eenbee-tar*
invoice la factura *fak-toora*
Ireland la Irlanda *eer-landa*
Irish irlandés/irlandesa *eerlan-des/eerlan-desa*
iron[1] *n* el hierro *yerro*; (*for clothes*) la plancha *plancha*
iron[2] *vb* planchar *planchar*
ironmonger's la quincallería *keenka-lyereea*
is: she's English es inglesa *es een-glesa*; **she's ill/on holiday** está enferma/de vacaciones *esta en-ferma/de baka-thyo-nes*
island la isla *eesla*
it lo/la *lo/la*
Italian italiano(a) *eeta-lyano(a)*
Italy la Italia *ee-talya*
itch la picazón *peeka-thon*
itemized bill la factura detallada *fak-toora deta-lyada*
ivory el marfil *marfeel*

J

jack el gato *gato*
jacket la chaqueta *cha-keta*
jam la mermelada *mer-mela-da*
jammed atorado(a) *ato-rado(a)*
January enero (*m*) *e-nero*
jar el tarro *tarro*
jaundice la ictericia *eek-teree-thya*
jaw la mandíbula *mandee-boola*
jazz el jazz *yas*
jeans los vaqueros *ba-keros*
jelly la gelatina *khela-teena*
jellyfish la medusa *me-doosa*
jersey el jersey *kher-sey*
jet (plane) el avión a reacción *a-byon a re-akthyon*
jeweller's la joyería *kho-yeree-a*
jewellery las joyas *khoyas*
Jewish judío(a) *khoo-deeo(a)*
jib el foque *fo-ke*
job el trabajo *tra-bakho*
jogging: to go jogging hacer footing *a-ther footeen*
join juntar *khoontar*; (*club*) hacerse socio de *a-ther-se sothyo de*
joint la articulación *artee-koola-thyon*
joint passport el pasaporte familiar *pasa-por-te famee-lyar*
joke la broma *broma*

journalist el/la periodista *peryo-deesta*

journey el viaje *bya-khe*

judge el juez *khweth*

jug el jarro *kharro*

juice el zumo *thoomo*

jukebox la máquina tocadiscos *ma-keena toka-deeskos*

July julio (*m*) *khoolyo*

jumbo jet el jumbo *yoombo*

jump saltar *saltar*

jump leads los cables para cargar la batería *ka-bles para kargar la ba-teree-a*

junction la bifurcación *beefoor-kathyon*; (*crossroads*) el cruce *kroothe*

June junio (*m*) *khoonyo*

just: just two solamente dos *sola-men-te dos*; **just a little** un poco nada más *oon poko nada mas*; **just there** ahí mismo *a-ee meesmo*; **I've just arrived** acabo de llegar *a-kabo de lyegar*

K

keep guardar *gwardar*

kettle la caldera *kal-dera*

key la llave *lya-be*

key ring el llavero *lya-bero*

kick el puntapié *poonta-pye*

kidney el riñon *reenyon*

kill matar *matar*

kilo el kilo *keelo*; **a kilo of** un kilo de *oon keelo de*

kilometre el kilómetro *keelo-metro*

kind[1] *n* (*sort*) la clase *kla-se*

kind[2] *adj* amable *a-ma-ble*

king el rey *rey*

kiosk el quiosco *kee-osko*

kiss el beso *beso*

kitchen la cocina *ko-theena*

knee la rodilla *ro-deelya*

knife el cuchillo *koo-cheelyo*

knit hacer punto *a-ther poonto*

knitting needle la aguja de hacer punto *a-gookha de a-ther poonto*

knock (*on door*) golpear *golpe-ar*

knot el nudo *noodo*

know (*facts*) saber *saber;* (*person*) conocer *kono-ther*

L

label la etiqueta *etee-keta*

lace (*fabric*) el encaje *enka-khe;* (*of shoe*) el cordón *kordon*

ladder la escalera de mano *eska-lera de mano*

ladle el cucharón *koocha-ron*

lady la señora *se-nyora;* **Ladies** los servicios *serbeethyos*

lager la cerveza *ther-betha*

lake el lago *lago*

lamb el cordero *kor-dero*

lamp la lámpara *lam-para*

lamp-post el farol *farol*

lampshade la pantalla *pan-*

talya

land¹ *vb* aterrizar *a-terree-thar*

land² *n* la tierra *tyerra*

landlady la propietaria *propee-e-tarya*

landlord el propietario *propee-e-taryo*

lane (*of road*) el carril *karreel*; (*in country*) el camino *ka-meeno*

language el idioma *eed-yoma*

large grande *gran-de*

larger más grande *mas gran-de*

laryngitis la laringitis *lareen-kheetees*

last¹ *vb* durar *doorar*

last² *adj* último(a) *ool-teemo(a)*; **last week** la semana pasada *la se-mana pasada*

late tarde *tar-de*

later más tarde *mas tar-de*

laugh reir *re-eer*

launderette la lavandería automática *laban-deree-a owto-matee-ka*

laundry la lavandería *laban-deree-a*; (*clothes*) la ropa para lavar *ropa para labar*

laundry room el lavadero *laba-dero*

laundry service el servicio de lavandería *ser-beethyo de laban-deree-a*

lavatory (*in house*) el wáter *bater*; (*in public place*) los servicios *ser-beethyos*

law la ley *le-ee*

lawyer el abogado *abo-gado*

laxative el laxante *laksan-te*

layby el área de aparcamiento *a-re-a de apar-kamyen-to*

layered (*hair*) en capas *en kapas*

lazy perezoso(a) *pe-re-thoso(a)*

lead¹ *vb* conducir *kondoo-theer*

lead² *n* (*electric*) el cable *ka-ble*; (*metal*) el plomo *plomo*

leaf la hoja *o-kha*

leak (*of gas, liquid*) la fuga *fooga*; (*in roof*) la gotera *go-tera*

learn aprender *apren-der*

least: at least por lo menos *por lo menos*

leather la piel *pyel*

leave salir (de) *saleer (de)*

leek el puerro *pwerro*

left izquierdo(a) *eeth-kyerdo(a)*; **on/to the left** a la izquierda *a la eeth-kyerda*

left-handed zurdo(a) *thoordo(a)*

left-luggage office la consigna *kon-seegna*

leg la pierna *pyerna*

legal legal *legal*

lemon el limón *leemon*; **lemon juice** el zumo de limón *thoomo de leemon*; **lemon squash** la limonada *leemo-nada*; **lemon tea** el té con limón *te kon leemon*

lemonade la gaseosa *ga-se-o-*

sa; **a Martini and lemonade** un Martini con gaseosa *oon mar-teenee kon ga-se-o-sa*

lend prestar *prestar*

length (*size*) la longitud *lonkhee-tood*; (*duration*) la duración *doora-thyon*

lens la lente *len-te*; **lens cover** la tapa de la lente *tapa de la len-te*

lentil la lenteja *len-tekha*

less menos *menos*

lesson la clase *kla-se*

let (*allow*) permitir *permeeteer*; (*hire out*) alquilar *alkee-lar*

letter (*written*) la carta *karta*; (*of alphabet*) la letra *letra*

letterbox el buzón *boothon*

lettuce la lechuga *le-chooga*

leukemia la leucemia *le-oothemya*

level plano(a) *plano(a)*

level-crossing el paso a nivel *paso a neebel*

library la biblioteca *beeblyoteka*

licence: driving licence el carné de conducir *kar-ne de kondoo-theer*

lick lamer *la-mer*

lid la tapa *tapa*

lie down acostarse *akos-tar-se*

life la vida *beeda*

lifebelt el cinturón salvavidas *theentoo-ron salba-beedas*

lifeboat el bote salvavidas *bo-*

te salba-*beedas*

lifeguard el vigilante *beekhee-lan-te*

life jacket el chaleco salvavidas *cha-leko salba-beedas*

lift el ascensor *as-thensor*

lift pass el forfait *for-fe*

light[1] *adj* (*colour*) claro(a) *klaro*; (*not heavy*) ligero(a) *lee-khero(a)*

light[2] *n* la luz *looth*; **light bulb** la bombilla *bom-beelya*; **light meter** el fotómetro *foto-metro*

light[3] *vb* encender *en-thender*

lighter el encendedor *enthen-dedor*

lightning el relámpago *relam-pago*

like[1] *prep* como *komo*; **like this** así *asee*

like[2] *vb* gustar *goostar*; **I would like to go** me gustaría ir *me goos-taree-a eer*; **I would like a newspaper** querría un periódico *kerree-a oon peree-o-deeko*

likely probable *proba-ble*

lime (*fruit*) la lima *leema*

line la línea *lee-ne-a*

linen el lino *leeno*

lip el labio *labyo*

lipstick la barra de labios *barra de labyos*

liqueur el licor *leekor*

liquid el líquido *lee-keedo*

list la lista *leesta*

listen (to) escuchar *eskoo-char*

litre el litro *leetro*

litter la basura *ba-soora*

little pequeño(a) *pe-kenyo(a)*; **a little** un poco *oon poko*

live vivir *beebeer*

liver el higado *ee-gado*

living room el cuarto de estar *kwarto de estar*

lizard la lagartija *lagar-teekha*

loaf el pan *pan*

loan prestar *prestar*

lobster la langosta *lan-gosta*

local local *lokal*

lock[1] *n* la cerradura *therra-doora*

lock[2] *vb* (*door*) cerrar con llave *therrar kon lya-be*

locker el casillero de consigna *kasee-lyero de kon-seegna*

log el tronco *tronko*

lollipop el piruli *peeroo-lee*; (*iced*) el polo *polo*

London Londres *lon-dres*

lonely solo(a) *solo(a)*

long largo(a) *largo(a)*; **for a long time** por mucho tiempo *por moocho tyempo*; **how long is it?** ¿cuánto tiene de largo? *kwanto tye-ne de largo*

look (at) mirar *meerar*

look after cuidar *kweedar*

look for buscar *booskar*

loose suelto(a) *swelto(a)*; (*clothing*) ancho(a) *ancho(a)*

loosen aflojar *aflo-khar*

lorry el camión *kamyon*

lorry driver el camionero *kamyo-nero*

lose perder *perder*

lost perdido(a) *per-deedo(a)*; **I have lost my wallet** he perdido mi cartera *e per-deedo mee kar-tera*; **I am lost** me he perdido *me e per-deedo*

lost property office la oficina de objetos perdidos *ofee-theena de ob-khetos per-deedos*

lot: a lot (of) mucho *moocho*

lotion la loción *lothyon*

lottery la loteria *lo-teree-a*

loud fuerte *fwer-te*

lounge (*in house*) el salón *salon*; (*at airport*) la sala de embarque *sala de embar-ke*

love querer *kerer*

lovely precioso(a) *pre-thyoso(a)*

low bajo(a) *bakho(a)*; **low tide** la baja marea *bakha ma-re-a*

lucky: to be lucky tener suerte *te-ner swer-te*

luggage el equipaje *ekee-pa-khe*

luggage allowance el equipaje permitido *ekee-pa-khe permee-teedo*

luggage rack la rejilla *rekhee-lya*

luggage tag la etiqueta *etee-keta*

luggage trolley el carrito

para el equipaje *ka-rreeto
para el ekee-pa-khe*
lump (*of sugar*) el terrón
terron; (*swelling*) el bulto
boolto
lunch el almuerzo *almwer-
tho*
lung el pulmón *poolmon*
luxury de lujo de *lookho*

M

macaroni los macarrones
maka-rro-nes
machine la máquina *ma-
keena*
mackerel la caballa *ka-balya*
mad loco(a) *loko(a)*
made-to-measure
hecho(a) a la medida *echo(a)
a la me-deeda*
magazine la revista *re-beesta*
magnetic magnético(a) *mag-
ne-teeko(a)*
maid la camarera *kama-rera*
maiden name el apellido de
soltera *a-pe-lyeedo de soltera*
main principal *preenthee-pal*;
main course el plato
principal *plato preenthee-pal*;
main road la carretera *ka-
rre-tera*; **main street** la calle
mayor *ka-lye mayor*
**mains: to turn the
electricity off at the
mains** cortar la electricidad
kortar la elek-treethee-dad
maize el maíz *ma-eeth*

Majorca Mallorca *ma-lyorka*
major road la carretera
principal *ka-rre-tera
preenthee-pal*
make hacer *a-ther*
make-up el maquillaje
makee-lya-khe
Malaga Málaga *ma-laga*
male masculino(a) *maskoo-
leeno(a)*
mallet el mazo *matho*
man el hombre *om-bre*
manager el gerente *kheren-
te*
managing director el
director gerente *deerek-tor
kheren-te*
manicure la manicura
manee-koora
many muchos(as)
moochos(as)
map el mapa *mapa*
marble el mármol *mar-mol*
March marzo (*m*) *martho*
margarine la margarina
marga-reena
marina el puerto deportivo
pwerto depor-teebo
mark la mancha *mancha*
market el mercado *mer-kado*
marmalade la mermelada de
naranjas amargas *mer-mela-
da de na-rankhas a-margas*
married casado(a) *ka-
sado(a)*
marrow el calabacín *kala-
batheen*
marry casarse *kasar-se*
marzipan el mazapán *matha-*

pan

mascara el rímel *ree-mel*

mass la misa *meesa*

mast el mástil *masteel*

match la cerilla *the-reelya*; (*sport*) el partido *par-teedo*

material la tela *tela*

matter: it doesn't matter no importa *no eem-porta*

mauve malva *malba*

May mayo (*m*) *mayo*

mayonnaise la mayonesa *mayo-nesa*

me me *me*; **for me** para mí *para mee*; **with me** conmigo *kon-meego*

meal la comida *ko-meeda*

mean querer decir *kerer detheer*

meaning el significado *seeg-nee-fee-kado*

meanwhile mientras tanto *myentras tanto*

measles el sarampión *sarampyon*; **German measles** la rubéola *roo-be-ola*

measure medir *medeer*

meat la carne *kar-ne*

mechanic el mecánico *meka-neeko*

medicine la medicina *medee-theena*

medieval medieval *medee-ebal*

Mediterranean el Mediterráneo *medi-terra-ne-o*

medium mediano(a) *me-dyano(a)*; (*wine*) semi-seco

semee-seko; **medium rare** medio(a) *medyo(a)*

meet encontrarse *enkon-trar-se*

meeting la reunión *re-oo-nyon*; (*appointment*) la cita *theeta*

melon el melón *melon*

melt derretir *de-rreteer*

member el miembro *myembro*

menu la carta *karta*

meringue el merengue *meren-ge*; **to make a mess** desordenar *desor-denar*

message el mensaje *mensa-khe*

metal el metal *metal*

meter el contador *konta-dor*

metre el metro *metro*

microwave oven el horno microondas *orno meekro-ondas*

midday el mediodía *medyo-dee-a*

middle el centro *thentro*

middle-aged de mediana edad *de me-dyana e-dad*

might: he might come podría llegar *podree-a lyegar*

migraine la jaqueca *kha-keka*

mild (*weather*) templado(a) *tem-plado*; (*flavour*) suave *swa-be*

mile la milla *meelya*

milk la leche *le-che*; **milk chocolate** el chocolate con leche *choko-la-te kon le-che*

milkshake el batido de leche

ba-teedo de le-che

millimetre el milímetro *meelee-metro*

million el millón *meelyon*

mince la carne picada *kar-ne pee-kada*

mind (*be careful*) tener cuidado *te-ner kwee-dado*; **do you mind?** ¿le importa? *le eem-porta*

mine: it's mine es mío *es mee-o*

mineral water el agua mineral *a-gwa mee-neral*

minimum el mínimo *mee-neemo*

minister el ministro *mee-neestro*

Minorca Menorca *me-norka*

minor road la carretera secundaria *ka-rre-tera sekoon-darya*

mint (*herb*) la hierbabuena *yerba-bwena*

minute el minuto *mee-nooto*

mirror el espejo *es-pekho*

miss (*a train etc*) perder *perder*

Miss la señorita *senyo-reeta*

missing perdido(a) *per-deedo(a)*

mist la neblina *ne-bleena*

mistake el error *e-rror*

misty nebuloso(a) *neboo-loso(a)*

mix mezclar *methklar*

mixture la mezcla *methkla*

model el modelo *mo-delo*

modern moderno(a) *mo-*
derno(a)

modest modesto(a) *mo-desto(a)*

mohair el mohair *mo-er*

moisturizer la leche hidratante *le-che eedra-tan-te*

monastery el monasterio *monas-teryo*

Monday el lunes *loo-nes*

money el dinero *dee-nero*; **money order** el giro postal *kheero postal*

monk el monje *mon-khe*

monkey el mono *mono*

month el mes *mes*

mood el humor *oo-mor*

moon la luna *loona*

moor amarrar *a-marrar*; **mooring line** la amarra *a-marra*

mop el fregasuelos *frega-swelos*

more más *mas*

morning la mañana *ma-nyana*

mosque la mezquita *meth-keeta*

mosquito el mosquito *mos-keeto*

most: most of la mayor parte de *la mayor par-te de*

motel el motel *motel*

moth la mariposa nocturna *maree-posa nok-toorna*

mother la madre *ma-dre*

motor boat la lancha motora *lancha mo-tora*

motorcycle la motocicleta

moto-thee-kleta

motorway la autopista *owto-peesta*

mountain la montaña *mon-tanya*

mountaineer el alpinista *alpee-neesta*

mouse el ratón *raton*

mousse la crema batida *krema ba-teeda*

moustache el bigote *beego-te*

mouth la boca *boka*

move moverse *mo-ber-se*

Mr el señor *senyor*

Mrs la señora *se-nyora*

much mucho *moocho*; **thank you very much** muchas gracias *moochas grathyas*; **that's too much** eso es demasiado *eso es demasyado*

mud el barro *barro*

mug el tazón *tathon*

mumps las paperas *pa-peras*

municipal municipal *moonee-theepal*

murder el asesinato *a-seseenato*

muscle el músculo *mooskoolo*

museum el museo *moo-se-o*

mushroom el champiñón *champee-nyon*

music la música *moo-seeka*

musician el músico *moo-seeko*

mussel el mejillón *mekhee-lyon*

must tener que *te-ner ke*; **I must go** tengo que ir *tengo ke eer*

mustard la mostaza *mos-tatha*

mutton el cordero *kor-dero*

my mi *mee*; **my friends** mis amigos *mees a-meegos*

N

nail el clavo *klabo*; (*on finger,toe*) la uña *oo-nya*; **nail brush** el cepillo de uñas *the-peelyo de oo-nyas*; **nail file** la lima de uñas *leema de oo-nyas*; **nail polish** el esmalte para uñas *esmal-te para oo-nyas*; **nail polish remover** el quita-esmalte *keeta-esmal-te*

naked desnudo(a) *des-noodo(a)*

name el nombre *nom-bre*; **what is your name?** ¿cómo se llama usted? *komo se lyama oos-ted*; **my name is...** me llamo... *me lyamo*

napkin la servilleta *serbee-lyeta*

nappy el pañal *panyal*

nappy liner la gasa *gasa*

narrow estrecho(a) *estrecho(a)*

national nacional *nathyo-nal*

nationality la nacionalidad *nathyo-nalee-dad*

native land la patria *pa-tree-a*

natural natural *natoo-ral*

naughty travieso(a) *tra-byeso(a)*

navy blue azul marino *a-thool ma-reeno*

near cerca *therka*; **near the station** cerca de la estación *therka de la esta-thyon*

nearer más cerca *mas therka*

nearest: the nearest post office la oficina de correos más cercana *la ofee-theena de ko-rre-os mas ther-kana*

neat ordenado(a) *or-dena-do(a)*

necessary necesario(a) *ne-the-saryo(a)*

neck el cuello *kwelyo*

necklace el collar *kolyar*

need necesitar *ne-thesee-tar*; **I need to go** tengo que ir *tengo ke eer*

needle: needle and thread aguja e hilo *a-gookha e eelo*

negative el negativo *nega-teebo*

neighbour el/la vecino(a) *be-theeno(a)*

neither ni *nee*

nephew el sobrino *so-breeno*

nervous nervioso(a) *ner-byoso(a)*

nest el nido *needo*

net la red *red*

never nunca *noonka*

new nuevo(a) *nwebo(a)*

news las noticias *no-teethyas*

newsagent el vendedor de periódicos *ben-dedor de peree-o-deekos*

newspaper el periódico *peree-o-deeko*

New Year el Año Nuevo *a-nyo nwebo*

New Zealand la Nueva Zelanda *nweba the-landa*

next próximo(a) *prok-seemo(a)*

nice (*person*) simpático(a) *seempa-teeko(a)*; (*place, holiday*) bonito(a) *bo-neeto(a)*

niece la sobrina *so-breena*

night la noche *no-che*; **at night** por la noche *por la no-che*

night club el nightclub *night-kloob*

nightdress el camisón *kamee-son*

night porter el portero de noche *por-tero de no-che*

nine nueve *nwe-be*

nineteen diecinueve *dyethee-nwe-be*

ninety noventa *no-benta*

no no *no*; **no, thank you** no, gracias *no grathyas*

nobody nadie *na-dye*

noise el ruido *rweedo*

noisy ruidoso(a) *rwee-doso(a)*

non-alcoholic no alcohólico(a) *no al-koleeko(a)*

none ninguno(a) *neen-goono(a)*

non-smoking no fumador *no fooma-dor*

noodles los tallarines *talya-reenes*

nor ni *nee*

normal normal *normal*

north el norte *nor-te*

nose la nariz *nareeth*

nosebleed la hemorragia nasal *emo-rrakhya nasal*

no-smoking *(sign)* prohibido fumar *pro-ee-beedo fumar; (area)* no fumador *no fooma-dor;* **no-smoking compartment** el compartimento no fumador *kompar-teemen-to no fooma-dor*

not no *no*

note *(bank note)* el billete de banco *bee-lyete de banko; (musical, letter)* la nota *nota;* **note pad** el bloc *blok*

nothing nada *nada*

notice *(sign)* el letrero *le-trero; (poster)* el anuncio *a-noonthyo*

novel la novela *no-bela*

November noviembre *(m) nobyem-bre*

now ahora *a-o-ra*

nowhere en ninguna parte *en neen-goona par-te*

nuclear nuclear *noo-kle-ar*

nuisance la lata *lata*

numb entumecido(a) *entoo-methee-do(a)*

number el número *noo-mero*

number plate la placa de matrícula *plaka de matree-koola*

nurse la enfermera *enfer-mera*

nursery slope la pista para principiantes *peesta para preenthee-pyan-tes*

nut la nuez *nweth; (for bolt)* la tuerca *twerka*

nutmeg la nuez moscada *nweth mos-kada*

nylon el nilón *neelon*

O

O negative/positive O negativo/positivo *o nega-teebo/posee-teebo*

oak el roble *ro-ble*

oar el remo *remo*

oats la avena *a-bena*

object el objeto *ob-kheto*

oblong rectangular *rektan-goolar*

obvious evidente *ebee-den-te*

occasionally de vez en cuando *de beth en kwando*

October octubre *(m) oktoo-bre*

octopus el pulpo *poolpo*

of de *de;* **of course** claro *klaro*

off *(light, TV, engine)* apagado(a) *apa-gado(a); (rotten)* pasado(a) *pa-sado(a);* **5 km off the main road** a 5 kilómetros de la carretera *a theenko keelo-metros de la ka-rre-tera*

offence la infracción *eenfrak-thyon*

offer ofrecer *o-fre-ther*

office la oficina *ofee-theena*
officer el policía *polee-thee-a*
official oficial *ofee-thyal*
often muchas veces *moochas be-thes*; **how often?** ¿cuántas veces? *kwantas be-thes*
oil el aceite *a-the-ee-te*
oil filter el filtro de aceite *feeltro de a-the-ee-te*
ointment el ungüento *oon-gwento*
O.K. de acuerdo *de a-kwerdo*; **it's O.K.** vale *ba-le*
old viejo(a) *byekho(a)*
olive la aceituna *athey-toona*; **olive oil** el aceite de oliva *a-the-ee-te de o-leeba*
omelette la tortilla *tor-teelya*
on (*light, TV*) encendido(a) *en-then-deedo(a)*; (*engine*) en marcha *en marcha*; **on the table** sobre la mesa *so-bre la mesa*
once una vez *oona beth*
one uno(a) *oo-no(a)*; **one-way street** la calle de dirección única *ka-lye de deerek-thyon oo-neeka*; **one-way ticket** el billete de ida *bee-lye-te de eeda*
onion la cebolla *the-bolya*
only sólo *solo*
open[1] *adj* abierto(a) *a-byerto(a)*
open[2] *vb* abrir *a-breer*
opera la ópera *o-pera*
operate (*machine*) hacer funcionar *a-ther foonthyo-*
nar
operation la operación *o-pera-thyon*
operator el/la telefonista *te-lefo-neesta*
opposite enfrente de *en-fren-te de*
optician el óptico *op-teeko*
or o *o*
orange la naranja *na-rankha*; (*colour*) color naranja *kolor na-rankha*
orange juice el zumo de naranja *thoomo de na-rankha*
orange squash la naranjada *naran-khada*
orchestra la orquesta *or-kesta*
order la orden *or-den*
ordinary normal *normal*
organize organizar *orga-neethar*
organized organizado(a) *orga-neetha-do(a)*
original original *oree-kheenal*
ornament el ornamento *orna-mento*
other otro(a) *o-tro(a)*
ought deber *de-ber*; **I ought to go** debería ir *de-be-ree-a eer*
ounce = 28 grams
our nuestro(a) *nwestro(a)*; **our rooms** nuestros cuartos *nwes-tros kwartos*
ours el/la nuestro(a) *el/la nwestro(a)*
out (*light etc*) apagado(a) *a-*

pa-gado(a); **he's out** ha salido *a sa-leedo*; **out of** fuera de *fwera de*
outdoors al aire libre *al ay-re lee-bre*
outside fuera *fwera*
outside lane el carril de la izquierda *karreel de la eeth-kyerda*
oval ovalado(a) *oba-lado(a)*
oven el horno *orno*
over (*on top of*) por encima de *por en-theema de*; **over there** allí *a-lyee*
overcharge sobrecargar la cuenta *so-bre-kargar la kwenta*
overheat recalentarse *reka-lentar-se*
overtake adelantarse a *a-delan-tar-se a*
owe deber *de-ber*
own propio(a) *propyo(a)*; **my own** el mío/la mía *el mee-o/la mee-a*
owner el/la propietario(a) *pro-pyeta-ryo(a)*
oxygen el oxígeno *oksee-kheno*
oyster la ostra *ostra*

P

package el paquete *pa-ke-te*
package tour el viaje organizado *bee-a-khe orga-neetha-do*
packed lunch el almuerzo frío *al-mwertho free-o*

packet el paquete *pa-ke-te*
paddling pool el estanque de juegos para los niños *estan-ke de khwegos para los neenyos*
padlock el candado *kan-dado*
page la página *pa-kheena*
paid pagado(a) *pa-gado(a)*
pail el cubo *koobo*
pain el dolor *dolor*
painful doloroso(a) *dolo-roso(a)*
painkiller el calmante *kalman-te*
paint[1] *n* la pintura *peen-toora*
paint[2] *vb* pintar *peentar*
paintbox la caja de pinturas *kakha de peen-tooras*
painter el pintor *peentor*
pair el par *par*
palace el palacio *pala-thyo*
pale pálido(a) *pa-leedo(a)*; (*colour*) claro(a) *klaro(a)*
pan la cacerola *ka-the-rola*
pancake la hojuela *o-khwela*
pane el cristal *kreestal*
panties las bragas *bragas*
pants los calzoncillos *kalthon-theelyos*
paper el papel *papel*
paperback el libro de bolsillo *leebro de bol-seelyo*
paper bag la bolsa de papel *bolsa de pa-pel*
paperclip el clip *klee*
paper handkerchiefs los pañuelos de papel *pan-nywelos de papel*
paprika la paprika *pa-preeka*

paraffin la parafina *parafeena*

paralysed paralizado(a) *para-lee-thado(a)*

parcel el paquete *pa-ke-te*

pardon ¿cómo? *komo*; **I beg your pardon** disculpe *deeskool-pe*

parents los padres *pa-dres*

park[1] *n* el parque *par-ke*

park[2] *vb* aparcar *apar-kar*

parking disk el disco de estacionamiento *deesko de esta-thyona-myento*

parking meter el parquímetro *parkee-metro*

parking ticket la multa por aparcamiento indebido *moolta por apar-kamyen-to ~en-debee-do*

parsley el perejil *pe-re-kheel*

part la parte *par-te*; **spare part** el repuesto *re-pwesto*

parting la raya *raya*

partly en parte *en par-te*

partner (*in firm*) el/la socio(a) *sothyo(a)*; (*sports, dance*) la pareja *pa-rekha*

party (*group*) el grupo *groopo*; (*celebration*) la fiesta *fyesta*

pass pasar *pasar*; (*overtake*) adelantar *a-delan-tar*

passenger el/la pasajero(a) *pasa-khero(a)*

passport el pasaporte *pasapor-te*

passport control el control de pasaportes *kontrol de pasa-por-tes*

pasta la pasta *pasta*

pastry la pasta *pasta*; (*cake*) el pastel *pas-tel*

pâté el paté *pa-te*

path el camino *ka-meeno*

patient el/la paciente *pathyen-te*

pattern (*on fabric*) el dibujo *dee-bookho*

pavement la acera *a-thera*

pay pagar *pagar*; **can I pay by cheque?** ¿puedo pagar con un cheque? *pwedo pagar kon oon che-ke*; **can I pay by credit card?** ¿puedo pagar con tarjeta de crédito? *pwedo pagar kon tar-kheta de kre-deeto*

payment el pago *pago*

peach el melocotón *melokoton*

peanut el cacahuete *kakawete*

pear la pera *pera*

pearl la perla *perla*

peas los guisantes *geesan-tes*

pebble el guijarro *gee-kharro*

pedal el pedal *pedal*

pedestrian el peatón *pe-a-ton*

peel pelar *pelar*

pen la pluma *plooma*

pencil el lápiz *lapeeth*

pencil sharpener el sacapuntas *saka-poontas*

penicillin la penicilina *penee-theelee-na*

penknife la navaja *na-bakha*

pension la pensión *pensyon*

pensioner el jubilado *khoobee-lado*

people la gente *khen-te*

pepper (*spice*) la pimienta *pee-myenta*; **green/red pepper** el pimiento verde/rojo *pee-myento ber-de/rokho*

peppermint (*herb*) la menta *menta*; (*sweet*) la pastilla de menta *pas-teelya de menta*

per por *por*; **per hour/person** por hora/persona *por o-ra/per-sona*

perfect perfecto(a) *per-fekto(a)*

performance la representación *re-presen-tathyon*

perfume el perfume *perfoo-me*

perhaps tal vez *tal beth*

period (*menstruation*) la regla *regla*

perm la permanente *perma-nen-te*; **to have a perm** hacerse una permanente *ather-se oona perma-nen-te*

permit el permiso *per-meeso*

person la persona *per-sona*

pet el animal doméstico *aneemal do-mes-teeko*

petrol la gasolina *gaso-leena*

petrol can el bidón de gasolina *beedon de gaso-leena*

petrol gauge el indicador del nivel de gasolina *eendee-*

kador del nee-**bel** de gaso-leena

petrol pump el surtidor de gasolina *soortee-dor de gaso-leena*

petrol station la estación de servicio *esta-thyon de ser-beethyo*

petrol tank el tanque de gasolina *tan-ke de gaso-leena*

petticoat las enaguas *e-nagwas*

phone[1] *n* el teléfono *te-le-fono*

phone[2] *vb* telefonear *te-le-fo-ne-ar*

phone box la cabina telefónica *ka-beena te-lefo-neeka*

phone call la llamada telefónica *lya-mada te-lefo-neeka*

photocopy[1] *vb* fotocopiar *foto-kopyar*

photocopy[2] *n* la fotocopia *foto-kopya*

photograph la fotografía *foto-grafee-a*

phrase book el libro de frases *leebro de fra-ses*

piano el piano *pyano*

pickle el encurtido *enkoor-teedo*

pick up (*collect*) recoger *reko-kher*; (*from floor*) levantar *leban-tar*

picnic la merienda *me-ryenda*

picture el cuadro *kwadro*

pie la tarta *tarta*

piece el pedazo *pe-datho*
pier el embarcadero *embar-ka-dero*
pig el cerdo *therdo*
pigeon la paloma *pa-loma*
pile el montón *monton*
pill la píldora *peel-dora*
pillar la columna *ko-loomna*
pillow la almohada *almo-a-da*
pillowcase la funda *foonda*
pilot el piloto *pee-loto*
pilot light la lámpara indicadora *lam-para eendee-kado-ra*
pin el alfiler *alfee-ler*
pine el pino *peeno*
pineapple la piña *peenya*
pingpong el ping-pong *peenpon*
pink rosa *rosa*
pint = 0.47 litres
pipe la pipa *peepa*
pipe cleaner el limpiapipas *leempya-peepas*
pipe tobacco el tabaco de pipa *ta-bako de peepa*
piston el pistón *peeston*
pity: it's a pity ¡qué pena! *ke pena*
place el lugar *loogar;* (*seat*) el asiento *a-syento*
plain (*fabric*) liso(a) *leeso(a)*
plan el plan *plan*
plane el avión *a-byon*
plant la planta *planta*
plaster (*sticking plaster*) el esparadrapo *es-para-drapo*
plastic el plástico *plas-teeko*
plastic bag la bolsa de plástico **bolsa de plas-**teeko

plate el plato *plato*
platform el andén *an-den*
play[1] *n* la obra de teatro *o-bra de te-a-tro*
play[2] *vb* jugar *khoogar*
playroom el cuarto de juego *kwarto de khwego*
pleasant agradable *agra-da-ble*
please por favor *por fabor*
pleased contento(a) *kon-tento(a)*
plenty: plenty of... bastante... *bas-tante*
pliers los alicates *alee-kates*
plug (*electrical*) el enchufe *enchoo-fe;* (*in bath*) el tapón *tapon*
plum la ciruela *thee-rwela*
plumber el fontanero *fonta-nero*
pneumonia la pulmonía *poolmo-nee-a*
poached egg el huevo escalfado *webo eskal-fado*
pocket el bolsillo *bol-seelyo*
point la punta *poonta*
pointed puntiagudo(a) *poontee-a-goodo(a)*
points (*in car*) los platinos *pla-teenos*
poisonous venenoso(a) *be-ne-noso(a)*
pole el palo *palo*
police la policía *polee-thee-a;* **police!** ¡policía! *polee-thee-a*
police car el coche patrulla *ko-che pa-troolya*

policeman el policía *polee-thee-a*

police station la comisaría de policía *komee-saree-a de polee-thee-a*

policewoman la mujer policía *moo-kher polee-thee-a*

polio la polio *polyo*

polish[1] *vb* (*shoes*) limpiar *leempyar*

polish[2] *n* (*for shoes*) el betún *betoon*

polite cortés *kor-tes*

political político(a) *polee-teeko(a)*

polluted contaminado(a) *konta-meena-do(a)*

polo neck el polo *polo*

polyester el polyester *polee-ester*

polystyrene el poliestireno *polee-estee-reno*

polythene el polietileno *polee-e-tee-leeno*

pond el estanque *estan-ke*

pony-trekking la excursión a caballo *exkoor-syon a ka-balyo*

pool la piscina *pees-theena*

poor pobre *po-bre*

Pope el papa *papa*

popular popular *popoo-lar*

population la población *pobla-thyon*

porcelain la porcelana *por-the-lana*

pork el cerdo *therdo*

port el puerto *pwerto;* (*wine*) el oporto *o-porto*

portable portátil *por-tateel*

porter el mozo *motho*

porthole la portilla *portee-lya*

portrait el retrato *re-trato*

Portugal el Portugal *portoo-gal*

Portuguese portugués (portuguesa) *portoo-ges* (*portoo-gesa*)

possible posible *posee-ble*

post[1] *n* el correo *ko-rre-o*

post[2] *vb* mandar por correo *mandar por ko-rre-o*

postage el franqueo *fran-ke-o*

postbox el buzón *boothon*

postcard la postal *postal*

postcode el código postal *ko-deego postal*

poster el cartel *kar-tel*

postman el cartero *kar-tero*

post office la oficina de correos *ofee-theena de ko-rre-os*

pot el tarro *ta-rro*

potato la patata *pa-tata*

pottery la cerámica *thera-meeka*

potty la bacinica *bathee-neeka*

poultry las aves de corral *a-bes de korral*

pound la libra *leebra*

pour echar *e-char*

powder el polvo *polbo*

powdered milk la leche en polvo *le-che en polbo*

power (*electrical*) la corriente *ko-rryen-te*

power cut el apagón *apa-gon*

power point el enchufe *enchoo-fe*

pram el cochecito de niño *kochethee-to de neenyo*

prawn la gamba *gamba*

prayer la oración *ora-thyon*

prefer preferir *pre-fereer*

pregnant embarazada *embaratha-da*

prepare preparar *pre-parar*

prescription la receta *retheta*

present el regalo *re-galo*

press apretar *a-pretar*

pretty bonito(a) *bo-neeto(a)*

price el precio *prethyo*

price list la lista de precios *leesta de prethyos*

priest el sacerdote *sa-ther-dote*

primary school la escuela primaria *es-kwela pree-marya*

print (*picture*) el grabado *grabado*; (*photograph*) la copia *kopya*

prison la cárcel *kar-thel*

private privado(a) *preebado(a)*

prize el premio *premyo*

probably probablemente *proba-ble-men-te*

problem el problema *problema*

profit la ganancia *ga-nanthya*

programme el programa *pro-grama*

promise prometer *pro-meter*

pronounce pronunciar *pronoonthyar*

pronunciation la pronunciación *pronoon-thya-thyon*

propeller la hélice *e-lee-the*

properly correctamente *ko-rrek-tamen-te*

Protestant protestante *protestan-te*

prune la ciruela pasa *theerwela pasa*

psychiatrist el siquiatra *seekyatra*

pub el pub *poob*

public público(a) *poobleeko(a)*

public holiday el día festivo *dee-a fes-teebo*

pudding el postre *postre*

pull tirar *teerar*

pullover el jersey *kher-sey*

pump[1] *n* la bomba *bomba*

pump[2] *vb:* **to pump up** inflar *eenflar*

puncture el pinchazo *peenchatho*

pupil (*in school*) el/la alumno(a) *a-loomno(a)*; (*of eye*) la pupila *poo-peela*

pure puro(a) *pooro(a)*

purple morado(a) *morado(a)*

purse el monedero *mo-nedero*

purser el contador de navío *konta-dor de nabee-o*

push empujar *em-pookhar*

push chair la sillita de ruedas *see-lyeeta de rwedas*

put poner *po-ner*; (*insert*) meter *me-ter*

put down dejar *dekhar*

puzzle el rompecabezas *rompe-ka-bethas*

pyjamas el pijama *pee-khama*

Pyrenees los Pirineos *peereene-os*

Q

quarantine la cuarentena *kwa-ren-tena*

quarter el cuarto *kwarto*; **quarter to 2** las dos menos cuarto *las dos menos kwarto*; **quarter past two** las dos y cuarto *las dos ee kwarto*

quay el muelle *mwe-lye*

question la pregunta *pregoonta*

queue¹ *n* la cola *kola*

queue² *vb* hacer cola *a-ther kola*

quick rápido(a) *ra-peedo(a)*

quickly rápidamente *rapeedamen-te*

quiet tranquilo(a) *trankeelo(a)*

quilt el edredón *e-dre-don*

quite (*completely*) completamente *kom-pletamen-te*; **quite expensive** bastante caro *bastan-te karo*

R

rabbi el rabino *ra-beeno*

rabbit el conejo *ko-nekho*

rabies la rabia *rabya*

race la carrera *ka-rrera*

rack (*for luggage*) la red *red*

racket la raqueta *ra-keta*

radiator el radiador *radya-dor*

radio la radio *radyo*

radio-cassette el radio-casete *radyo-kaset*

radishes los rábanos *ra-banos*

raft la balsa *balsa*

railway el ferrocarril *ferrokarreel*

railway station la estación de ferrocarril *esta-thyon de ferro-karreel*

rain la lluvia *lyoobya*

raincoat el impermeable *eemper-me-a-ble*

raining: it's raining está lloviendo *esta lyo-byendo*

raisin la pasa *pasa*

rally el rallye *ralee*

ramp la rampa *rampa*

rare raro(a) *raro(a)*; (*steak*) poco hecho(a) *poko e-cho(a)*

rash el sarpullido *sarpoo-lyeedo*

raspberry la frambuesa *frambwesa*

rat la rata *rata*

rate la tasa *tasa*; **rate of exchange** el tipo de cambio *teepo de kambyo*

rather bastante *bastan-te*

raw crudo(a) *kroodo(a)*

razor la maquinilla de afeitar

*makee-**neel**ya de a-fe-ee-**tar***
razor blades las hojas de afeitar *o-khas de a-fe-ee-**tar***
reach llegar a *lyegar a*
read leer *le-**er***
ready listo(a) *leesto(a)*
real verdadero(a) *berda-dero(a)*
realize darse cuenta de *dar-se kwenta de*
really de verdad *de berdad*
rear la parte trasera *par-te tra-sera*
reason la razón *ra-thon*
receipt el recibo *re-theebo*
receiver el auricular *owree-koolar*
recently recientemente *rethyen-temen-te*
reception la recepción *re-thepthyon*
receptionist el/la recepcionista *re-thepthyo-neesta*
recipe la receta *re-theta*
reclining seat el sillón recostable *seelyon rekos-ta-ble*
recognize reconocer *reko-no-ther*
recommend recomendar *reko-mendar*
record (*music*) el disco *deesko*
recover reponerse *reponer-se*
red rojo(a) *rokho(a)*
redcurrant la grosella roja *gro-selya rokha*
reduction la rebaja *re-bakha*

reel el carrete *ka-rre-te*
refill (*for pen*) el recambio *re-kambyo;* (*for lighter*) el repuesto *re-pwesto*
refund el reembolso *re-embolso*
regional regional *re-khyonal*
registered certificado(a) *thertee-feeka-do(a)*
regulation la norma *norma*
reimburse reembolsar *re-em-bolsar*
relation el pariente *paryen-te*
relax relajarse *re-lakhar-se*
relaxing relajante *rela-khan-te*
reliable (*method*) seguro(a) *se-gooro(a)*
religion la religión *relee-khyon*
remain permanecer *perma-nether*
remember acordarse de *akor-dar-se de*
remove quitar *keetar*
rent alquilar *alkee-lar*
rental el alquiler *alkee-ler*
repair reparar *repa-rar*
repeat repetir *re-peteer*
reply responder *respon-der*
reply coupon el cupón-respuesta *koopon-res-pwesta*
rescue salvar *salbar*
reservation la reserva *re-serba*
reserve reservar *re-serbar*
reserved reservado(a) *reser-bado(a)*
rest[1] *n* el descanso *des-kanso;*

the rest los/las demás *los/las demas*

rest[2] *vb* descansar *deskan-sar*

restaurant el restaurante *restow-ran-te*

restaurant car el vagón-restaurante *bagon-restow-ran-te*

retail price el precio al público *prethyo al poo-bleeko*

retired jubilado(a) *khoo-bee-lado(a)*

return volver *bol-ber*; (*give back*) devolver *debol-ber*

return ticket el billete de ida y vuelta *bee-lye-te de eeda ee bwelta*

reverse dar marcha atrás *dar marcha a-tras*

reversed charge call la conferencia a cobro revertido *kon-ferenthya a kobro reber-teedo*

reverse gear la marcha atrás *marcha a-tras*

reversing lights las luces de marcha atrás *loo-thes de marcha a-tras*

rheumatism el reumatismo *re-oo-ma-teesmo*

rib la costilla *kos-teelya*

ribbon la cinta *theenta*

rice el arroz *a-rroth*

rich (*person etc*) rico(a) *reeko(a)*; (*food*) sabroso(a) *sa-broso(a)*

ride (*on horse*) montar a caballo *montar a ka-balyo*; **to go for a ride** dar un paseo *dar oon pa-se-o*

riding la equitación *ekee-tathyon*

rigging la jarcia *kharthya*

right[1] *n* (*side*) la derecha *de-recha*; **on/to the right** a la derecha *a la de-recha*

right[2] *adj* correcto(a) *korrekto(a)*; **is this the right way to...?** ¿por aquí vamos bien para...? *por akee bamos byen para*

ring el anillo *a-neelyo*

rink la pista de patinaje *peesta de patee-na-khe*

ripe maduro(a) *ma-dooro(a)*

river el río *ree-o*

road la carretera *ka-rre-tera*; (*street*) la calle *ka-lye*

road conditions las condiciones de la circulación *kondee-thyo-nes de la theerkoo-lathyon*

road map el mapa de carreteras *mapa de ka-rre-teras*

road sign la señal de tráfico *senyal de tra-feeko*

road works las obras *o-bras*

roast asado(a) *a-sado(a)*

rob: I've been robbed me han robado *me an ro-bado*

roll (*bread*) el panecillo *pa-ne-theelyo*

roof el tejado *te-khado*

roof-rack la baca *baka*

room el cuarto *kwarto*

room service el servicio de habitaciones *ser-beethyo de*

abee-tathyo-nes
rope la cuerda **kwer**da
rose la rosa *rosa*
rosé el rosado ro-**sado**
rotten podrido(a) po-**dreedo(a)**
rough (*surface*) áspero(a) **as**-pero(a); (*sea*) agitado(a) akhee-**tado(a)**
round (*shape*) redondo(a) redon-do(a); **round the house** alrededor de la casa alre-de**dor** de la **kasa**; **round the corner** a la vuelta de la esquina a la **bwelta** de la es-**keena**
roundabout (*at fair*) el tiovivo tee-o-**beebo**; (*traffic junction*) el cruce giratorio **kroo**-the kheera-**toryo**
route la ruta **roota**
row[1] *n* (*line*) la fila **feela**
row[2] *vb* (*boat*) remar re**mar**
rowing boat la barca **barka**
royal real re-**al**
rub frotar fro**tar**
rubber (*material*) la goma **goma**; (*eraser*) la goma de borrar **goma** de bor**rar**
rubber band la gomita go**meeta**
rubbish la basura ba-**soora**
ruby el rubí roo-**bee**
rucksack la mochila mo-**cheela**
rudder el timón tee**mon**
rude grosero(a) gro-**sero(a)**
rug la alfombrilla alfom-**breelya**

ruin arruinar a-rwee**nar**
ruins las ruinas rwee**nas**
ruler (*for measuring*) la regla **regla**
rum el ron *ron*
run[1] *vb* correr ko-**rrer**; (*machine*) funcionar foonthyo-**nar**; **I've run out of petrol** se me acabó la gasolina se me aka-**bo** la gaso-**leena**
run[2] *n* (*skiing*) la pista **peesta**; (*outing in car*) el paseo en coche pa-**se**-o en **ko**-che
rush hour las horas puntas o-ras **poontas**
rusty oxidado(a) oxee-**dado(a)**
rye bread el pan de centeno pan de then-**teno**

S

saccharin la sacarina saka-**reena**
sad triste **trees**-te
saddle (*of horse*) la silla de montar **seelya** de mon**tar**; (*of bicycle*) la silla **seelya**
safe[1] *adj* seguro(a) se-**gooro(a)**
safe[2] *n* la caja fuerte **kakha** **fwer**-te
safety pin el imperdible eem-per**dee**-ble
sage (*herb*) la salvia **salbya**
sail la vela **bela**
sailing la vela **bela**

sailing boat el velero *be-lero*

sailor el marinero *ma-ree-nero*

salad la ensalada *ensa-lada*

salad dressing la vinagreta *beena-greta*

sale (*in general*) la venta *benta;* (*bargains*) la liquidación *leekee-dathyon*

salmon el salmón *salmon*

salt la sal *sal*

salty salado(a) *sa-lado(a)*

same mismo(a) *meesmo(a);* **the same as...** igual que... *eegwal ke*

sample la muestra *mwestra*

sand la arena *a-rena*

sandals las sandalias *sanda-lyas*

sandwich el bocadillo *boka-deelyo*

sandy (*beach*) de arena *de a-rena*

sanitary towels las compresas *kom-presas*

sapphire el zafiro *tha-feero*

sardine la sardina *sar-deena*

satin el satén *sa-ten*

Saturday el sábado *sa-bado*

sauce la salsa *salsa*

saucepan la cacerola *ka-thero-la*

saucer el platillo *pla-teelyo*

sauna la sauna *sowna*

sausage la salchicha *sal-cheecha;* (*salami*) el chorizo *cho-reetho*

sautéed salteado(a) *sal-te-a-.do(a)*

save (*rescue*) salvar *salbar;* (*not spend*) ahorrar *a-o-rrar*

savoury salado(a) *sa-lado(a)*

say decir *detheer*

scales la balanza *ba-lantha*

scallop la vieira *byey-ra*

scarce escaso(a) *es-kaso(a)*

scarf la bufanda *boo-fanda*

scenery el paisaje *paysa-khe*

scheduled flight el vuelo normal *bwelo normal*

school la escuela *es-kwela*

science la ciencia *thyenthya*

scientist el científico *thyen-tee-feeko*

scissors las tijeras *tee-kheras*

Scotch el whisky escocés *weeskee esko-thes*

Scotland la Escocia *es-kothya*

Scottish escocés(cesa) *esko-thes(thesa)*

scrape rozar *rothar*

scratch la raya *ra-ya*

screen la pantalla *pan-talya;* (*partition*) el biombo *bee-ombo*

screw el tornillo *tor-neelyo*

screwdriver el destornillador *destor-neelya-dor*

scuba-diving el buceo con escafandra autónoma *boo-the-o kon eska-fandra owto-noma*

sculpture la escultura *eskool-toora*

sea el mar *mar*

seafood los mariscos *ma-reeskos*

sea front el paseo marítimo *pa-se-o maree-teemo*

seaside la playa *pla-ya*

season (*of year*) la estación *esta-thyon*; (*hunting etc*) la temporada *tempo-rada*

season ticket el abono *a-bono*

seat (*in bus, train*) el asiento *a-syento*; (*chair*) la silla *seelya*

seat belt el cinturón de seguridad *theentoo-ron de segoo-reedad*

seat reservation: I have a seat reservation tengo reservado un asiento *tengo reser-bado oon a-syento*

seaweed las algas *algas*

second[1] *adj* segundo(a) *se-goondo(a)*

second[2] *n* (*of time*) el segundo *se-goondo*

second class de segunda clase *de se-goonda kla-se*

second-hand de segunda mano *de se-goonda mano*; (*car*) usado(a) *oo-sado(a)*

secret el secreto *se-kreto*

secretary el/la secretario(a) *se-kreta-ryo(a)*

sedative el calmante *kalman-te*

see ver *ber*

seem parecer *pa-re-ther*

self-catering sin pensión *seen pensyon*

self-service de autoservicio *owto-serbee-thyo*

sell vender *ben-der*

Sellotape la cinta adhesiva *theenta a-de-seeba*

send enviar *en-byar*

senior citizen el/la pensionista *pensyo-neesta*

sensible sensato(a) *sen-sato(a)*

sentence la frase *fra-se*

separate separado(a) *sepa-rado(a)*

September setiembre (*m*) *se-tyembre*

serious grave *gra-be*

serve servir *serbeer*

service el servicio *ser-beethyo*

service charge el servicio *ser-beethyo*

set (*of golf clubs*) el juego *khwego*; (*of plates*) el equipo *e-keepo*

set menu el menú *menoo*

settle pagar *pagar*

seven siete *sye-te*

seventeen diecisiete *dye-theesye-te*

seventy setenta *se-tenta*

several varios(as) *baryos(as)*

Seville Sevilla *see-beelya*

sew coser *ko-ser*

sex (*gender*) el sexo *sekso*; (*intercourse*) las relaciones sexuales *rela-thyo-nes sekswa-les*

shade (*of colour*) el tono *tono*; (*shadow*) la sombra *sombra*

shadow la sombra *sombra*

shake agitar *a-kheetar*; **to shake hands with somebody** estrechar la mano con alguien *es-trechar la mano kon al-gyen*

shallow poco profundo(a) *poko pro-foondo(a)*

shampoo el champú *shampoo*

shampoo and set lavar y marcar *labar ee markar*

shape la forma *forma*

share repartir *repar-teer;* (*have in common*) compartir *kompar-teer*

sharp (*edge*) afilado(a) *afee-lado(a)*; (*pain*) agudo(a) *a-goodo(a)*

shave afeitarse *a-fe-eetar-se*

shaver la máquina de afeitar *ma-keena de afe-eetar*

shaving cream la crema de afeitar *krema de afe-eetar*

she ella *e-lya*

sheet la sábana *sa-bana*

shelf el estante *estan-te*

shell (*seashell*) la concha *koncha;* (*of egg, nut*) la cáscara *kas-kara*

shellfish los mariscos *ma-reeskos*

shelter el abrigo *a-breego*

sherry el jerez *khe-reth*

shiny brillante *breelyan-te*

ship el barco *barko*

shirt la camisa *ka-meesa*

shiver temblar *temblar*

shock el golpe *gol-pe*

shock absorber el amortiguador *amor-teegwa-dor*

shoe el zapato *tha-pato*

shoot tirar *teerar*

shop la tienda *tyenda*

shopping: to go shopping ir de compras *eer de kompras*

shopping bag la bolsa de compras *bolsa de kompras*

shore la orilla *o-reelya*

short corto(a) *korto(a)*

short-cut el atajo *a-takho*

shorts los pantalones cortos *panta-lo-nes kortos*

should deber *de-ber;* **I should go** debería ir *de-beree-a eer*

shoulder el hombro *ombro*

shout gritar *greetar*

shovel la pala *pala*

show[1] *n* el espectáculo *espek-takoo-lo*

show[2] *vb* mostrar *mostrar*

shower la ducha *doocha*

shrimp el camarón *kama-ron*

shrink encoger *enko-kher*

shut cerrar *therrar*

shutter (*outer*) la contraventana *kontra-benta-na;* (*inner*) la persiana *per-syana*

sick (*ill*) enfermo(a) *en-fermo(a)*; **I feel sick** tengo náuseas *tengo now-se-as*; **to be sick** vomitar *bomee-tar*

side el lado *lado*

sidelights las luces de posición *loo-thes de posee-thyon*

side street la calle secundaria *ka-lye sekoon-darya*

sieve el colador *kola-dor*

sightseeing el turismo *too-reesmo*

sign la señal *senyal*

signal la señal *senyal*

signature la firma *feerma*

silencer el silenciador *see-lenthya-dor*

silent silencioso(a) *see-lenthyo-so(a)*

silk la seda *seda*

silver la plata *plata*; **a silver ring** un anillo de plata *oon a-neelyo de plata*

similar parecido(a) *pa-re-theedo(a)*

simple sencillo(a) *sen-theelyo(a)*

since desde *des-de*; (*because*) ya que *ya ke*; **since I arrived** desde que llegué *des-de ke lye-ge*

sincerely: Yours sincerely le saluda atentamente *le sa-looda a-tenta-men-te*

sing cantar *kantar*

single (*unmarried*) soltero(a) *sol-tero(a)*

single bed la cama individual *kama eendee-beedwal*

single room la habitación individual *abee-ta-thyon eendee-beedwal*

single ticket el billete de ida *bee-lye-te de eeda*

sink[1] *n* el fregadero *frega-dero*

sink[2] *vb* hundirse *oondeer-se*

sir el señor *senyor*; **Dear Sir** Muy señor mío *mooy senyor mee-o*

sister la hermana *er-mana*

sister-in-law la cuñada *koo-nyada*

sit sentarse *sentar-se*

site el sitio *seetyo*

six seis *seys*

sixteen dieciséis *dyethee-seys*

sixty sesenta *se-senta*

size (*of clothes*) la talla *talya*; (*of shoes*) el número *noo-mero*

skate patinar *patee-nar*

skates los patines *patee-nes*

skating el patinaje *patee-na-khe*

skewer la broqueta *bro-keta*

ski[1] *n* el esquí *eskee*

ski[2] *vb* esquiar *eskee-ar*

ski boot la bota de esquí *bota de eskee*

skid patinar *patee-nar*

skimmed milk la leche desnatada *le-che desna-tada*

skin la piel *pyel*

skindiving el escafandrismo *eska-fandrees-mo*

ski pants los pantalones de esquí *pan-talo-nes de eskee*

ski pole el palo de esquí *palo de eskee*

skirt la falda *falda*

ski run la pista de esquí *peesta de eskee*

ski suit el traje de esquí *tra-khe de eskee*

skull el cráneo *kra-ne-o*

sky el cielo *thyelo*
slack flojo(a) *flokho(a)*
sledge el trineo *tree-ne-o*
sleep dormir *dormeer*
sleeper (berth) la litera *lee-tera*
sleeping bag el saco de dormir *sako de dormeer*
sleeping car el coche-cama *ko-che-kama*
sleeping pill el somnífero *som-neefero*
sleeve la manga *manga*
slide (photo) la diapositiva *dee-a-posee-teeba*; (in park) el tobogán *tobo-gan*
sling el cabestrillo *ca-bestreelyo*
slip resbalarse *resba-lar-se*
slipper la zapatilla *thapa-teelya*
slippery resbaladizo(a) *resbala-deetho(a)*
slope (up) la cuesta *kwesta*; (down) el declive *de-klee-be*
slow lento(a) *lento(a)*
small pequeño(a) *pe-kenyo(a)*
smell[1] vb oler *o-ler*
smell[2] n el olor *o-lor*
smile sonreír *son-re-eer*
smoke[1] n el humo *oomo*
smoke[2] vb fumar *foomar*
smoked ahumado(a) *a-oomado(a)*
smooth suave *swa-be*
smuggle pasar de contrabando *pasar de kontra-bando*

snack bar la cafetería *ka-fe-te-ree-a*
snail el caracol *kara-kol*
snake la serpiente *ser-pyen-te*
sneeze estornudar *estor-noodar*
snore roncar *ronkar*
snorkel el tubo *toobo*
snow[1] n la nieve *nye-be*
snow[2] vb nevar *nebar*; it's snowing está nevando *esta nebando*
snowplough el quitanieves *keeta-nye-bes*
so tan *tan*; **so much** tanto(a) *tanto(a)*
soap el jabón *khabon*
soapflakes el jabón en escamas *khabon en es-kamas*
soap powder el jabón en polvo *khabon en polbo*
sober sobrio(a) *sobryo(a)*
socket el enchufe *enchoo-fe*
socks los calcetines *kal-thetee-nes*
soda la soda *soda*
soda water la soda *soda*
soft blando(a) *blando(a)*
soft-boiled egg el huevo pasado por agua *webo pasado por agwa*
soft drink la bebida no alcohólica *be-beeda no alko-leeka*
sole (fish) el lenguado *lengwado*
solid sólido(a) *so-leedo(a)*
soluble soluble *soloo-ble*
some algunos(as) *al-*

*goo*nos(as); **some friends** algunos amigos *al-goo*nos a-*mee*gos; **some coffee** un poco de café *oon poko de ka-fe*

somehow de alguna manera *de al-goo*na ma-*ne*ra

someone alguien *algyen*

something algo *algo*

sometimes a veces *a be*-thes

somewhere (*be*) en alguna parte *en al-goo*na par-*te*; (*go*) a alguna parte *a al-goo*na par-te

son el hijo *ee-kho*

song la canción *kanthyon*

son-in-law el yerno *yerno*

soon pronto *pronto*

sooner más temprano *mas tem-prano*

sore doloroso(a) *dolo-ro*so(a); **sore throat** el dolor de garganta *dolor de gar-ganta*

sorry: sorry! ¡perdón! *perdon*; **I'm sorry** ¡lo siento! *lo syento*

sort: what sort of ...? ¿qué tipo de ...? *ke teepo de*

soufflé el soufflé *soo-fle*

sound el sonido *so-nee*do

soup la sopa *sopa*

sour agrio(a) *a-gree-o*(a)

south el sur *soor*

souvenir el recuerdo *re-kwerdo*

space el espacio *es-pathyo*

spade la pala *pala*

spanner la llave inglesa *lya-be een-glesa*

spare (*left over*) sobrante *sobran-te*; (*available*) disponible *deespo-nee-ble*

spare part la pieza de recambio *pyetha de re-kambyo*

spare wheel la rueda de recambio *rweda de re-kambyo*

sparkling espumoso(a) *espoo-mo*so(a)

spark plug la bujía *bookhee-a*

speak hablar *a-blar*

special especial *es-pethyal*

speciality la especialidad *es-pethya-leedad*

special menu el menú especial *menoo es-pethyal*

special rate la tarifa especial *ta-reefa es-pethyal*

speed la velocidad *belo-thee*dad

speed limit la velocidad máxima *belo-theedad mak-seema*

speedometer el velocímetro *belo-thee-metro*

spell deletrear *de-le-tre-ar*; **how do you spell it?** ¿cómo se escribe? *komo se es-kree-be*

spend (*money*) gastar *gastar*; (*time*) pasar *pasar*

spice la especia *es-pethya*

spicy picante *peekan-te*

spill derramar *derra-mar*

spinach las espinacas *espee-nakas*

spin-dryer el secador centrifugo *seka-dor thentree-foogo*

spine el espinazo *espee-natho*

spirits el alcohol *alkol*

spit escupir *eskoo-peer*

splint la tablilla *ta-bleelya*

splinter la astilla *as-teelya*

split hender *en-der*

spoil estropear *estro-pe-ar*

sponge la esponja *es-ponkha*

sponge bag la bolsa de aseo *bolsa de a-se-o*

spoon la cuchara *koo-chara*

sport el deporte *depor-te*

sprain la torcedura *tor-thedoo-ra*

spring (*season*) la primavera *preema-bera*; (*metal*) el resorte *resor-te*

sprinkle salpicar *salpee-kar*

square (*shape*) el cuadrado *kwa-drado*; (*in town*) la plaza *platha*

squash (*drink*) el zumo *thoomo*

squeeze (*press*) apretar *a-pretar*; (*lemon*) exprimir *ekspree-meer*

stain la mancha *mancha*

stainless steel el acero inoxidable *a-thero eenok-seeda-ble*

stairs la escalera *eska-lera*

stall el puesto *pwesto*

stalls (*in theatre*) la butaca *boo-taka*

stamp la estampilla *estam-peelya*

stand[1] *vb* estar de pie *estar de pye*; (*tolerate*) aguantar *a-gwantar*

stand[2] *n* (*at exhibition*) la caseta *ka-seta*

standard standard *es-tandar*

staple la grapa *grapa*

stapler la grapadora *grapa-dora*

star la estrella *es-trelya*

starboard el estribor *estree-bor*

start[1] *n* el comienzo *ko-myentho*

start[2] *vb* comenzar *ko-menthar*; (*car, engine*) poner en marcha *po-ner en marcha*

starter (*in restaurant*) el entremés *en-tre-mes*; (*in car*) el motor de arranque *motor de a-rran-ke*

station la estación *esta-thyon*

stationer's la papelería *pa-pe-leree-a*

statue la estatua *es-tatwa*

stay[1] *n* la estancia *estan-thya*

stay[2] *vb* quedarse *kedar-se*; (*as guest*) hospedarse *os-pedarse*

steak el filete *fee-le-te*

steel el acero *a-thero*

steep escarpado(a) *eskar-pado(a)*

steeple la aguja *a-gookha*

steering la dirección *deerek-thyon*

steering column la columna de dirección *ko-loomna de deerek-thyon*

steering wheel el volante *bolan-te*

step el escalón *es-ka-lon*

step-father el padrastro *padrastro*

step-mother la madrastra *ma-drastra*

stereo el equipo estereofónico *e-keepo es-te-reo-foneeko*

sterling: pounds sterling las libras esterlinas *leebras ester-leenas*

stern la popa *popa*

stew el estofado *esto-fado*

steward el camarero *kamarero*

stewardess la azafata *athafata*

stick[1] n el palo *palo*

stick[2] vb pegar *pegar*

sticking plaster el esparadrapo *espa-radra-po*

sticky pegajoso(a) *pega-khoso(a)*

stiff rígido(a) *ree-kheedo(a)*

still todavía *toda-bee-a*

sting[1] vb picar *peekar*

sting[2] n la picadura *peeka-doora*

stir remover *remo-ber*

stitch coser *ko-ser*

stockings las medias *medyas*

stolen: my passport has been stolen me han robado el pasaporte *me an ro-bado el pasa-por-te*

stomach el estómago *esto-mago*

stomach upset el trastorno estomacal *tras-torno esto-makal*

stone la piedra *pyedra;* (in fruit) el hueso *weso*

stop[1] n (of bus) la parada *parada*

stop[2] vb parar *parar;* **stop thief!** ¡al ladrón! *al ladron*

stoplights las luces de detención *loo-thes de deten-thyon*

stopover la escala *es-kala*

stopping train el tren ómnibus *tren omnee-boos*

storm la tormenta *tor-menta*

story la historia *ees-torya*

straight derecho(a) *de-recho(a);* **straight on** todo recto *todo rekto*

strange extraño(a) *eks-tranyo(a)*

stranger el/la forastero(a) *foras-tero(a)*

strap la correa *ko-rre-a*

straw la paja *pakha;* (for drinking) la pajita *pa-kheeta*

strawberry la fresa *fresa*

streaks (in hair) las mechas *mechas*

stream el arroyo *a-rroyo*

street la calle *kalye*

street plan el plano de la ciudad *plano de la thyoodad*

stretch estirar *estee-rar*

stretcher la camilla *ka-meelya*

strike la huelga *welga;* **to be on strike** estar en huelga *estar en welga*

string la cuerda *kwerda*

strip la tira *teera*

striped rayado(a) *ra-yado(a)*

strong fuerte *fwer-te*

struggle luchar *loochar*

stuck: it is stuck está atorado *esta ato-rado*

student el/la estudiante *estoo-dyan-te*

stuffing el relleno *re-lyeno*

stun aturdir *atoor-deer*

stung picado(a) *pee-kado(a)*

stupid tonto(a) *tonto(a)*

style el estilo *es-teelo*

styling mousse el fijador *feekha-dor*

suburb el suburbio *sooboorbyo*

success el éxito *ek-seeto*

successful: to be successful tener éxito *te-ner ek-seeto*

such tal *tal*

suck sorber *sor-ber*

suddenly de repente *de re-pen-te*

suede el ante *an-te*

suet el sebo *sebo*

sugar el azúcar *a-thookar*

suit el traje *tra-khe*

suitable (time) conveniente *kon-be-nyen-te*; (fitting) apropiado(a) *a-pro-pyado(a)*

suitcase la maleta *ma-leta*

summer el verano *be-rano*

sun el sol *sol*

sunbathe tomar el sol *tomar el sol*

sunburn la quemadura del sol *kema-doora del sol*

Sunday el domingo *domeen-go*

sunglasses las gafas de sol *gafas de sol*

sunhat el sombrero ancho *som-brero ancho*

sunny: it's sunny hace sol *a-the sol*

sunshade la sombrilla *sombree-lya*

sunstroke la insolación *eenso-lathyon*

suntan el bronceado *bron-the-a-do*

suntan cream la crema bronceadora *krema bron-the-a-do-ra*

suntan oil el aceite bronceador *a-the-ee-te bron-the-a-dor*

supermarket el supermercado *soo-permer-kado*

supper la cena *thena*

supplement el suplemento *soo-ple-mento*

suppose suponer *soo-poner*

suppository el supositorio *soopo-seeto-ryo*

sure seguro(a) *se-gooro(a)*

surface la superficie *sooperfee-thye*

surface mail: by surface mail por vía terrestre *por bee-a te-rres-tre*

surfboard la plancha de surf *plancha de soorf*

surfing el surf *soorf*

surname el apellido *ape-*

Iyeedo

surprised: to be surprised
estar sorprendido(a) *estar
sorpren-deedo(a)*
suspension la suspensión
soos-pensyon
sweat el sudor *soodor*
sweater el suéter *swe-ter*
sweep barrer *barrer*
sweet dulce *dool-the*
sweets los caramelos *kara-
melos*
swerve desviarse *desbyar-se*
swim nadar *nadar*
swimming la natación *nata-
thyon*
swimming pool la piscina
pees-theena
swimming trunks el
bañador *banya-dor*
swimsuit el traje de baño
tra-khe de banyo
swing (*seat*) el columpio *ko-
loompyo*
switch el interruptor *een-
terroop-tor*
switch off (*engine*) parar
parar
switch on (*engine*) encender
en-then-der
swollen hinchado(a) *een-
chado(a)*
symptom el síntoma *seen-
toma*
synagogue la sinagoga *seena-
goga*
system el sistema *sees-tema*

T

table la mesa *mesa*
tablecloth el mantel *mantel*
table d'hôte el menú *menoo*
tablespoon la cuchara *koo-
chara*
tablet la pastilla *pas-teelya*
table tennis el ping-pong
peen-pon
table wine el vino de mesa
beeno de mesa
tail la cola *kola*
take tomar *tomar*; **how long
does it take?** ¿cuánto
tiempo lleva? *kwanto
tyempo Iyeba*
take out sacar *sakar*; (*stain*)
quitar *keetar*; **may I take
you out?** le invito a salir *le
een-beeto a saleer*
talc los polvos de talco *polbos
de talko*
talk[1] *vb* hablar *a-blar*
talk[2] *n* la conversación *kon-
bersa-thyon*
tall alto(a) *alto(a)*
tame manso(a) *manso(a)*
tampons los tampones
tampo-nes
tap el grifo *greefo*
tape la cinta *theenta*
tape-measure la cinta
métrica *theenta me-treeka*
tape-recorder el
magnetofón *mag-neto-fon*
tart la tarta *tarta*
tartar sauce la salsa tártara

salsa tar-tara

taste[1] *vb* saborear *sabo-re-ear*

taste[2] *n* el sabor *sabor*

tax el impuesto *eem-pwesto*

taxi el taxi *tak-see*

taxi rank la parada de taxis *pa-rada de tak-sees*

tea el té *te*

teabag la bolsita de té *bolseeta de te*

teach enseñar *en-se-nyar*

teacher el/la profesor/ profesora *pro-fesor/pro-feso-ra*

team el equipo *e-keepo*

teapot la tetera *te-tera*

tear (*rip*) el rasgón *ras-gon*; (*crying*) la lágrima *la-greema*

teaspoon la cucharilla *koocha-reelya*

teat la tetilla *te-teelya*

technical técnico(a) *tek-neeko(a)*

teddy bear el osito de felpa *o-seeto de felpa*

teenager el/la adolescente *ado-lesthen-te*

teeshirt la camiseta *kamee-seta*

teeth los dientes *dyen-tes*

telegram el telegrama *tele-grama*

telephone el teléfono *te-le-fono*

telephone call la llamada telefónica *lya-mada te-lefo-neeka*

telephone directory la guía telefónica *gee-a te-lefo-neeka*

television la televisión *te-lebee-syon*

telex el télex *teleks*

tell decir *detheer*; (*story*) contar *kontar*; **I will tell him** se lo diré *se lo dee-re*

temperature la temperatura *tem-pera-toora*; **to have a temperature** tener fiebre *tener fye-bre*

temporary provisional *probee-syonal*

ten diez *dyeth*

tender tierno(a) *tyerno(a)*

tennis el tenis *te-nees*; **tennis ball** la pelota de tenis *pe-lota de te-nees*; **tennis court** la pista de tenis *peesta de te-nees*; **tennis racket** la raqueta de tenis *ra-keta de te-nees*

tent la tienda de campaña *tyenda de kam-panya*

tent peg la piqueta de tienda *pee-keta de tyenda*

tent pole el mástil *masteel*

terminus la estación terminal *esta-thyon termee-nal*

terrace la terraza *te-rratha*

terrible terrible *terree-ble*

terylene el terylene *teree-le-ne*

textbook el libro de texto *leebro de texto*

than que *ke*; **more than that** más que eso *mas ke eso*; **less than 9** menos de 9 *menos de nwe-be*

thank you gracias *grathyas*

that eso *eso*; **that book** ese libro *e-se leebro*; **that table** esa mesa *esa mesa*; **that one** ése/ésa *e-se/e-sa*; **the book that you bought** el libro que compraste *el leebro ke kompras-te*; **I know that...** sé que... *se ke*

thaw: it's thawing deshiela *dez-yela*

the el/la *el/la*; (plural) los/las *los/las*

theatre el teatro *te-a-tro*

their su *soo*; **their children** sus chicos *soos cheekos*

theirs el/la suyo(a) *el/la sooyo(a)*; **they're theirs** son suyos *son sooyos*

them los/las *los/las*; **I will send them a letter** les enviaré una carta *les enbya-re oona karta*; **with them** con ellos(as) *kon elyos(as)*

then después *des-pwes*

there allí *a-lyee*

therefore por lo tanto *por lo tanto*

thermometer el termómetro *termo-metro*

these estos/estas *estos/estas*; **these ones** éstos(as) *estos(as)*

they ellos/ellas *e-lyos/e-lyas*

thick grueso(a) *grweso(a)*

thief el ladrón *ladron*

thigh el muslo *mooslo*

thin delgado(a) *del-gado(a)*

thing la cosa *kosa*

think pensar *pensar*; (be of opinion) creer *kre-er*

third[1] *adj* tercero(a) *ter-thero(a)*

third[2] *n* el tercio *terthyo*

thirsty: I am thirsty tengo sed *tengo sed*

thirteen trece *tre-the*

thirty treinta *tre-eenta*

this esto *esto*; **this book** este libro *e-ste leebro*; **this table** esta mesa *e-sta mesa*; **this one** éste/ésta *e-ste/e-sta*

those esos/esas *e-sos/e-sas*

thousand mil *meel*

thread el hilo *ee-lo*

three tres *tres*

throat la garganta *gar-ganta*

throat lozenge la pastilla para la garganta *pas-teelya para la gar-ganta*

throttle el acelerador *a-the-le-rador*

through por *por*

throw lanzar *lanthar*

thumb el pulgar *poolgar*

thunder el trueno *trweno*

Thursday el jueves *khwe-bes*

thyme el tomillo *to-meelyo*

ticket el billete *bee-lye-te*

ticket collector el revisor *rebee-sor*

ticket office el despacho de billetes *des-pacho de bee-lye-tes*

tide la marea *ma-re-a*

tidy ordenado(a) *or-de-nado(a)*

tie[1] *n* la corbata *kor-bata*

tie² vb atar *atar*

tight ajustado(a) *akhoostado(a)*

tights las pantimedias *panteemedyas*

till¹ n la caja *kakha*

till² conj (until) hasta *asta*

time el tiempo *tyempo*; (occasion) la vez *beth*; **what time is it?** ¿qué hora es? *ke o-ra es*; **three times** tres veces *tres be-thes*

timetable el horario *o-raryo*

tin la lata *lata*

tinfoil el papel de estaño *papel de es-tanyo*

tin-opener el abrelatas *a-brelatas*

tinted teñido(a) *te-nyeedo(a)*

tip la propina *pro-peena*

tipped con filtro *kon feeltro*

tired cansado(a) *kan-sado(a)*

tissues los pañuelos de papel *panyoo-e-los de papel*

T-junction el cruce en T *kroo-the en te*

to a *a*; **I want to go** quiero ir *kyero eer*

toast el pan tostado *pan tostado*

toaster la tostadora *tosta-dora*

tobacco el tabaco *ta-bako*

tobacconist's el estanco *estanko*

today hoy *oy*

toe el dedo del pie *dedo del pye*

together juntos(as) *khoontos(as)*; (at the same time) a la vez *a la beth*

toilet los servicios *serbeethyos*; **where are the toilets?** ¿dónde están los servicios? *don-de es-tan los ser-beethyos*

toilet paper el papel higiénico *pa-pel ee-khyeneeko*

toilet water el agua de colonia *a-gwa de ko-lonya*

toll el peaje *pe-a-khe*

tomato el tomate *toma-te*

tomato juice el zumo de tomate *thoomo de toma-te*

tomb la tumba *toomba*

tomorrow mañana *ma-nyana*; **tomorrow morning** mañana por la mañana *ma-nyana por la ma-nyana*

ton la tonelada *to-nela-da*

tongue la lengua *lengwa*

tonic water la tónica *to-neeka*

tonight esta noche *esta noche*

tonsillitis la amigdalitis *ameeg-dalee-tees*

too también *tambyen*; (too much) demasiado *demas-yado*

tool la herramienta *erra-myenta*

tooth el diente *dyen-te*

toothache el dolor de muelas *dolor de mwelas*

toothbrush el cepillo de dientes *the-peelyo de dyen-tes*

toothpaste la pasta de

dientes *pasta de dyen-tes*

top (*highest point*) la cima *theema*; **on top of** sobre *so-bre*

top floor el último piso *ool-teemo peeso*

torch la linterna *leen-terna*

torn rasgado(a) *ras-gado(a)*

total el total *total*

touch[1] *vb* tocar *tokar*

touch[2] *n* el contacto *kon-takto*

tough (*meat*) duro(a) *dooro(a)*

tour (*trip*) la vuelta *bwelta*; (*of museum etc*) la visita *bee-seeta*

tourism el turismo *too-reesmo*

tourist el/la turista *too-reesta*

tourist office la oficina de turismo *ofee-theena de too-reesmo*

tourist ticket un billete turístico *bee-lye-te toorees-teeko*

tow remolcar *remol-kar*

towards hacia *a-thya*

towel la toalla *to-a-lya*

tower la torre *to-rre*

town la ciudad *thyoodad*

town centre el centro de la ciudad *thentro de la thyoodad*

town plan el plano de la ciudad *plano de la thyoodad*

tow rope el cable de remolque *ka-ble de remol-ke*

toy el juguete *khoo-ge-te*

track el camino *ka-meeno*;

(*sports*) la pista *peesta*

tracksuit el chandal *chandal*

trade fair la feria de muestras *ferya de mwestras*

trade union el sindicato *seendee-kato*

traditional tradicional *tradee-thyonal*

traffic la circulación *theerkoo-lathyon*

traffic jam el embotellamiento *embo-telya-myento*

traffic lights el semáforo *sema-foro*

traffic offence la infracción de tráfico *eenfrak-thyon de tra-feeko*

traffic warden el guardia de tráfico *gwardya de tra-feeko*

trailer el remolque *remol-ke*

train el tren *tren*; **to change trains** cambiar de tren *kambyar de tren*

tram el tranvía *tran-beea*

tranquillizer el tranquilizante *trankee-leethan-te*

transfer transferir *trans-fereer*

transfer charge call la conferencia a cobro revertido *kon-feren-thya a kobro rebert-eedo*

transistor (*radio*) el transistor *transees-tor*

translate traducir *tradoo-theer*

translation la traducción

tradook-*thyon*
transparency la diapositiva
dee-*apo*-seetee-ba
transparent transparente
transpa-*ren*-te
travel viajar byakhar
travel agency la agencia de
viajes a-*khen*-thya de *bya*-
khes
traveller's cheque el
cheque de viajero *che*-ke de
bya-khero
tray la bandeja ban-*dekha*
treat tratar *tratar*; **I'm
treating you** te invito te
een-*beeto*
treatment el tratamiento
trata-*myento*
tree el árbol arbol
trick el truco trooko
trim el recorte rekor-*te*
trip la excursión exkoor-*syon*
tripe los callos ka-*lyos*
tripod el trípode *treepo*-de
trouble los problemas pro-
blemas
trousers los pantalones panta-
lo-*nes*
trout la trucha *troocha*
true verdadero(a) berda-
dero(a)
trunk el baúl ba-*ool*
trunks el bañador banya-*dor*
try intentar een-*tentar*
try on probarse probar-*se*
t-shirt la camiseta kamee-*seta*
tube el tubo toobo
Tuesday el martes *mar*-tes
tuna el atún a-*toon*

tune la melodía melo-*dee*-a
tunnel el túnel *too*-nel
turbot el rodaballo roda-*balyo*
turkey el pavo *pabo*
turn[1] n el turno *toorno*
turn[2] vb volver bol-*ber*;
(*rotate*) girar kheerar; **to
turn left** torcer a la
izquierda tor-*ther* a la eeth-
kyerda; **to turn off** (*light*)
apagar a-*pagar*; (*tap*) cerrar
therrar; (*engine*) parar *parar*;
to turn on (*light, engine*)
encender en-*thender*; (*tap*)
abrir a-*breer*
turning (*side road*) la
bocacalle boka-*ka*-lye
turnip el nabo *nabo*
turquoise turquesa toor-*kesa*
TV la tele te-*le*; **TV lounge** la
sala de televisión *sala* de te-
lebee-*syon*
tweezers las pinzas *peenthas*
twelve doce *do*-the
twenty veinte be-*een*-te
twice dos veces dos be-*thes*
twin el/la gemelo(a) khe-
melo(a); **twin beds** las
camas gemelas *kamas* khe-
melas
twist torcer tor-*ther*
two dos dos
type escribir a máquina
eskree-*beer* a ma-*keena*
typewriter la máquina de
escribir ma-*keena* de eskree-
beer
typical típico(a) tee-
peeko(a)

typist la mecanógrafa *mekanogra-fa*

tyre el neumático *ne-oo-matee-ko*

tyre pressure la presión de los neumáticos *presyon de los ne-oo-matee-kos*

U

ugly feo(a) *fe-o(a)*

ulcer la úlcera *ool-thera*

umbrella el paraguas *paragwas*

uncle el tío *tee-o*

uncomfortable incómodo(a) *een-komodo(a)*

unconscious inconsciente *eenkons-thyen-te*

under debajo de *de-bakho de*

underclothes la ropa interior *ropa een-te-ryor*

underdone poco hecho(a) *poko echo(a)*; (steak) medio asado(a) *medyo a-sado(a)*

underground el metro *metro*

underground station la estación de metro *esta-thyon de metro*

underpass el paso subterráneo *paso soobte-rra-ne-o*

understand comprender *kom-prender*

undone desabrochado(a) *des-a-brochado(a)*

unemployed parado(a) *pa-rado(a)*

unfortunate desgraciado(a) *desgra-thyado(a)*

unfortunately desgraciadamente *desgra-thyada-men-te*

uniform el uniforme *oo-nee-forme*

United States of America los Estados Unidos de América *es-tados oo-needos de a-meree-ka*

university la universidad *oo-neeber-seedad*

unless a menos que *a menos ke*

unlock abrir con llave *a-breer kon lya-be*

unpack deshacer las maletas *desa-ther las ma-letas*

unpleasant desagradable *desa-grada-ble*

unscrew destornillar *destor-neelyar*

unusual poco común *poko komoon*

up arriba *a-rreeba*; (out of bed) levantado(a) *lebantado(a)*; **to go up** subir *soo-beer*

upside down al revés *al re-bes*

upstairs arriba *a-rreeba*

urgent urgente *oor-khen-te*

urine la orina *o-reena*

us nos *nos*; **for us** para nosotros(as) *para no-sotros(as)*

use[1] vb usar *oosar*

use[2] n el uso *ooso*

used : I used to do it solía
hacerlo *solee-a-a-therlo*; **I'm
used to it** estoy
acostumbrado *es-toy akos-
toombra-do*
useful útil *oo-teel*
usual acostumbrado(a) *akos-
toombra-do(a)*
usually por lo general *por lo
khe-neral*
U-turn el vuelta en U *bwelta
en oo*

V

vacancy la habitación libre
abee-tathyon lee-bre
vaccination la vacunación
bakoo-nathyon
vacuum cleaner la
aspiradora *aspee-rado-ra*
vacuum flask el termos
termos
vague vago(a) *bago(a)*
valid válido(a) *ba-leedo(a)*
valley el valle *ba-lye*
valuable de valor de *balor*
value el valor *balor*
valve la válvula *bal-boola*
van la camioneta *kamyo-neta*
vanilla la vainilla *ba-ee-
neelya*
vase el florero *flo-rero*
VAT el IVA *eeba*
veal la ternera *ter-nera*
vegetables las verduras *ber-
dooras*
vegetarian vegetariano(a)
be-kheta-ryano(a)

vehicle el vehículo *be-ee-
koolo*
veil el velo *belo*
vein la vena *bena*
velvet el terciopelo *terthyo-
pelo*
vending machine el
distribuidor automático
*deestree-bweedor owto-
matee-ko*
venison la carne de venado
kar-ne de be-nado
ventilator el ventilador
bentee-lador
vermouth el vermut
bermoot
vertical vertical *berteekal*
very muy *mwee*; **it's very
hot** hace mucho calor *a-the
moocho kalor*
vest la camiseta *kamee-seta*
vet el veterinario *be-teree-
naryo*
VHF la muy alta frecuencia
mwee alta fre-kwenthya
via por *por*
video el vídeo *beede-o*
view la vista *beesta*
villa (*in country*) la casa de
campo *kasa de kampo*; (*by
sea*) la casa en la playa *kasa
en la pla-ya*
village el pueblo *pweblo*
vinaigrette la vinagreta
beena-greta
vinegar el vinagre *beena-gre*
vineyard la viña *beenya*
vintage la cosecha *ko-secha*
virus el virus *beerus*

visa el visado *bee-sado*
visit la visita *bee-seeta*
visitor el/la visitante *beeseetan-te*
vitamin la vitamina *beeta-meena*
V-neck el cuello en pico *kwelyo en peeko*
vodka la vodka *bodka*
voice la voz *both*
voltage el voltaje *bolta-khe*
vomit vomitar *bomee-tar*
vote votar *botar*

W

wage el sueldo *sweldo*
waist la cintura *theen-toora*
waistcoat el chaleco *cha-leko*
wait (for) esperar *es-perar*
waiter el camarero *kama-rero*
waiting room la sala de espera *sala de es-pera*
waitress la camarera *kama-rera*
wake up despertarse *despertar-se*
Wales el País de Gales *pa-ees de ga-les*
walk[1] *vb* andar *andar*
walk[2] *n* el paseo *pa-se-o*
walking shoes los zapatos para andar *tha-patos para andar*
walking stick el bastón *baston*
wall (*inside*) la pared *pa-red*; (*outside*) el muro *mooro*
wallet la cartera *kar-tera*

walnut la nuez *nweth*
want querer *ke-rer*
war la guerra *gerra*
warm[1] *adj* caliente *ka-lyen-te*; **it's warm** hace calor *a-the kalor*
warm[2] *vb* calentar *ka-lentar*
warning triangle el triángulo de avería *tree-angoo-lo de a-beree-a*
wash lavar *labar*; (*oneself*) lavarse *labar-se*; **to wash one's hands** lavarse las manos *labar-se las manos*
washable lavable *laba-ble*
washbasin el lavabo *la-babo*
washing el lavado *la-bado*
washing machine la lavadora *laba-dora*
washing powder el jabón en polvo *khabon en polbo*
washing-up liquid el lavavajillas *laba-bakhee-lyas*
washroom el lavadero *laba-dero*
wasp la avispa *a-beespa*
waste gastar *gastar*
waste bin el cubo de la basura *koobo de la ba-soora*
waste-paper basket la papelera *pa-pe-lera*
watch[1] *n* el reloj *relo*
watch[2] *vb* mirar *meerar*; (*luggage etc*) vigilar *beekhee-lar*
watchstrap la pulsera de reloj *pool-sera de relo*
water el agua *a-gwa*
water heater el calentador

de agua *ka-len-tador de a-gwa*
watermelon la sandía *sandee-a*
waterproof impermeable *eemper-me-a-ble*
water-skiing el esquí acuático *eskee a-kwatee-ko*
watertight hermético(a) *er-me-teeko(a)*
wave (*on sea*) la ola *o-la*
wax la cera *thera*
way el camino *ka-meeno;* (*method*) la manera *ma-nera;* **this/that way** por aquí/por ahí *por a-kee/por a-ee;* **which is the way to...?** ¿cuál es la carretera de...? *kwal es la ka-rre-tera de*
WC el váter *bater*
we nosotros(as) *no-sotros(as)*
weak débil *debeel;* (*coffee, tea*) flojo(a) *flokho(a)*
wear llevar *lyebar;* (*shoes*) calzar *kalthar*
weather el tiempo *tyempo*
wedding la boda *boda*
Wednesday el miércoles *myerko-les*
week la semana *se-mana;* **this/next/last week** esta semana/la semana próxima/la semana pasada *esta se-mana/la se-mana prok-seema/la se-mana pa-sada*
weekday el día laborable *deea labo-ra-ble*
weekend el fin de semana *feen de se-mana*

weekly cada semana *kada se-mana*
weigh pesar *pesar*
weight el peso *peso*
welcome bienvenido(a) *byen-be-needo(a)*
well[1] *n* el pozo *potho*
well[2] *adv* bien *byen*
well done (*steak*) muy hecho(a) *mwee e-cho(a)*
wellington boot la bota de goma *bota de goma*
Welsh galés/galesa *ga-les/ga-lesa*
went: I went fui *fwee;* **he went** fue *fwe;* **you went** Ud fue *oo-sted fwe*
west el oeste *o-es-te*
western occidental *okthee-dental*
wet mojado(a) *mo-khado(a);* (*weather*) lluvioso(a) *lyoo-byoso(a)*
wetsuit el traje de bucear *tra-khe de boo-the-ar*
what ¿qué? *ke;* **what is it?** ¿qué es? *ke es;* **what I did** lo que hice *lo ke ee-the*
wheat el trigo *treego*
wheel la rueda *rweda*
wheel brace el berbiquí *berbee-kee*
wheelchair la silla de ruedas *seelya de rwedas*
where donde *don-de;* **where?** ¿dónde? *don-de*
which cuál *kwal;* **which books?** ¿cuáles libros? *kwa-les leebros*

while mientras *myentras*
whip batir *bateer*
whisky el whisky *weeskee*
whisper cuchichear *koochee-che-ar*
whistle el silbato *seel-bato*
white blanco(a) *blanko(a)*
white coffee el café con leche *ka-fe kon le-che*
who: who is it? ¿quién es? *kyen es*; **the boy who came** el niño que vino *el nee-nyo ke beeno*
whole entero(a) *en-tero(a)*
wholemeal bread el pan integral *pan een-tegral*
wholesale price el precio al por mayor *el prethyo al por mayor*
whooping cough la tos ferina *tos fe-reena*
whose: whose is this? ¿de quién es esto? *de kyen es esto*
why ¿por qué? *por ke*
wide ancho(a) *ancho(a)*
widow la viuda *byooda*
widower el viudo *byoodo*
width el ancho *ancho*
wife la esposa *es-posa*
wild salvaje *salba-khe*
will[1] *vb:* **I will go** iré *ee-re*; **she will go** ella irá *e-lya ee-ra*
will[2] *n* el testamento *testa-mento*
win ganar *ganar*
wind el viento *byento*
windmill el molino de viento *mo-leeno de byento*

window la ventana *ben-tana*; (*in shop*) el escaparate *eska-para-te*; (*in car, train*) la ventanilla *benta-neelya*
window seat el asiento junto a la ventanilla *a-syento khoonto a la benta-neelya*
windscreen el parabrisas *para-breesas*; **windscreen washer** el lavaparabrisas *laba-para-breesas*; **windscreen wiper** el limpiaparabrisas *leempya-para-breesas*
windsurfing el surf de vela *soorf de bela*
windy: it's windy hace viento *a-the byento*
wine el vino *beeno*; **red wine** el vino tinto *beeno teento*
wine list la carta de vinos *karta de beenos*
wine waiter el escanciador *eskan-thyador*
wing el ala *a-la*
wink guiñar *geenyar*
winner el ganador *gana-dor*
winter el invierno *een-byerno*
winter sports los deportes de invierno *depor-tes de een-byerno*
wipe limpiar *leem-pyar*
wire el alambre *a-lam-bre*; (*electrical*) el cable *ka-ble*
with con *kon*
without sin *seen*
witness el testigo *tes-teego*

woman la mujer *moo-kher*
wonder: I wonder if... me pregunto si... *me pre-goonto see*
wonderful maravilloso(a) *mara-beelyo-so(a)*
wood el bosque *boske*; (*material*) la madera *ma-dera*
wool la lana *lana*
word la palabra *pa-labra*
work (*person*) trabajar *traba-khar*; (*machine*) funcionar *foon-thyo-nar*
world el mundo *moondo*
worried preocupado(a) *pre-okoo-pado(a)*
worse peor *pe-or*
worst el/la peor *el//la pe-or*
worth: 2000 pesetas worth of petrol 2000 pesetas de gasolina *dos meel pe-setas de gaso-leena*; **it's worth...** vale... *ba-le*
would: I would like... quisiera... *kees-yera*
wrapping paper el papel de envolver *pa-pel de enbol-ber*
wrap (up) envolver *enbol-ber*
wreck arruinar *aroo-eenar*
wrist la muñeca *moo-nyeka*
write escribir *eskree-beer*
writer el autor *owtor*
writing paper el papel de escribir *pa-pel de eskree-beer*
wrong equivocado(a) *ekee-boka-do(a)*; **you're wrong** está equivocado *esta ekee-bo-kado*

XYZ

X-ray la radiografía *radyo-grafee-a*
yacht el yate *ya-te*
yawn bostezar *bos-tethar*
year el año *a-nyo*; **this/next/last year** este año/el año próximo/el año pasado *es-te a-nyo/el a-nyo prok-seemo/el a-nyo pa-sado*
yeast la levadura *leba-doora*
yellow amarillo(a) *ama-reelyo(a)*
yes sí *see*; **yes please** sí por favor *see por fabor*
yesterday ayer *a-yer*; **yesterday morning** ayer por la mañana *a-yer por la ma-nya-na*; **yesterday evening** anoche *ano-che*
yet todavía *toda-bee-a*
yoga el yoga *yoga*
yoghurt el yogur *yogoor*
you usted *oos-ted*; (*familiar*) tú *too*
young joven *kho-ben*
your su *soo*; **your friends** sus amigos *soos a-meegos*
yours el/la suyo(a) *el//la sooyo(a)*; **is this yours?** ¿éste es suyo? *e-ste es sooyo*
youth la juventud *khoo-bentood*
youth hostel el albergue de juventud *alber-ge de khoo-bentood*
zero el cero *thero*
zip la cremallera *krema-lyera*
zoo el zoo *tho*